MW00437833

Creation of the World

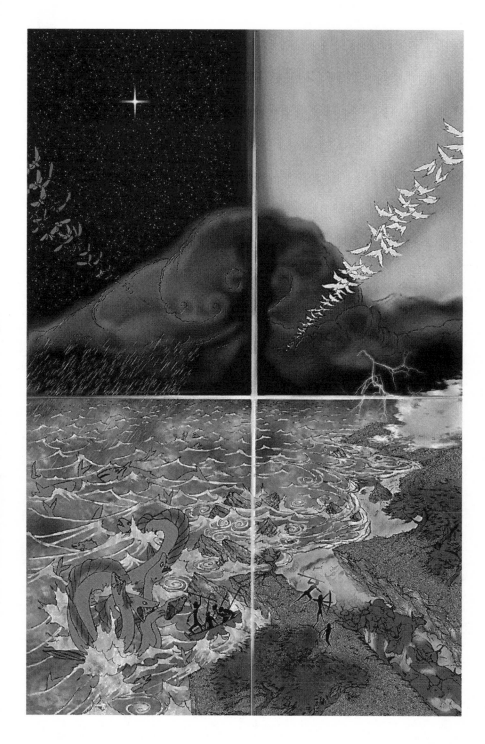

Creation of the World

(Il Mondo Creato)

by

Torquato Tasso

Translated by

Dario Rivarossa, Salwa Khoddam, and Carter Kaplan

Illustrated by

Dario Rivarossa, Eva Nieri, and Tiziana Grassi

international authors
brookline, massachusetts

Published by International Authors: Brookline, Massachusetts.

© Copyright 2016 by Dario Rivarossa, Salwa Khoddam and Carter Kaplan

All materials in this publication are under the exclusive copyright of the contributing writers and artists. All rights reserved.

ISBN: 978-1534983526

Library of Congress Control Number: 2016946742

Cover illustrations: The Magic Trio. Cover design: Carter Kaplan with Gareth Jackson and Ruud Antonius.

Contents

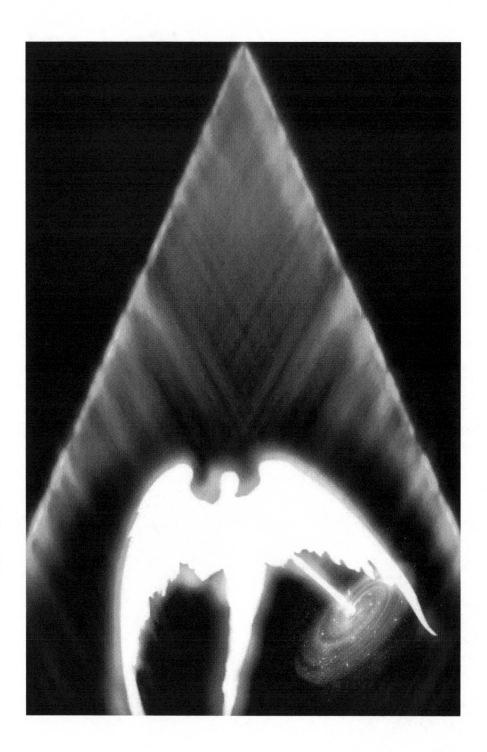

Preface

I FEEL VERY FORTUNATE to have been invited by Professor Khoddam and Mr. Rivarossa to participate in the project of translating into English Torquato Tasso's great poem *Il Mondo Creato* (*Creation of the World*). Their proposal described a long poem combining experimental syntactical structures, stream-of-consciousness, Counter-Reformation politics, early-modern science, post-Aristotelian *Weltanschauung*, geographical explor-ation, a paradoxical and "restless" theology—and many of these features pointed in various ways to connections with John Milton. Obviously, this was a capital project for International Authors. Not so obvious, however, was that my role would grow from being an editor (as originally proposed) to becoming a member of the translation team. All very well, but my Italian is limited. Fortunately, this was no obstacle for translators Khoddam and Rivarossa, and I found myself in the stimulating position of walking their manuscript those final steps into the English of a native speaker. Moreover, by engaging in the close reading of the poem demanded by the task, I was brought into a gratifying intimacy with a sensibility that is significant to the field of philosophy and literature. Tasso has broadened my appreciation for the philosophical antecedents to the modern world. This poem is material evidence that the modern grammatical techniques and the development of a new mythopoeic "epistemology"—elements of a project that I had long associated with John Milton—are anticipated in this earlier work, which antedates *Paradise Lost* by a couple of generations. Identifying the advent of nascent modernity is an assemblage fraught with complications—one could argue that the marks of such sensibility are present even in the *Epic of Gilgamesh*—but suffice it to say that after turning from Milton to Tasso, and then back to Milton, it is evident that the emergence of modern reflexive methods of conceptualization—the rational employment of bizarre imaginative constructions, syntactical experimentation, skeptical-empirical inquiry, scholastic parody, critical historiography, philological analysis, encyclopedic warehousing, and other signs of a "higher" or collective human consciousness—are common artifacts found in the work of both authors.[1] Tasso, like Milton, seizes upon the point-counterpoint of hard

---

[1] See p. xii, n. 7; p. 209, n. 5.

ratiocination within the context of a world of artifice, and transforms the phenomenon into a principle of anthropological insight. As such, *Creation of the World*[2] demonstrates that the Counter-Reformation was as vital as the Reformation in forcing the emergence of the modern world in which we are epistemological equals, where we are members of a "grammatical commons." The shared understanding that is made possible by such syntax could very well be the definitive feature of our modern world, and Tasso's descriptions of human beings who are conscious of each other while also seeing each other as parts of a larger world neatly underscore this idea, which is rooted to the very center of his exposition. We are awakened to the audaciousness of these features when considering the personal obstacles (described in the Introduction) which Tasso overcame by expressing his modern, experimental insights through figurative language and suggestive exuberance. Indeed, I am sensitive to a "meta-exuberance" that drives his ideas yet further into the realm of modernity, into a forceful awareness of our *immediacy*. In more grounded terms, Tasso's achievement is significant because of his indefatigable flare for considering the multifaceted character of things, raising the eyebrow of circumspection, asking questions, and speaking of reality—which in poetry is oftentimes enhanced in a milieu of fossilized institutions and political censure. Truth takes on colors appropriate to the character of the darkness through which it radiates.

Our methodology in pursuing the project can be described as eclectic, enquiring, and lively. Reflecting the poem's character, we felt our way ahead through realms of sensation and spectacle, but what we found was knowledge. A variety of traditional scholarly footnotes combining critical and historical matter are presented, as well as less formal notices communicating divers speculations, critical inferences, philosophical queries, cultural mentions, comparisons, commentary, and observations. Pertinent source material is documented fully, while other notes are set forth in an anecdotal fashion for readers to pursue as they wish. Our desire to bring together a broad body of ideas also has been the rule in selecting the illustrations, where it has been our philosophy to present a farrago of styles and perspectives in order to reflect the complexity of Tasso's conception. Overall, we have achieved remarkable consensus. Differences of opinion do emerge, however, and Professor Khoddam wishes to be identified ex-

---

[2] An alternative translation of the title, *The Created World*, underscore this theme of artifice.

clusively for her role as a translator, though I would be remiss (and I would feel unappreciative) if I did not thank her for the valiant effort she put forth in offering suggestions and refinements that have done so much to enhance our introduction and our footnotes. Each member of our group has gone over the material of this volume exhaustively; however, as the final arbiter of what appears between these covers, I accept responsibility for any errors or omissions.

My chief role in the effort of bringing *Creation of the World* into modern English has been to examine the poem prepared by translators Khoddam and Rivarossa, and strictly, indeed sometimes vigorously, thrust the manuscript into a language that maintains fidelity to Tasso's text while recreating the excitement and immediacy of the emotional texture that is so brilliantly animated by his fine character. As the three of us steadily worked closely together, over what has now been a span of two years, we were repeatedly surprised by the protean elasticity of the English language, and, notwithstanding our dedication to an absolute line-by-line fidelity to the text, we discovered ourselves continually awakening to the expository precision (and temptations) that English affords. We trust that our production is—in deed if not in fact—an exact and full rendering of *Il Mondo Creato*. Where disappointments invariably show themselves and blemishes are quite plainly recognizable, nevertheless Tasso's intellectual genius and the supple clarity of his otherwise madly complex vision represent adequate consolations. Here, we believe, are rewards that should prove satisfying to the most discriminating and demanding reader. Here, indeed, are new expressions, new delights, and new possibilities for poetry in English. It is a project we now convey (it feels *suddenly*) to our colleagues the scholars and to our friends the poets, and one that we offer in the determined spirit of confusion, enthusiasm, contention and humility that such an effort must entail. The result is this shining gem you hold in your hand.

CK

A Technical Introduction

THE ONLY DIFFERENCE between Torquato Tasso and a madman is that he was not a madman.[1] He spent seven years (1579-1586) in an asylum in Ferrara, in central-northern Italy, not because he *was* crazy, but in order to *drive* him crazy, so as to make his declarations unreliable, because he had become politically dangerous. He knew too much about the local Court's and Church's corruption, and he seriously meant to speak up. Compare the methods that would be employed in the twentieth century by the USSR. The propagandistic machine fueled by Duke Alphonse II of Este worked so well that, still today, many Italian scholars and readers think that he "was" mad; but it will suffice to read the essays he wrote during those years to realize that there is something very wrong in that version.[2]

Tasso surely was a victim of the irony of history. His long poem here translated for the first time in a line-by-line form,[3] *Il Mondo Creato*, "The Seven Days of the World's Creation," proved a great success all over Europe, even leading, according to one hypothesis, an Englishman called John Milton to sing the following *Genesis* chapter in a long poem called *Paradise Lost*. But *Il Mondo Creato* was published in 1607, after Tasso's death; whereas he had spent his entire life and consumed all his energies writing *another* long poem dealing with the First Crusade.[4] It is celebrated as *Gierusalemme*[5] *Liberata*, "Jerusalem Delivered," on the basis of a 1581 edition that was not precisely the "official" version, but perhaps the "less unofficial." Many drafts of the poem, at different stages of editing, circulated throughout Italy, and many pirate editions—with all kinds of

---

[1] Paraphrasing a famous joke by Salvador Dalí.

[2] We will not dwell on Tasso's biography. The best book on this subject has been written by Fabio Pittorru, *Torquato Tasso: L'Uomo, il Poeta, il Cortigiano*, Milan (Italy): Gruppo Editoriale Fabbri, 1982. Biographical details linked with the poem will be indicated in the footnotes. As to his political essays, see Luigi Firpo (ed.), *Torquato Tasso: Tre Scritti Politici*, Turin (Italy): UTET, 1980.

[3] Joseph Tusiani has published an admirable translation (Center for Medieval and Renaissance Studies, 1982), but it sometimes condenses groups of lines, and is sometimes misled by Tasso's quirky vocabulary and syntax. Cited in this text as "JT", Tusiani's translation is several times mentioned when sources or explanations conflict. The field of Tassology is fraught with contradictions, alternative possibilities and "shape-shifting" interpretations, as the translators can readily attest.

[4] Where Tasso does not omit to praise the Muslim heroes too.

[5] Spelled *Gerusalemme*, without "i," in current Italian.

mistakes—had been published. Not even the title had been chosen by the author. Tasso more or less accepted the 1581 version as a lesser evil, but meanwhile went on reworking the text, and thoroughly so, until 1593, two years before he died, when at last he published it as he really wanted it; and it was almost completely different from the *Liberata*. It was called *Gierusalemme Conquistata*, "Jerusalem Conquered" or "Regained." And it was a supreme flop from the beginning.

Now we can understand why: the *Conquistata* was more than four centuries before its time, what with its website structure, its super-heroic comic-strip action scenes, its bold updating of classical themes, and its crazy mix of fantasy, science fiction, refined symbols, sheer violence, eroticism, homosexuality, archeology, technology, magic, Christian spirituality, Celtic war values... But this is a story worth telling on another occasion.[6]

Il Mondo Creato, though dealing with subjects that Tasso had been pondering for a decade or more (see his *Dialogues*), was written "in a hurry" after conversations in Naples with the devout mother of a friend of his, Count Giovanni Battista Manso, who would later host Milton in Italy during November and December of 1638.[7] Tasso started work on *Il Mondo Creato* in 1592 and gave it the final touches in 1594—it was eventually published in a partial edition in 1600, and complete in 1607. Throughout this period he was plagued by many personal and health troubles, and meanwhile he was working very diligently upon another project, namely *Gierusalemme Conquistata*. Despite these occupations, however, *Il Mondo Creato* is no light effort. It is 8,815 lines long, comparable in length to Dante's *Inferno* and *Purgatorio* put together. Basing his poem on St. Basil's *Sermons on Genesis* (or, *on the Six Days of Creation*), which had recently

---

[6] The blog *tassonomia.blogspot.it*, in English, is almost entirely devoted to it.

[7] In the Latin poem "Mansus" dedicated to his host, Milton gives Tasso significant mentions—artifacts of allusion and of parody—which in a careful and sympathetic reading appear to indicate "Tasso the author of *Il Mondo Creato*." Tasso's influences upon Milton have been explored in Judith A. Kates' *Tasso and Milton: The Problem of Christian Epic*, Lewisburg: Bucknell UP, 1983; and David Quint's *Epic and Empire: Politics and Generic Form from Virgil to Milton*, Princeton UP, 1993. Unfortunately, neither study examines *Il Mondo Creato* (*MC*), and instead these writers underscore the influences of the *Liberata*, classic epic, and Italian romance. We believe this translation will help build the possible case that *MC* was influential not only upon Milton's subject matter in *Paradise Lost*, but, in considering Tasso's analysis of knowledge, it was influential upon Milton's satire as well. See p. 209, n. 5.

been translated into Latin,[8] Tasso adds literature to Basil's multidisciplinary approach, i.e. theology, philosophy, and science; updates the geographic and sociological descriptions by taking the New World into account; and adds detailed analyses of special issues: astronomy, "monsters," the "poem of the phoenix" at the end of Day Five, the whole Day Seven, etc. The outcome is a mazy "stream of consciousness" (another novelty, because in the Church Father's *Genesis Sermons* the passages from one subject to another were clearer). *Il Mondo Creato* abounds with references to Greek philosophy, Latin literature, the *Divine Comedy,* [9] Renaissance poetry, astronomy, astrology, the natural sciences, folk legends, exploration, classical and Egyptian mythology, the Church Fathers, Medieval theology, the Jewish Rabbis' *midrashim* (Bible interpretations)… and includes then non-existent disciplines like geology and ecology. This richness alone can let us perceive something of Tasso's amazing genius—an amazing genius his con-temporaries knew well.

The year 1592 marked one century after the "official" date of the discovery of America. Although he is not expressly overt in his assessment of the effects of exploration and the "enlarging" world (and worldview), Tasso is not insensitive to the situation of Western civilization after the impact of a century of intercourse with the New World. And, what has happened? Most social and cultural elements are still the same as in Dante's era, but beneath the surface the whole psychological structure has collapsed and shattered. *Il Mondo Creato* reminds us of the experimental movies of the Russian director Dziga Vertov in the early twentieth century, or those in the United States in the 1960s: movies with "no plot, no screenplay, no actors." *Il Mondo Creato* loosely follows the sequence of the six plus one days of creation as they are told in *Genesis* 1. The more the poem proceeds, however, the more the pieces fall apart, moreover psychologically, just below the surface. From this point of view, *Paradise Lost* is a more traditional poem; it gives us a powerful Satan, the very interesting Eve and Adam, angels who may be liked or not, and who are endowed with personalities, and all these actors operate within the bounds of a consistent

---

[8] Basil, St., "the Great" (c. 330-79) is the most important Church Father in the Eastern European Christian tradition, but plays a secondary role in the Western history of thought and spirituality. Tasso' use of Basil is another original and remarkable feature of *Il Mondo Creato*.

[9] In *Il Mondo Creato*, probably for the first time ever, Dante appears as a character in a poem by another author.

and well-structured plot. The case is quite different in *Il Mondo Creato*. Adam appears when the poem is basically through, and he will not say one word, except a brief quotation from the Bible (his comment when he first sees Eve). Tasso is interested in him as an anatomical specimen, e.g., describing the shape and function of his ears, nostrils, etc.

The actual protagonist is the World itself, as "projected" in a long and detailed avant-garde film. Tasso reveals a cosmos with its lights and shadows, its joys and fears, its void and life, and its frightening and fascinating complexity. Here is history with its thrilling discoveries and its bloodbaths; humankind being created, saved, and loved by God in Christ, and continuously under the menace of being destroyed. Nature is pregnant with marvels and monsters. Ancient traditions convey deception or wisdom. Moreover, it is not a silent film. It has a soundtrack in which learned quotations and visceral cries mix as themes ebb and flow, tumble down mountainsides, reverse, and swirl like whirlpools.

This leads us directly to the "matter" with which the poem has been built: language and the text of that language.

* * *

The Italian text of *Il Mondo Creato* that has been used for the translation is the book edited by Professor Bruno Basile (in this text referred to as "BB").[10] The Basile edition is especially valuable insofar as it makes a full immersion into everything that Tasso had read.[11] A long list of *Il Mondo Creato* sources is provided by the poet himself in his *Postille*.[12] Tasso drew materials from many other books that Professor Basile also retrieved on the basis of the poet's biographical data and cultural milieu.

We sought to cannibalize BB as little as possible, but certain specific sources would have been impossible to discover without his notes. Some concrete examples will point out the novelties contained in BB, here offered in the footnotes of this English version. The BB text offers many quotations

---

[10] Torquato Tasso, *Aminta. Il Re Torrismondo. Il Mondo Creato*, ed. by Bruno Basile, Rome: Salerno Editrice, 1999.

[11] The same—often disapproved—approach that had been adopted by Giovanni Pascoli in 1899-1901 for his interpretation of the *Divine Comedy*.

[12] Hand-written notes; though the sheets kept in the *Biblioteca Palatina* (Palatine Library) in Parma are not the original notes but a copy made by Tasso's skilled editor, Angelo Ingegneri, the same who edited the 1581 version of *Gierusalemme Liberata* and the 1607 version of *MC*.

from Dante, but many more have been added, sometimes on the basis of *one* rare or unusual word taken from the *Divine Comedy*, which Tasso employed in a different context; but that Dantean echo gives a deeper meaning to the verse, opening into a second level of interpretation. Regrettably missing in BB—as is often the case with contemporary Italian criticism—are the references to *the* Source, that is, the Bible; many quotations have been supplied here. Other concerns such as literature and society in the Renaissance, analogies and differences with Ludovico Ariosto's *Orlando Furioso*, Tasso's biography, and others, have been indicated in our version. Professor Basile was obviously not interested, as we are, in examining the possible effects, either direct or indirect, of Tasso's poetry on Milton's *Paradise Lost*, and on an English author who may be termed the "last Renaissance writer," namely Clive Staples Lewis. Original parallels and comparisons among these authors are offered in our footnotes.

On some occasions, the BB text has typographical errors, or, in a half dozen cases, even missing words: it was possible to fix these problems thanks to a nineteenth century edition of *Il Mondo Creato* available on the Internet.[13] When we happen to give a problematic translation of a certain *MC* passage, the respective footnote explains why.

* * *

As already mentioned, in comparison to Tasso's other long works, *Il Mondo Creato* was written in a hurry. Precisely this marks its surprising modernity. Tasso abandons the stanzas, the octaves that rhythmically structure his Jerusalem-poems, and runs off Cantos whose length varies from 700 to 1,900 lines, more or less. He writes in hendecasyllables, but *sciolti*, "untied," not rhyming. At first sight, the poem flows like a "stream of consciousness," with repetitions, inconsistencies, twisted lines that sometimes leave the subject or the verb implied. In appearance, some passages deserve a bit more editing, but the case is very much the opposite: the de-structured flow of the text is meant to match a de-structured universe; or, to put it more accurately, a universe that, through its de-structuring, is revealed to be an artifice. A close inspection shows that Tasso's "spontaneous" sentences are full of pondered words and ingenious

---

[13] Vincenzo Antinori, *Il Mondo Creato* (Pisa: Presso Niccolò Capurro, 1823). Google Books.

syntactical configurations. It may be inappropriate to apply the phrase "avant-garde" to such phenomena, but when considering Tasso's possible influence on Milton we find the phraseology rewarding.

Our translation did not adopt one specific meter but nonetheless carefully aimed at being poetical. We did not simply render *Il Mondo Creato* into prose and cut the result into lines. By tuning the sounds and rhythm by ear, lines from 9 to 12 syllables usually came out, with a certain number of hendecasyllables, either slightly irregular of fully regular. The result is a musical effect that evokes, as Professor Kaplan names it in the Preface, Tasso's "fine character."

The main problems in the process of translation have been basically five:

1. *Syntax*

Though not specifically referring to this poem, Tasso's critics said that, because of the wording and syntax he employed, he should have written his verses in Latin. Since he is no longer "tied" to stanzas, Tasso in *Il Mondo Creato* builds sentences whose length varies whimsically, and, what is "worse," the word order is shaped after the manner of classical epic, but with a great difference: in Greek and in Latin, the word endings ("cases") help the reader link, say, an adjective in line 1 with a noun "far away" in line 2. Not so in Italian; as a consequence, some passages—in Italian—may need to be read two or three times before the whole syntactical picture becomes clear. Unlike Ariosto's *Orlando Furioso* or Tasso's own juvenile play *Aminta*, *Il Mondo Creato* was not conceived in order to be recited. Nevertheless, we have discovered that in the case of our translation—perhaps because of the peculiarities of English, which Anthony Burgess has styled "a language without a grammar" with words "simply" grouped together in respect to their relevance to each other—the oral recitation is wonderfully effective.

This English translation seeks a difficult balance between following the text as closely as possible and being reader-friendly. The general rule is that the translation should correspond to the original text line-by-line. When the Italian structure was incompatible with English grammar, or could have been adapted only in a very clumsy way, a device that was often adopted was to turn an active verb into a passive one. On other occasions, it was necessary to rephrase a whole section. In these cases, in a group formed by, say, lines from 10 to 15, it may well be that the wording in line 12 in English does not correspond to the Italian wording in the same line, but the contents in the 10-to-15 block are the same in both languages. An example can be found in Day Three, lines 827-830, where, because of a Latinizing phrasing in the original text, the subject and the verb appear three lines below the objects they refer to.

Again in order to make the text as clear as possible while also preserving its complexity, the punctuation has been completely redone according to current American English standards, without taking the Renaissance rules, as well as Tasso's and/or his publishers' choices, into account.

2. Gender

This was a major crux. As it is well known, all Italian nouns and adjectives are either masculine or feminine; this turned out to create thorny questions in some cases. A good example is provided by the moon (or, the Moon? See below). The Italian word *luna* is feminine, with all the consequent psychological associations. To choose regularly the pronoun "she" would have had an unnatural and annoying effect in English when the moon is described as a "planet" (according to the Ptolemaic astronomy) with its light, spots, and course across the sky; on the other hand, to keep using "it," even when the Moon as the goddess Diana/Artemis in involved, would have completely spoiled the ambiance. So, "it" has been used in the first instance, "she" in the second, but with a slightly puzzling side effect in English, when Tasso suddenly switches from the one nuance of the word to the other. Nevertheless, the charming authority of the poetry "smooths" over the perception of such shifts, and indeed when the reader is in this mode the confluence of Tasso's vision and this English text is wonderfully sustained.

And so with the animals. They are usually referred to as "it," or "they" by changing the sentence into a plural form, but they are dealt with as "he" or "she" when the gender is important, and when the poet paints delightful or tragic scenes in which the animals' feelings are described in terms of human sympathies.

When treating Tasso's animals, the most complicated task has been translating the gender of the phoenix in Day Five. The Italian word *fenice* is feminine, but Tasso also refers to the bird in the masculine as *augello* (*uccello*, bird). In the phoenix section, Tasso begins by describing the bird as she/her following the gender of the Italian word *fenice*, but then at line 1417 the subject *augel* (later also in the form *augello*, i.e. *uccello* in current Italian: "bird") appears, and from that point Tasso maintains a masculine representation except in lines 1470-1474, where he describes the bird in the stages of infancy. At line 1561 ff., however, the poet clearly states that the phoenix has no sex at all. Rather than hermaphroditic, he/she is neither. Proclaiming that the phoenix has no sex allows Tasso to enter into an exaltation of the bird as a symbol of Christ in His incarnation, death, and resurrection, "the father and son of himself" (line 1417). Further complicating matters, the gender of any given pronoun could be construed as arbitrary because it is determined by the gender of the noun which it accompanies. Since Italian words always have a gender, Tasso necessarily used them as such; as he changed grammatical subjects, genders varied accordingly. A neutral "it" is too weak, as the poem will show. Tasso could have kept *"fenice"* (feminine) as the subject of the whole phoenix section, but this would have appeared clumsy in the long and sophisticated section, and all the more so for Tasso, who loved variations. But there are other considerations. The symbolism of the bird's rebirth is clearly central to the meaning of the myth, and this metamorphosis is grammatically reflected in the passages beginning at lines 1417 and 1561. For all these reasons, the feminine has been chosen for continuity in the lines prior to 1417, while masculine is maintained in the lines which follow; and readers are invited to reflect upon Tasso explaining the bird actually has no sex (again, 1561 ff.). The matter of Tasso's admonition to the ladies in lines 1270 ff. also has bearing on the selection of the feminine in the initial passage of the section, as the phoenix story can be read as underscoring his apostrophe to them, but this is conjecture. We respectfully turn the matter over to commentary.

3. *M/m*

Let us go back to the moon… or the Moon? Baroque writers and publishers were fond of capitalized words for the sake of emphasis and pomp—while Milton's use of them in *Paradise Lost* had a significance of its own. Currently in Italy, the trend is to write as many words as possible in small letters, and this also applies to Tasso's works; therefore, BB does not reflect the typographic rules followed in the late sixteenth century. Also, Tasso, as his manuscripts show, had his personal idiosyncrasies, but he set free his favorite editor Angelo Ingegneri to standardize the final text as he liked best, not only as far as initials were concerned, but also regarding spelling. Ingegneri could even choose among two different words or two different lines when Tasso could not make up his mind.

We used more capitalized words than BB, especially for such terms as the Moon, the Sun, the Earth, Nature, etc., when they are described as protagonists, as living beings, or when a scientific section lists all the elements involved. God's pronoun is always "He." As to the adjectives and titles referring to Him, they are usually capitalized ("His," "heavenly Father,"…), except "his" in lines that are already loaded with capitalized divine words. "Man" has a capital M when it means Adam, or when some fundamental statement on our nature is made.

4. *Synonyms*

Two words are better than one, or so Tasso apparently believed. Often in the poem, one concept is expressed by two words linked by "and." It is not precisely about a hendiadys, because the two terms do not complete each other, as when a poet uses "night and darkness" to mean "a very dark night." Very often, the two words employed by Tasso are simply the same word in two variants, of which the one is often a now outdated form, and the other a more modern one. Latinizing words often—but not always—belong to the former class.

The translation choices varied according to several factors: the verse length in English, the sound and rhythm, the actual necessity—or not—to use two words, and the actual existence of two English synonyms in such a case. Quite often, the two terms have been reduced to one.

For example, *Il Mondo Creato* 5: 441 deals with *'l serpente e l'angue*, both words meaning "snake," but the more refined *angue* (also used by Dante, see *Inferno* 7: 84), from Latin *anguis*, has disappeared from the commonly used language. On the other hand, *serpente*, that has a Latin root as well—*serpens*—is the word still in use. This leads us to the fifth issue.

5. *"What?"*

Even when Tasso does not link two synonyms by means of "and," he very often employs sequences of synonyms in one and the same section. The problem is that English does not always provide two or three words corresponding to the Italian terms. A telling example may be the snow, described as *bianca* (white) in one line, and as *candida* a little later in another. Now, according to the dictionary, *candida neve* should be tautologically translated as "snow-white snow." Things get worse when *candida* refers to a dove, meaning both its whiteness and its being a symbol of pureness and innocence—which, moreover, is not the same thing as "candor," in its turn.

The most "frightening" adjective has proved to be *vago* (and the declined forms: *vaga, vaghi, vaghe*), a "must" of Italian landscape poetry up until the nineteenth century. It means something beautiful in a graceful, gentle way, and at the same time—not as an alternative, but at the same time— something shifting in the distance; practically and *par excellence*: stars and birds.

The words belonging to this group have been translated after weighing each case. In general, the most interesting occurrences of all five types of linguistic problems have been indicated in the footnotes.

* * *

The initial author of this introduction—summarizing many months of collaboration—has been Dario Rivarossa, who thanks Professor Salwa Khoddam and Professor Carter Kaplan for believing in this "crazy" project from the beginning, as well as for their great support and painstaking commitment in editing the text.

Special thanks to Eva Nieri (Nivalis) and Tiziana Grassi (Selkis), namely the other two members of the Magic Trio, for their wonderful contribution to the illustrations. During the Middle Ages and the Renaissance, illustrated books were not "for kids." They were the books that really mattered.

As to this literary operation as a whole, we initially conceived a middle way between popularization and scholarship. Professor Kaplan, however, objected to this "compromise" and insisted the poem should be presented in in the manner that best evokes Tasso's voice and vision for the con- temporary manifestation of the "timeless" audience. We deferred to his Platonic views, and every aspect of the production was subject to careful negotiation, close revision, and precise refinement. Scholars will find a wealth of historical and critical details in the quotations, references, and sources represented in the footnotes. An examination of the translation itself will reward the specialist interested in unpacking the unique and oftentimes crafty solutions we discovered for solving a range of linguistic problems. Contemporary poets, we believe, will discover in Tasso a source for inspiration and invention. In any event, this book is not a finish line, it is a starting point. It is our hope that it may be of some help in promoting the re-discovery of a "huge" and too often ignored poet.

DR, CK

Creation of the World

Day One

F ather of heaven—and You, of the eternal Father[1]
  the eternal Son, and the uncreated Issue,
the only birth of the immutable Mind,
the divine Image, equal to your divine
Pattern, and blazing Light out of Light—
and You, from both blowing and shining,
the Spirit lighted out of that twin Light,
You also a sacred lamp and a sacred flame,
like a bright river from a clear spring,
and again, true Image of the true Image[2]   10
in which the Primal Pattern matches himself
(if one can say so), and tripled Sun
lighting souls, enlightening pure minds,
holy Gift, holy Envoy, holy Knot[3]
linking three holy Persons into One
—non-solitary God, in whom the Whole unites,
which then lowers[4] and spreads itself into many—
you the term of the high infinite Thought[5]
and, of His order,[6] the divine Love;   20
from the Father and Son, now come descend in me
and inhabit my heart, and from Both to me
bring graces, and inspire both senses[7] and verses
to let me sing of that first, high effort
by the Three of You—and out of You it shines
wonderfully, together with the rich craftsmanship
of this world then created by You-Three
in distinct six days. Or You-One teach this,
Who in one point hold the spaces and the route

---

[1] The duplication of "Father" already hints at the Son as Image ("copy").

[2] Calling the Spirit "Image of Image" is unusual in Western theology.

[3] All about the Spirit in three words: His divine essence *ab intra* (knot); His role *ad extra* with reference to humankind (envoy); His effect (gift, grace).

[4] A Neoplatonic perspective.

[5] "Termine d'infinito alto consiglio" echoes Dante's "termine fisso d'eterno consiglio" (*Paradiso* 33: 3); Dante, however, meant the Virgin Mary. In this case, the Catholic Tasso "de-catholicizes" Dante by bringing back the concept from Mary to the Holy Spirit as "love and order."

[6] *Ordo, dharma, rta.* On this topic, see e.g. Raimon Panikkar.

[7] The inner, spiritual senses of Neoplatonism; see also the Church Fathers.

that, ever-rotating along oblique paths,
swift time follows with a thousand turns.   30
May it also please You[8] that in the aura of your fire
I may sing the seventh day, of soft and sweet
eternal rest, in which You promise—and keep—
not only luminous seats and joy and feast,
but after a brief, earthly, uncertain war,[9]
certain, at last, crowns and palms on high,
and heavenly triumph. And may, meanwhile,
this quiet in which I grow old and cry
(if any quiet is here below, in tears and anger)
be like that one to which the high hope   40
of an unerring promise invites and calls us,
enticing the heart with words of eternal glory.
Remind me of the reasons why this new[10] world
was made—You, the first eternal Cause
of those things created before the turns
of the volatile[11] and running aeons.[12]
And what reason moved You, the unmoved,
the supreme Mover, towards the amazing work,
then brand new on Your outside, now old,[13]
which gathers and carries all in its womb   50
and still keeps its first, ancient laws
as it keeps shining with light and gold
and with various colors and various forms,
wonderfully figured to our senses.
Tell me what kind of work or rest
was in Your divine and holy mind
in that blessed state of eternity;
in what unknown place, in what Idea
your model was, You heavenly craftsman,
in making your own palace and temple.   60
You know: reveal! Make clear and known
to me, too, the works, the ways, the arts.

---

[8] Here again specifically the Spirit.
[9] This line suggests Tasso's deepest moods—and his biography in brief—in an otherwise perfectly Baroque victory. See also below, lines 38-39.
[10] After heaven, the "homeland" of angels, and/or the very ideas in God's mind. See lines 45 and 85-86.
[11] "Volubile" in Italian, that preserves the Latin root *volu-*, "flight." In current Italian, *volubile* means fickle.
[12] "Secoli" (centuries) in the stronger sense of the Latin *saeculum* = aeon (cf. Panikkar).
[13] Another typical Tassean concept.

Lord, You are the hand, and I the lyre
which, moved by You, with sweet tempering[14]
of soft harmony resounds and softens
even the hardest of adamant feelings.
Lord, You are the breath, I a hoarse trumpet
—by myself—to Your glory, and my voice
and sound languish if You are not inspiring.
Let your marvels echo inside me,   70
Lord, and let my new song be a fruit of grace;
so that it may be heard not only by the Tiber,
by fine Sebeto, and Arno, and the King of Rivers,[15]
by Mincius, Brembo, the icy Rhine, and Danube,
but also where the Nile deafens the folks around;
and those[16] who are deafer with error and fault may be
awakened by You, and hear at last these sacred notes.

Before God made the earth and heaven,
there were neither gods nor monarchs
to oppose the making of a new world.   80
Nor did, all alone in an eternal silence,
the supreme Father dwell in darkness,
but together with his Son and divine Spirit
He had his seat and kingdom in himself,
the high monarch of his conceived worlds:
for a divine inner work it was, that thought.
Nor did He need any armies and arms,
nor a theater for his glory, in which He shines
to himself only, meanwhile hidden to all.
But it cannot be told nor can the intellect   90
of man comprehend, so narrow and slow,
how He, in himself, out of himself, begot
the Word[17] from eternity; and the sacred way

---

[14] "Dolci temper," from Dante's *Paradiso.*

[15] The Po River, crossing a great part of Northern Italy. Most rivers here mentioned are in Italy.

[16] Non-Christians in general, i.e. Jews, Muslims, and Native Americans. Muslim won't be expressly mentioned anywhere in this poem (but abundantly, of course, in *Gerusalemme Liberata*, 1581, and in its reboot, *Gerusalemme Conquistata*, 1593); Jews and "Indians" will. It is worth noting that Tasso conceived *Il Mondo Creato* as a great Apologia of Christianity, but it wasn't appreciated even by his fellow Christians. The protagonists of Tasso's Shakespearean tragedy *Il Re Torrismondo*, 1587, set in Scandinavia in the seventh century AD, are not obviously Christian nor heathen, as in *Beowulf*, set in the same area in more or less the same era.

3

of his generation; and the ineffable birth
of his Son, whom in that sublime majesty
He makes equal to himself—sitting on his right.
So let that old, lying[18] Greece be silent[19]
about the progeny of Sky[20] and Saturn
and the mutilated parts of expelled gods;[21]
and Giants and Titans bound at the bottom   100
of the Tartarean and shadowy night;
and the usurped seats and the unjust son,[22]
unclean for outraging his own father;
and that fabled goddess he produced out
of his head, with her shield and spear;
and so with Osiris and the barking Anubis[23]
let dark[24] Egypt be silent about its monsters,
that darkens truth with its ancient lies.
Or, if they[25] deserve it, may they hear the clear sound
of Wisdom,[26] who came out of the divine mouth   110
of the most high Father before the time
of all created things, and dwells with Him
on the lofty mounts of old eternity:
His first-born in that sublime light
to which the human mind aspires in vain.

---

[17] "Il Verbo" has inadvertently been explained as "the Holy Spirit" in the Italian edition of *Il Mondo Creato* used for this translation (see Foreword; henceforth, it will be indicated as BB, in reference to Bruno Basile).

[18] Somewhat misleading: Tasso was a great admirer of Greek culture.

[19] "Taccia…" A figure of speech also be found in Dante, see *Inferno* 25: 94, 97.

[20] "Celo" (Cielo) in Tasso's text, translating from the Greek *Ouranos*, Uranus.

[21] Uranus' genitals were cut off by Saturn.

[22] Zeus/Jove, who rebelled against Saturn in his turn. A reference to Athena/Minerva follows. The same Tartarean atmospheres and the head-birth of Athena will be used by Milton in *Paradise Lost* for his Satan and Sin. In general, the fact of identifying the classical gods with devils, rather than denying their existence, is present in the *Tanakh* (the Hebrew scriptures), the Church Fathers, and John Milton and William Blake.

[23] The topical—and rough—phrase "the barking Anubis" comes from Virgil's *Aeneid* (8: 946-947).

[24] Another half-truth. During the Renaissance, thanks to the study of classical sources, Ancient Egypt regained recognizable features (with its gods, the hieroglyphs, the names of Pharaohs, etc., much before Napoleon's campaigns), while in the Middle Ages it was virtually *terra incognito*, except for the episodes described in the Bible. Later in the poem, Tasso will mention the places and religions of America on the basis of the explorers' reports. All of this marks a clear cultural difference with the *Divine Comedy*.

[25] Egypt was already a Muslim country at that time. See Tasso's two Jerusalem-poems.

[26] Divine Wisdom, Word, Logos; here unusually woman-like since the implied term *Sapienza* (cf. Sapience in English) is feminine in Italian, as well as the Greek *Sophia* and Latin *Sapientia*.

This eternal Daughter,[27] born of Him,
has always been with Him, untouched by
the turning of decades,[28] the varying of years.
And the dark abysses did not yet exist,
nor had the first springs broken the earth,   120
when She was conceived, nor had the Pyrenees
and Alps raised their steep ridges,
nor had Ossa, Pelion, Olympus, hard Atlas,
or other mounts; and from their open sides
the rivers did not run rippling into the sea
from the four opposite world quarters yet,
when the high Father begot Her.
She was with Him in drawing the dark
circle and *vallum* around the blind abysses.
With Him, when He struck stars through the sky   130
and hung His waters[29] in balance above.
With Him when fixing a limit to the deep
Ocean, and giving His laws to waves;
and when He set the foundations of the
wide earth, with Him She was co-working.
She shaped with Him the Whole, day by day,
almost as a game, and work was then delight.
And[30] all was made into the golden home,
adorned and strewn with bright stars and gold,
for that created wisdom,[31] partaking   140
in that happy and blessed eternity.
But that home, by its own nature, turns and changes
itself into soon-to-be-abandoned shapes,
and in its varying, already half-frozen,
it would partly get darker and darker

---

[27] In this section Tasso partly translates, partly paraphrases from *Proverbs*, ch. 8, and other Biblical texts (from the Latin *Vulgate*). Apparently, as he got old he discovered that his "calling" was as a translator. Many of the new episodes he added to his main poem—just reworked, and powerfully—were verses by Homer and Virgil. In *MC*, whole sections consist of translations from the Bible, the Church Fathers, and both ancient and modern scholars. Tasso prepared a list indicating which parts of the poem were based on which works by which authors. The list is included in BB.

[28] "Lustri," literally a period of five years. A word that is almost exclusively used in poetry.

[29] The clouds, according to BB; but more probably the "waters above the firmament," see Day 2.

[30] Literally "but." Often used by Tasso in the sense of the Greek *dé*: "on the other hand, to be sure," or simply "and."

[31] Angels. The translation of lines 138-141 is partly conjectural because of Tasso's puzzling syntax.

and, as a falling and ruining mass,
already it would reel; thus One comes near
and reaches to it, One who sustains and supports[32]
and enlightens and inflames it by His love,
One who won't dissolve, who won't ever   150
fear death or ruin, nor fall nor collapse
for the succession of times or any rebellion
—although some may cite Ixion's wheel
and the tired Mauritanian's weight,[33]
but the heavenly home, that will be our own, rests
in Him, and by gazing at Him, it achieves eternity.
And She, next to God from the beginning,
even before He made his fine work,
was with Him in the beginning, when He willed
to shape amazing things with his words.   160

 God is good: a quiet, clear water spring,
indeed a sea of goodness, deep and wide,
not diminished or upset by any envy.
And what is good and fully perfect in itself
shares: pours its goodness onto others as well.[34]
So He, full and fertile of His own goodness,
spread beneficence like a sea shedding its waves,
unfolded like a sun unfolding its rays,
joining His nature and will into one.[35]
The created things were then like buds   170
or births, in which you can glimpse Him
more or less clearly; and in the highest
to the lowest[36] He still gleams and shines.
And in all creatures did the Creator imprint
a high sign of goodness, and figured them inside;
but of His goodness the true image
appears elsewhere,[37] and they, noble-featured,
can properly raise their heads towards the sky,[38]

---

[32] One of the most interesting cosmic/scientific views in Tasso. We may call it *the dynamism of Entropy* (see especially lines 144-145) *and Negentropy*. We are here light-years away from Dante's cosmology.

[33] Atlas, identified with a mountain in Northern Africa.

[34] A concept that passed from Plotinus to the Church Fathers, to the Medieval and Renaissance theologians.

[35] God is both good-natured and good-willed; out of His *intrinsic* goodness, He *decides* to *communicate* it.

[36] Paraphrasing the very beginning of Dante's *Paradiso*.

[37] In humankind.

showing in themselves a part of His divinity.
Indeed, among all created things, none[39]   180
is so low in value or appearance, or so far
from the pure, shining forms in the sky;
none moves or slithers along a tiring path,
or clings to the earth, or to a hard rock
washed by the sea is seen adhering,
or lying in a swamp or a deep valley,
that one may not find and admire
the wonderful art of its eternal Master,[40]
who out of nothing made both art and artworks.

   This[41] was, of the created world, the one   190
high Cause, that fulfills the many effects
of Himself while infinitely transcending them;
and never mean or sparing with his gifts
does He his abundance share. To this still
add His glory, that must not remain in hiding.[42]
And, as in heaven among starry cloisters
in that eternal temple sacred to His name
are those[43] who worship Him, with perpetual sound
praising and singing Him with high immortal voice,
making the East, West, North, and South   200
happily resound with the honor of Him,
and the ancient mountains of eternity
all resound in that celestial harmony
—so must the Earth here below have His
worshipers and those who, in sonorous hymns,
devote to God their sacrifice of praise.
So that with the high, supreme divine goodness
fulfilled, His glory may also full-fill,

---

[38] Not only Biblical but also classical anthropology, see Ovid's *Metamorphoses*, the very first lines. It must also be remembered that the Italian word "cielo" means both sky and heaven, with easy interchanges. Dante's *Paradiso*, i.e. supposedly the supernatural heaven, is in fact the physical universe.

[39] An Aristotelian teaching seeps into a basically Platonic worldview. Tasso will always oscillate between the love and the hate of this world. So did Dante, though less evidently, cf. Dario Rivarossa, *Dante Was a Fantasy Writer* (International Authors, 2013). For the praise of reptiles, insects, etc., see also William Blake, another paradoxical example of a poet and thinker who was a pantheist and a (dualistic) Gnostic at the same time.

[40] Cf. Dante, *Inferno* 19: 10-11; *Purgatorio* 10: 99, etc.

[41] The communication of God's goodness.

[42] A general opinion, but more specifically echoing Dante, *Paradiso* 29: 14-15.

[43] The angels. Cf. the words "on earth as it is in heaven" in the Lord's Prayer, already referred to the angelic and human liturgies by Dante, *Purgatorio* 11: 10-12.

and fill the Whole, and with His rays
illumine the middle and the extremes.   210
     And now: what God, who is without beginning
and end, had fixed to himself from eternity,
was due to begin, and the time had come
together with the advent of time: As out of
a vortex or out of a quiet, deep lake,
still and stagnant without motion or waves,
a quick stream sometimes springs;
similarly, out of Eternity revolving enclosed
around itself, its own center and sphere,[44]
now Time took its motion and route;   220
when its Creator made room for its passing
and eternal Stillness gave a measure to it.
Just the invisible, nearly unperceivable objects
were before (provided "before" makes sense),
along with the seeds of the sensible ones.
Then it all began, when the high Father
(who doesn't leave the Son and Spirit behind
in the external works, all common to Them)[45]
gave the chosen beginning to the new world,
He, older and prior to every created thing,   230
by creating the sky above, the Earth below.
     But[46] as in a sublime and beautiful building
matching the tops of the highest hills
and hiding its golden roofs among the clouds,
its base, its firm foundation, is not yet
the building we see; and in a steep path
the starting point is not the same as the path;
so is the fixed point, in which "Time in itself"[47]
turns, not the same as the space or time

---

[44] A well-known metaphor, used and reused from the times of Plotinus and Proclus (see BB) to the Medieval *Book of the Twenty-Four Philosophers* (see Panikkar), to Blaise Pascal.

[45] A common tenet of Scholastic theology: every action happening *outside* God (creation, history of salvation, grace) is the work of the three Persons together, although we tend to ascribe some things to the Father, others to the Son, etc.

[46] Several of the following examples come from St. Basil's *Hexaemeron* ("The Six Days" of Creation), "read by Tasso in his *Complete Works* published in Venice in 1548" (BB). *Il Mondo Creato* is replete with quotations from St. Basil, a fourth century Cappadocian monk who is one of the mainstays of theology for the East European Orthodox Churches, but was—and is—much less known in the Western world, and even less in Catholically-monopolized Italy.

[47] "Time in itself," as opposite to the flux of time, is a Platonic concept known by Tasso through St. Basil (BB).

9

that starts from a beginning and returns there.   240
In the beginning, God made the outer circle;
and this,[48] appearing to us as a firm and still
seat, He made in the center of the wide wheel.
Nor was this just a shadowy effect of His
power, nor disjoined from His eternal will
(as sometimes a shadow belongs to the opaque,
thick body, and light and rays to the shining one),
but His will turned into power and precious work.

And, as a good craftsman in Lesbos or Samos
makes thousands of pots in clay, and in a thousand   250
ways he then colors and paints them,
nor does his endless art performing those
works exhaust its own power and skill;
so the World-Maker has not a power just
for one world, since He surpasses the Whole
and transcends a thousand worlds[49] and the infinite.

He[50] who, in the various and immeasurable fields
where no high and no low place can be found
nor can the left or right side be marked,
out of[51] the casual meeting of tiny bodies   260
moved by Chance and flying in long wanderings
—like those that, where the sun shines,
we can see in varying, mixed multitude—
He makes various worlds, and reforms and
destroys, all different in place and shape,
while He unites or divides them...
He weaves, like Arachne's web, a frail tissue,

---

[48] The Earth.

[49] "Thousand/endless worlds" may hint at the controversial cosmological doctrines of Giordano Bruno, who was sent to the stake in Rome in the year 1600 during the papacy of that same Clement VIII to whom *Il Mondo Creato* is dedicated. But Tasso couldn't know this, as the poem was composed in 1592 and he died in 1595. According to Tasso, God could create a thousand universes, to be sure—but He did not. We shouldn't take the value of infiniteness for granted. According to the Greek philosophers, in fact, "in-finite" meant "indefinite," therefore "im-perfect." Among Christian thinkers, Origen, e.g., said that God's perfect power was shown precisely in the fact that He created *one* universe. The positive meaning of the infinite was a modern shift, see Paolo Zellini, *A Brief History of Infinity* (Penguin Books, 2005).

[50] A hypothetical "God," Force, etc., as it was conceived by Democritus, Lucretius, and others. Even when Tasso disagrees with a doctrine or social habit, he can nevertheless describe it with sympathy and effect. Cf. (on the basis of the same sources, rather than for a direct influence) Dante, *Paradiso* 14: 112-117, and Milton's description of Chaos in *Paradise Lost*, bk. 2.

[51] To be linked with "makes" in line 264.

then so easily dispersed or dissolved
by the blow and breeze of errant Fortune
or by a capricious breath of uncertain path.   270
    But He[52] plants these—say—high columns
on a very solid base, on which the deepest Earth,
according to His will, finds a support;
and no storm and no twister can shake it,
but His will alone can move and shake it
—His will, that of endless abysses
has shadowy, dark, profound recesses.[53]
If *this* had been seen by the blind eyes
of him[54] who erased the boundaries of Cosmos
and knocked down its fiery walls   280
and crossed the Void with his thought, he would
not give the scepter and reign of heaven
and earth to an unseeing, misleading Goddess.[55]
Fool! Unable to recognize the way and art
by which creation follows the primal scheme
drawn by the divine Architect in himself:
much greater than the work then offered
as an object to be admired by our senses.
So, as an earthly master sculpts and shapes
the sky in precious stone, in a small circle,   290
together with its bright, splendid signs,
so did the immortal smith imprint in these
errant spheres strewn with many lights
His inner Idea, unparalleled by the Whole
—Matter being defeated by this, and losing.
And Matter was created by the first Master
who made the work, not made elsewhere,
and in vain is a different origin searched for.
She[56] turns to her Creator, she gets dressed for Him,
glad of her own beauty, and in her rough womb   300

---

[52] Now Tasso means the "true" God.

[53] The Christian tradition, especially in Neoplatonic and mystical milieus, Dante included, spoke of God's "abysses," but Tasso's abysses are more uncanny.

[54] Epicurus.

[55] Reason, according to BB; and in fact, Tasso will often stress the limits of human intellect. But "Goddess Reason" is a 18th century phrase. A reference to Fortune (see already line 269) seems more likely. Cf. Dante, *Inferno* 7: 77 ff., but among the two Christian poets more differences than similarities surface here. In *Gerusalemme Conquistata*, Canto 18, Tasso even creates a huge, powerful fighting devil, a Poseidon-like "sea Satan," whose name is precisely Fortune.

[56] Matter, a feminine noun in Italian.

11

she colors a thousand forms, ignites a thousand
lamps out of light,[57] in all kinds of ways.
    Those[58] who pose two Principles and a double source,
deriving goodness from one side, from the other
originating just wide streams of evil,
must either divide the Reign or double it,
and imagine a King of darkness, to adorn
and impose on him a crown of evilness.
If it were so, Matter would be a rebel
in contrast, or maybe shy and slow   310
she would appear under a contrary garb
to Him who enamored and pleased her.
But we see that she, all longing and ready,
welcomes the forms, and transmutes and varies
them so as to please Him who adorns her so.
She looks steadier in her most beautiful works,[59]
and meets her own wishes for the sake of them,
so she refuses to lose them, at least before
the precarious world staggers, and the oblique
run of the sun and wandering stars cease forever.   320
Regardless, let Matter in sky be this or another
of a different kind, never could she boast
eternity, nor dare to liken herself, as to
her old age and age-honored status, to the
ancient Father of her and of everything,
and the ancient Lord, and the ancient God.
    His exhaling Spirit did create her
not *after* nor *before* but *with* her forms;
and He of His divine beauty and goodness
inspired her with a desire deep within,   330
a vague, indistinct, indeed a pleasant love,
that put an end to the native, dreadful[60] war
in which she, reluctant, wicked and rebellious,
in her fury was at variance with herself
—provided we can say earth and fire were

---

[57] In Italian, "sua luce," that may mean either "her own light" or "His" (God's).

[58] "The Manichees" in Tasso's notes, i.e., Gnostic thinkers. Tasso had the old arguments of the Church Fathers handy, but these and other ancient religious worldviews had surfaced again in his own times.

[59] A concept that will play a basic role much later, in Day 6, in dealing with hybrids and monsters.

[60] "Orrida," one of Tasso's favorite adjectives (cf. "orribil" in line 336), that he uses with a lot of meanings: dreadful, hideous, horrible, dark, bristling... like *horridus* in Latin.

mixed in that hideous confusion.
There wasn't fire, nor earth; and air and water
destroyed one another in their contrary natures.
And each of them amid that uncertain
acquisition lost itself,[61] and a fierce death   340
was its victory; and the *below* badly adapted
to the *above*, and was badly confused with it.
Therefore that rough, upset mass was not
the Whole; not Nothing but looked like nothing.
This was maybe just an imagined war,
the image and shadow of another[62] war-to-be,
and the simulacrum of that evil battle
that made Nature the enemy of her Maker.
But the high God almost suddenly created
both matter and forms; and which first,   350
these or that, I will not boast of being
able to prove in a perilous harangue like
a disciple from the Academy or the Lyceum.
For the divine art[63] comes first, and beats
any other by dignity, and defeats Time;
while human art just childishly plays[64]
around its own works as if it were a joke.

First[65] must the white wool clothe the docile
lambs, then it will be woven and dyed
by a skilled dyer; and from inside wet shells   360
people from Sidon and Tyre pick purple
like sea flowers. And first the tall pine tree
with sharp needles on green mountains
grows—or the fir, the manna-ash, the oak—
then technique makes ships and spears.
The reluctant earth first in her wide womb
hides the iron, thence drawn and shaped
by human industry as swords or shiny helms

---

[61] Echoing the dreadful, hideous, etc., metamorphoses in Dante's *Inferno*, see especially 25: 72, 110. Tasso's description of Chaos is as powerful as Milton's, although the former pretends not to "believe" in any Chaos before creation. See line 345.

[62] That of—Gnostic—Nature against God, according to BB; or rather it could be identified with Satan's rebellion, see the two following lines. In this case, "Nature" in line 348 should be rendered as "nature," uncapitalized, i.e. a created nature, a creature. But, all in all, it is only a matter of nuances, given the nature of Nature in Gnostic dualism.

[63] In the Latin/Medieval/Renaissance broader sense of art, technique, skills, craftsmanship, see e.g. line 365.

[64] "Pargoleggia," a verb invented by Dante (*Purgatorio* 16: 87).

[65] The following examples come from St. Basil, except for that of mining (BB).

14

or harmless plows for man's hard fields.[66]

Now Divine Art, existing before time   370
and before the world, made heaven and earth,
and everything whole, with no part being
left behind, filling the extremes and the core;
and it there set fire, and air, and Water[67]
which all around the heavy, still[68] earth
spread her arms murmuring, ever-
wandering but heavy; and in a circle
surrounded by lighter and more variable air;
and He put the lightest fire as a crown
to it, setting it closer to the sky.   380
So the divine art tied together,
like a solid many-ringed chain,
the various and clashing elements;
and between the opposite extremes
placed—partly contrary, partly friendly—
the middle two, and by this He created
a steady, firm, indissoluble bond.

Still invisible was the bare earth, just then
created, without any ornaments,
like a new theater[69] with empty seats,   390
without anyone watching or struggling;
for the wretched mortals weren't born yet
to see her,[70] and a vast and absolutely
waste loneliness filled the fields,
massifs, and desert sands with horror.
The high-reaching trees hadn't displayed yet
their shadowy foliage, their leaves and shadow
did not make a fine scene of green hills.

---

[66] Cf. *Isaiah* 2: 4. Tasso, as it often happens, mixes contemporaneity and literary/Biblical references.

[67] The water element was the one that most fascinated Tasso, see both Jerusalem-poems, e.g. *Gerusalemme Liberata*, Canto 14 (the origin of all waters), and *Gerusalemme Conquistata*, Canto 8 (the five symbolic rivers).

[68] Tasso sticks to the Earth-centered pattern of universe. At that time, the "Galileo Affair" had not broken out yet, though discussions about the shape of the universe were already going on. Ludovico Ariosto liked joking on this topic. Tasso shifts the question to a more interesting level: the universe as something *interdisciplinary* being *told*.

[69] Another of Tasso's favorite images.

[70] The earth was invisible *because* nobody saw it: this recalls such philosophical concepts as Berkeley's *esse est percipi* (being is being perceived) or Arthur Schopenhauer's World as *Vorstellung*/Representation. See also Owen Barfield's *Saving the Appearances* (Wesleyan UP, 1988), ch. 1.

Roses and privets didn't flower yet,
nor did hyacinths, narcissuses, and others,   400
nor did they paint the grassy meadows within,
nor did they wreathe the clear springs.
She was still nearly all underwater,
for the veil was dark and shadowy
which hid her then dismal[71] face
and dreary limbs and rough womb:
still astonished was the Ancient Mother.
And the sublime sky was unadorned yet,
nor did its distinct, wonderful work[72]
shine with a serene clearness, golden frills   410
and bright signs. And the revolving Sun
didn't shake his burning, immortal lamp.
And in her full circle, the white Moon was not
in opposition to him, nor with silver horns
turned her route along a twisted path.
The dances and voices and choirs[73] were missing,
and of both fixed and wandering stars
no high crowns encircled him[74] yet.
The sweet[75] light hadn't been created either,
but on the face of the dark abysses   420
there were dark shadows. That way,
while being born, the world was unseen.
    But what were (if we can look into this)
those ancient shadows, those abysses,
when no Sun yet brought the day to other
peoples,[76] to us the night and shadows,
out of the opaque and dense womb
of the Earth, reaching as far as the sky?
Neither those abysses were many contrasting
Powers, as some[77] wrongly maintain.   430

---

[71] Again "orrida."

[72] The Zodiac.

[73] The "music of the spheres" (rotating skies) and/or the angels, who—according to Tasso and his sources—were created together with the light.

[74] The Sun, that was considered the primal source of all the light of the stars.

[75] "Vaga," an almost untranslatable Italian adjective. Its root conveys the idea of vagueness or wandering (cf. "vagabond"), but in 16th-19th century poetry it meant a sweet, sublime beauty. The Hazon-Garzanti English-Italian Dictionary suggests "graceful, pretty," but they don't work very well here. The most famous quote in Italian literature is Giacomo Leopardi's 1830 poem starting with: *Vaghe stelle dell'Orsa*, "You, sweet stars of Ursa…"

[76] Another hint, in passing, at the discovery of America, or other lands.

[77] Gnostics. Basil mentions Marcion and Valentine in his *Hexaemeron* (BB).

Nor was Darkness against Goodness,
and an evil Archon[78] of great strength,
for, if Evil were equal to Goodness
in power and valor, a perpetual war
there would be, perpetual death indeed,
both victors and defeated dying together.
But, if Goodness is more powerful, and wins,
why doesn't this eradicate, destroy Evil?

Ha, will there ever be an evil-less world
abounding in good only, with no part   440
or place left to unbearable Death?
So that Life may triumph, killing Death[79]
in its victory, and of the ancient fraud[80]
no trace or vestige may be left among us.

Now, let no insulting tongue dare—
no profane, dirty tongue aiming at God
by darting and shooting blasphemies—
dare ever affirm that evil comes as
begotten by Him, who's the great source
from which all good pours down onto us.[81]   450
In fact (mark well) no contrary can be
begotten or produced by the other;
indeed,[82] if one chances to fall
dead, the other would rise and live.
Further, things are produced and begotten
by similar things, as fire is by fire.
So, out of bright Light man tries in vain
to give a beginning to evil darkness,
and out of death to originate life,
or out of illness yield health to us weak[83]   460
and wretched mortals. Don't be deceived
by any false likeness and mask of truth!

Evil is not nature, is not actual substance:
Neither search for it in any faraway place,

---

[78] Tasso uses a more general term, "podestà": power, authority.
[79] Cf. *I Corinthians* 15: 54-55.
[80] Original sin, the "channel" through which death reached humankind. See e.g. *Romans* 7: 11-13; *James* 1: 15.
[81] Cf. *James* 1: 17.
[82] *Benché* usually means "even though," but here the context would suggests *ben che*, "it may *well* be that…," therefore, "it *does* happen that…"
[83] Possibly a half-hidden attack against (black) magic. Herb healers were seen quite positively in *Gerusalemme Liberata*, but less positively in the later *Conquistata*.

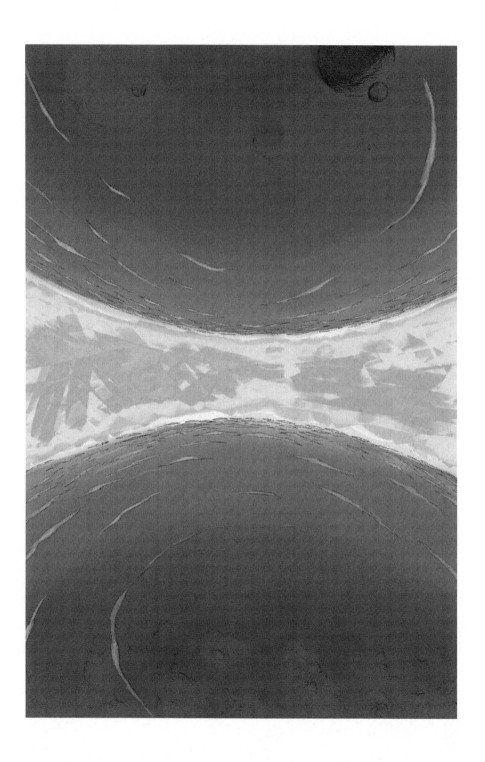

nor look around you or outside, as if
it were a thing, grounded in itself and firm;
but find it in yourself, inside your own soul
just gaze at it, the stain or shadow
of a voluntary and welcome fault.
You are constantly to yourself the smith   470
of your evils,[84] that you color and embellish,
and attracted by them with vain affections, you
worship them like beloved idols in yourself.

    But a life of shame, or in sad exile,
and hateful poverty,[85] and that—what
frightens us so much—hideous death,
are not true evils (so may fear now cease,
or flee away!). But in vain you search or hope
for true goods among their contrary here,
though it *is* an evil, when most needed,   480
to be deprived of them. So, a place bereft
of good may well symbolize Evil,
and those shadows (unless I rave) were,
in that blind and light-less atmosphere,
an old or rather new quality, or effect.
But if those shadows were older than the newborn
universe, Evil would be ancient and prior;
but it is improper for the worst things to be older.
Before the world, then, was eternal Light,
with external darkness[86] around the cosmos: 490
Light only shining to the blessed minds,
not to senses, but to what enlightens senses.
And this adorned mass exposed to our senses,
this visible light, is only an image of Light;[87]
an image adorning itself by the Primal Pattern;
a Pattern from which far are the sunbeams
often jammed by clouds or shadow.
    Before the world, there was uncreated[88] light,

---

[84] The significant overturning of an optimistic Latin saying: *Faber est suae quisque fortunae*, "Each of us is the smith of their own luck."

[85] Tasso knew these things all too well, as Dante did (see *Paradiso* 17: 55-60, etc.). As for "shame," in 1579-1586 Tasso had been shut up in a private asylum.

[86] A New Testament phrase meaning hell (see *Matthew* 22: 13, etc.; see below, line 524) but here apparently mixing with a physical *outer* space, outside of the borders of the cosmos, like Chaos in *Paradise Lost*.

[87] The fascinating topic of the relationship between divine/spiritual and material light: see Robert Grosseteste, Dante, Milton… Tasso here equalizes cosmic *mass* and *light*.

20

perhaps, and created; and not only a thousand
and a thousand decades, but flying aeons   500
kept on turning before the world was.
And near-eternities (if I may speak so)
came before the cosmos and our time,[89]
since the creation, in the first Light,
of the second splendors—the holy angels.
The heavenly Principalities could not, in fact,
nor could the sublime Dignities and Virtues
—so many formations above, armed in gold
and *electrum*, glorious, immortal, noble,
so many of His armies[90]—live such a long   510
shadowy life, dim in darkness.
    So, if at first there were created minds,
there was created light; and with joy and songs
they already lived a shining life
in the likeness of Him, who is Life and Light,
performing holy dances and happy choirs
and sacrifices of most high praise
to the splendor of His eternal glory
in that serene and luminous temple.[91]
And this very light did the old Fathers[92]   520
promise to the righteous; and they will have
immortal light forever, called to partake
in the light of Saints—while the unrighteous
spirits will have pain in the external darkness.
    However, in the shadows of blind abysses
and over the waters, the divine Spirit

---

[88] BB interprets as "not (yet) created," but here the ambivalent Italian word *increata* probably makes reference to God's own "non-created" light. Tasso, following St. Basil and in general the Eastern European Orthodox theologies, says that *maybe* a spiritual universe—made up by God and angels—came before the material one, and it lasted a very long time. This goes against Dante's angelology (*Paradiso* 29: 37-45), that, in fact, will be refuted by Tasso later on. This is not a futile debate, it touches on the perception of the role of (corporeal, material) humanity in the universe. Tasso is much less anthropocentric than Dante, as this very de-structured *MC* shows.

[89] Properly speaking—according to Scholastic theologians, at least—angels don't perceive our time, or time as we do, but *aevum*, which is not based on the passing of "things" but on one's own states of consciousness. It may still be called "time," in the sense the word has for Kant and Schopenhauer.

[90] In the *Divine Comedy*, angels were luminous messengers. In Ariosto's *Orlando Furioso*, they started to play military roles, but with parodic outcomes. With Tasso, and then Milton, the militarization of angels is complete.

[91] Vaguely echoing Dante, *Paradiso* 28: 53.

[92] The writers of the Bible.

21

already had flown to prepare the wet
element; He also sharing the work
by inspiring strength and virtue[93] in the waves,
like a bird who, out of a frail shell   530
brooded and filled with her vital heat,
draws her featherless, nearly shapeless son.[94]
And He said, "Light be made!"[95] and His *word*
was *work*, as soon as the eternal Father spoke.
His speech was not the sound of a tongue
being moved or blown, imprinting the air
with itself, "in-forming"[96] it by its voice;
but of the holy Will, inclined to His works,
the very inclination is the inner word.[97]

    Thus, the primal voice and command   540
of the great Father of heaven suddenly made
the most clear, pure, and beautiful light
which was at first gathered, then divided
into many lamps on the fourth day.[98]
He cleared horror, He dispersed darkness,
He illumined the blind world from many sides,
He showed the sweet face of the sky,
He revealed, with serene, noble features,
the other graceful shapes;[99] and everywhere
He led forward the dear, happy Sight,   550
the joy of Nature, the noble delight
of heaven and earth, the pleasure and glory
of mind and senses, almost the proof[100]

---

[93] In the sense of "generating power," see Dante, *Purgatorio* 25: 52, etc.

[94] As explained by BB, this beautiful paraphrase of *Genesis* 1: 2 has a long tradition in Biblical commentaries. See also Milton's account of the creation in *Paradise Lost*, Book 7.

[95] "Fatta sia luce" in the Italian text, modifying its more usual rendering, "*Sia la luce!*" By following closely the former wording in the translation, we can avoid the somewhat misleading formula "Let there be light!" since, in fact, there was no one "letting" God do what He did.

[96] In the Scholastic sense of the verb "to inform," the inner principle giving shape to anything. Here the Latin word *forma* translates the Aristotelian concept of μορφη.

[97] The "inner word" being expressed, in man, by the "external word" is an Augustinian theme.

[98] According to Tasso and his sources, as well as Milton afterwards, the light of the sun and the stars was "inserted" into them by God by using the "general" light created on the first day.

[99] What? There was nothing to see yet. Tasso probably anticipates future events, as he often does.

of both mortal and eternal things.
And in a trice, the North and the South
as well as the West and the East
were all irrigated by the golden light.
It looked like a wonderful chariot
much faster than time and thought,[101]
shedding and giving divine virtue.   560
 And what faster or more beautiful cart
—O most beautiful light, O light, friend
of Nature and of the human mind,
you serene image of the Godhead,
comforting and calling us to heaven—[102]
could bring virtues and heavenly gifts
all around to us wretched mortals
from those eternal treasuries and realms;
to us dispensed with generous hand
by the Father of lights,[103] the bountiful Giver?   570
 As a powerful Persian or Indian king
from the dark womb of a reluctant earth
draws the most precious metals,
and from sands sprinkled with gold
and from the sea depths he gathers
pearls and purple, and adds the rubies,
beautiful emeralds, bright amethysts,
and the most valuable luminous gems[104]
that in the Orient harden and petrify;
so the High King of the universe,   580
hidden in Empyrean to our vague senses[105]
and unknown to the minds of geniuses[106]
who measured the turns and tracks of stars,
owns eternal and rich treasures of divine
light, that He either shares or keeps.

---

[100] The Italian words "a prova" are not very clear. BB interprets them as *a gara*, "in competition," as it is often the case in *MC*, but it does not fit the context here. By rendering it as "[providing] a proof" we have *Romans* 1: 20 in mind.

[101] A fascinating pre- (or post-?) Relativity view. Cf., in part, John Milton, *Paradise Lost* 6: 752 and 8: 110-114.

[102] This brief and wonderful Hymn to Light will be developed in *Paradise Lost* 3: 1-55 by Milton, who will have even more profound and tragic reasons to do so.

[103] *James* 1: 17.

[104] Amber.

[105] Cf. *I Timothy* 6: 16.

[106] A cutting remark against the "too daring" astronomers of his times. Unlike Dante and Milton.

Heaven itself is indeed pure light,
in which nothing ever darkens or mixes.
Light is His adorned temple, His high palace;
made of light are the crowns and weapons
with which He covers his chosen ones.   590
    But, seeing his created light here below,
He said it was good, adding the testimony
of his voice—his clear judgment, indeed.
And since Light is good and beautiful,[107] no source
of pride[108] for the beauty of co-joined parts
being composed with exact measures[109]
is left to earthly nature, though sublime;
nor can it, in a green, deep valley, be found
by an incautious shepherd's erring judgment
and false sentence. So, Hesperus[110] in the sky,   600
may the lustful eyes admire Hesperus in the sky,
then becoming Lucifer[111] in bringing the day
together with the clear, longed-for light;
she may satisfy the senses with her[112] purity,
and the mind may ascend to its primal objects.[113]
    Therefore God divided the bright light
from the dark shadows, and gave them names
calling the latter "night," the former "day."
And He made one day, morning to evening,[114]
between dark and luminous borders limited   610
on both sides; a day to which the rotating
Sun did not set its lofty goal—while
turning and coming back to itself—
as the Sun had yet no shape or path.
But He, the eternal forger of time,
gave time both space and measure and signs;

---

[107] "Good and beautiful" are the two meanings of the Hebrew adjective *tov* (*Genesis* 1: 4, etc.), usually translated as "good." There is no evidence that Tasso knew Hebrew, but the study of this language flourished in the Renaissance, so he might have received some notions from the scholars in the Courts he was in touch with.

[108] A typo in BB: " ...bella, e non si vanti," where "e" (= and) must be deleted.

[109] The Renaissance ideal of Beauty, especially with reference to the human—and more specifically, female—body; in line 599 the judgment of Paris is mentioned.

[110] The evening star, that is the *true* Venus to be admired, Tasso says.

[111] The morning star, again Venus; nothing to do with the devil here.

[112] The heavenly, not the sexy, Venus. C. S. Lewis' *Perelandra* comes to the mind, where "Perelandra" is precisely Venus (planet and "goddess").

[113] The supreme truths/realities, according to Scholastic theology.

[114] But in the Bible, and in Jewish culture in general, the day begins with the evening.

and with the *four* and the *three* He turned
its measures, filling with one day
—seven times turning and coming back—
by that number the whole space.   620
   This figure[115] has its own beginning and end,
and it does fit eternity, not only time,
indeed it is like a very mainstay of time;
so it still boasts[116] being the first day
since its Creator divided it from the others,
as dispelled and obscure, and marked it with
His own seal, and it proceeds on its own.
This is the Lord's Day, named after Him,
as it disdains being named after the Sun;[117]
chasing away the wretched profane ones[118]   630
busy with tiring and base works.
This is the Lord's Day, great and illustrious;
in the end, whenever it may be, it will be cut
from the number of days, of years indeed,
and decades, and of running centuries;
nor any day will be second or third to it.
   Thus to you, who wait for the Lord's Day:[119]
don't follow old dreams, and the shadows
of such a day in any frightful darkness.
Follow, rather, that eighth,[120] new light   640
that now gleams and shines for you; the one
that doesn't laboriously run to vesper,
that has no evening or dark limits, nor
is it followed, turning alternatively,
by another day bounded by the enemy night;

---

[115] The Seven, as well as the seventh day and the first day (line 624) in the weekly calendar. But this whole section is all too laborious as to syntax and contents.

[116] Conjectural translation of a verb, "si sdegna," that's hardly understandable in this context (it is clearer in line 629). Unless—see the following three lines—Tasso makes hidden reference to himself; cf. Dante, *Paradiso* 17: 69. "And what's much more, much more than this, I did it my way."

[117] The Latin name of the seventh day was *(dies) dominica*, the Lord's Day, hence the Italian "domenica." Tasso apparently doesn't approve of the "heathen" name "Sunday," although the Sun was a symbol of Christ.

[118] "Miseri profani," a literal quotation from Dante, *Inferno* 6: 21. A powerful rendition of the concept of the weekly day of rest, seeing human life as mud and useless toil. Plus Virgil's famous warning *procul O procul este profani* (*Aeneid* 6: 258).

[119] Eschatological movements were not lacking in the Renaissance.

[120] The "eighth day," the eternal... Sunday (*oops*). The *dies dominica* can be either the seventh or the first, and therefore the eighth, day; according to one's way of considering sacred times.

26

and there will be a constantly happy state,
at last; and it[121] will remain one, solely one.
One day, or one century, becoming eternal:
this you were shown in the primal times
by the clear voice of prophetical spirit.[122]   650
This He then showed when He[123] rose
like a lion,[124] He, the heavenly King,
and triumphed over the shadowy hell.
And the one struggling and winning for Him,
the Holy Roman Church, teaches you this,
which celebrates this day with holy notes,
amid endless sacred and golden furnishings.[125]
And from his highest throne of prayer
he[126] also blesses and points this day out;
he whose holy kingdom in heaven and earth   660
has no limits or borders. And rightly will
the eighth Clement on the eighth day
enlighten the very choirs[127] of divine light
—as well as the rough, dark, and slow minds.[128]

---

[121] The eighth day.

[122] "Di/del profetico spirito" quotes Dante, *Paradiso* 12: 141, who however, more daringly, referred to a heretical thinker, Joachim of Fiore.

[123] Christ, see *John* 20: 26.

[124] See *Revelation* 5: 5—and C. S. Lewis' character Aslan in *The Chronicles of Narnia*.

[125] Catholic Baroque liturgies. "Furnishings" translates *spoglie*, an unusual word in this context, but absolutely usual in war poems, where it means "spoils." In both of his *Jerusalems*, Tasso described their choreographic—and in a way also sacred—effect.

[126] Pope Clement VIII. Tasso plays with the number 8 in his name.

[127] The angels. Each liturgy is (supposed to be) a cosmically-blessing event.

[128] An indirect and conventionally humble call for sponsorship. Not in vain, as the Pope and his noble family, the Aldobrandini, actually helped poor Tasso during the last years of his life.

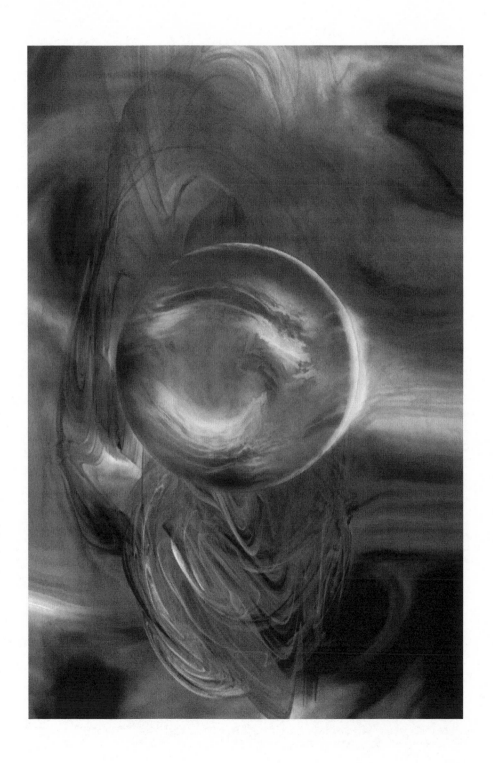

Day Two

B efore the doors of that wonderful temple[1]
that was moved from one place to another,
the open areas remaining in the open air,
uncovered by a roof, unshadowed by a veil,
were exposed to frost, exposed to ice,
to the turbid blowing of irritating winds,
and to the summer rays of the burning Dog;[2]
and out there the profane crowds gathered,
and the herds and flocks doomed to the blade.
Such are the places in which the world   10
houses us, in its deep and darkest part.[3]
    After speaking of the temple and earthly things,
now, from the misty, obscure darkness already
passing to the serene clearness, we are
where the candelabrum[4] appears divided
into seven lights: inextinguishable,
joyful, safe from the blowing Auster, a lamp
here lighted to God, and the pure dwelling
keeps its sacred parts uncontaminated
by filthy feelings and brute desires.   20
    Away, away, O profane ones, stand aside![5]
Who will remove the veil[6] from the great mysteries,
so that we may see, flaming on high,
the winged Cherub as it appeared then?
Already had the Father created—in the Son,
Son who is the Principle[7]—the first heaven,[8]

---

[1] The tent containing the Ark of Covenant during the Exodus.

[2] The so-called "dog days," in fact. Tasso was a great "painter" of landscapes, though he often set the events of the Holy Land in a European-like climate; see both Jerusalem-poems.

[3] Implying that the *whole* world is a hellish, deep (at the bottom of the universe), and dark place.

[4] Cf. the *Menorah*, here—in my opinion—used as a symbol of the seven Upper Angels in Jewish, Patristic and Renaissance traditions. Tasso's wording recalls *Revelation* 1: 12, 20, and also Dante, *Purgatorio* 29: 50, 76, referring to the seven gifts of the Holy Spirit. "Seven Spirits" anyway.

[5] A plain translation of Virgil's *procul O procul este profani* (cf. above, 1: 630).

[6] A spiritual/moral interpretation of the *Sancta Sanctorum*; cf. the *Letter to the Hebrews*, especially ch. 9. But the "flaming Cherub" comes indirectly from *Genesis* 3: 24.

the one beyond the beautiful[9] starry circles;
already a quiet, steady peace was enjoyed,
undisturbed, unchanged by motions on the right
nor, on the left, by any round routes.   30
And with the Empyrean heaven[10] of pure minds
the angelic splendors being lighted together,
the Supreme Sun's rays already spread about.
And if other angels were created elsewhere,
they were of a lesser rank, and less high
were their seats and duties and works.
Already their knowledge[11] passes from
morning to evening; as in a luminous dawn,
each brightens in truth by gazing at God;
but in material things that knowledge darkens   40
and nearly sets; while grace and merit[12] already
make them blessed, and fill them, and adorn.

    The eternal Forger, in continuing
his holy wonders day by day,
said, "*Be*, and be solid and firm
between the waters, O star-strewn sky,[13]
dividing the waters from the waters!"
And He made a clear sky sprinkled with stars,
of great strength against the passing time
and firm in the turning of a long route,   50
so that, as the other skies keep moving,

---

[7] In addition to *John* 1: 1 ff., see *John* 8: 25 in the *Vulgate* version, when Jesus is asked, "Who are you?" and he answers: *Principium, qui et loquor vobis* ("The Principle, now even talking to you").

[8] The Empyrean, therefore more "heaven" than "sky"—but both have the same name in Italian, "cielo."

[9] Once again, the polysemous Italian adjective "vaghi," see above, Day 1.

[10] "Empireo ciel," echoing Dante, *Inferno* 2: 21. "Of pure minds" can refer either to "heaven" or to "splendors," given Tasso's fanciful syntax; or rather a Latinizing one, but since Italian has no grammatical cases, his sentences are often quite thorny.

[11] The double knowledge angels supposedly have of things: *cognitio matutina* (in the morning) and *vespertina* (in the evening), reinterpreting the verses of *Genesis* 1—a famous doctrine by St. Augustine. Morning knowledge, the superior one = of all things in God; evening knowledge = of all things according to the things themselves.

[12] That Is The Question! But Tasso simply mentions the topic. Dante ventures something more in the parallel text of *Paradiso* 29: 61-66; perhaps Tasso takes Dante's explanation for granted.

[13] The Biblical "firm-ament," a sort of immense transparent dome dividing the waters of the Earth from the mysterious "heavenly" ones; see below (lines 53-57). But Tasso is a bit inconsistent, as he will later say that the stars were created after the sun in the fourth day. Another inconsistency is the simultaneous adoption of the Greek cosmic pattern (the spheres) and the Biblical one (the firmament as a solid vault).

it may be their certain rule and law.
By density, He distinguished waters:
either wandering,[14] thin, fine, quick, nimble,
or waters of a waving, or icy, solid
condensed nature. And He divided them,
leaving some of them below, some above.

    God did so, and giving a name to the sky
for its firmness, He called it "firmament"
—what man would then call starry sphere   60
or starry circles. And with this, the second
day was made, morning to evening.

    As Daedalus, or Skopas, or some other
ancient renowned master of noble craftsmanship
first gathers precious types of marble
and the glossy metals and select cedars,
which the envious teeth of time and age
will not be able to consume and erode;
he then shapes the whole, dividing, completing
the superb mass; and grounds its vaults   70
and its arches on high marble columns,
or he supports them by statues of Carya,[15]
making theaters and arcades, inside and around,
with works from Ionia or from Corinth—
so does the eternal Forger, out of matter,
first shape the universe; He then differentiates
the parts, and embellishes, and adorns.

    Neither is it true what has been claimed and described
by those sages of whom Greece is still so proud:
that He consumed all matter in the making   80
of one world and that would be the reason why
He made just one, encircling everything
and housing everything in its vast womb.

    Nor are endless the worlds and the skies
(as someone[16] says) which from the opposite side
the literary fury hurls in the quarrel.
But God, who begot the forms and produced,
at the same time, the matter of this world,

---

[14] "Vaghe." With a bit of happy non-philological imagination, these cosmic waters might be identified with plasma.

[15] Caryatids. Line 74 refers to the Ionian and Corinthian architectonic styles.

[16] Possibly, another reference to the doctrines of Giordano Bruno (see note at 1: 256), who spoke of endless worlds. The phrase "literary fury," *furor letterato*, would echo Bruno's *eroici furori*, heroic furies.

could make many of them, like bubbles
the wind blows out of foamy waters.   90
Yes: compared to the all-surpassing Power,
the worlds and skies are just bubble-like.[17]
    The eternal Forger nonetheless made *one*
world, as one was the Pattern, one the Master;[18]
and He shaped it by impressing his own power.
And one is its order; and as one it rotates,
though it divides into many spheres,[19] and turns.
The highest sphere, or supreme heaven,
with no motion—through which only man's weak
senses can know the eternal substances—   100
is no celestial body, but a pure form
burning and flaming with serene light;
that is called Empyrean heaven by us.
The other, being a bodily, wandering mass,
and being known by our errant senses,
divides into nine circles, and turns;
but about its matter there's quarrel and war,[20]
so that the dialectical quiver is full
of sharp syllogisms in competition,
arming the opposite enemy parties.   110
    Someone[21] forms and shapes it from the formless,
rough mixture whence the elements came:
a frail and transient sky, exposed to death.
But with an all-fulfilling form
an inner sweet desire keeps it alive,
a nearly eternal one, making it like
the eternal things with such a wonderful sight.[22]
Someone else[23] gathers and selects the noblest,
purest element out of filth and dregs,

---

[17] A paraphrase of Biblical passages like *Isaiah* 40: 15.

[18] A Platonic concept conveyed by St. Basil (BB).

[19] The nine concentric skies/spheres, as the universe was modelled: seven spheres—of Greek origin—rotating around the Earth, then the sphere of the Fixed Stars, and lastly—and last added—the invisible *Primo Mobile*, the First Mover, the origin of all cosmic movements.

[20] This pluralism was healthier than the scientific mono-morphism of nowadays; see Panikkar. The sources of the different hypotheses are listed in BB following Tasso's own hand-made notes (*Postille*).

[21] Johannes Gramaticus of Alexandria (JT), or Giovanni Filipino (BB).

[22] Egidius Romanus, or (according to JT) Egidio Colonna in *Contra gradus et pluralitates formarum*, XIV.

[23] Plato.

and by it he models the starry courts[24]   120
which receive their serene light from fire
and constancy and firmness from earth.
He frees the newly born world, like
a friendly judge, from frightful death;
though not by nature, forcefully subject
to the sad fate of shadowy death,
but because its Maker[25] holds and sustains
it, and by His will keeps it eternally.
    Another,[26] much closer to the primal times,
by alternating the turns of the world's four   130
different principles, makes and destroys it
according to Discord, according to Love:
if Discord is the winner in the war
against Love, the sensible world arises;
if vice versa Discord is defeated,
the victor Love then reshapes the world[27]
to the intellects,[28] and triumphs and reigns.
    Another[29] vexes and tires his vain awareness
in a turbid confusion, and mixes it with
endless parts, therefore in vain does   140
that crazy mind attempt all things
to divide them again. Another[30] creates
a bodily mass out of different figures
—thin fire from a sharp-peaked pyramid,
the firm earth out of square forms,
and with twenty faces the wandering, light,
blowing, floating air is made by him,
with eight[31] the water, wanting vain figures,
still and weightless—to give weight and body
to the four elements in so many fashions.   150
    Yet another[32] gives the sky a fifth essence,
free from all human qualities, and he
defends the sky from death and shields it

---

[24] Literally, "cloisters," as before.

[25] The Platonic Demiurge.

[26] Empedocles.

[27] This process had already been described by Dante, through Virgil, in *Inferno* 12: 41-43.

[28] Possibly, just a filler, i.e. "in the eyes of those who think about it."

[29] Anaxagoras.

[30] Pythagoras.

[31] But, in Pythagoras, the air corresponded to eight faces, the water to twenty (BB).

[32] Aristotle. The "quinta [fifth] essenza" is, in one word, the "quintessenza," quintessence.

33

against any lethal damage; eternal in its route,
turning and again turning in many circles,
like a longing lover, around its Mover.
    You know what?[33] Reason is short-winged[34]
behind deceiving senses, and no certain path
is shown us and pointed out by varying motions.
Why heavy bodies tend towards the center,   160
but the light ones ascend upwards,
and why non-light, non-heavy bodies[35]
turn and rotate around the center:
in any case, the human mind finds
no way open to unseen objects and it is
often darkened by the seen things too
—the others, too beamy, dazzle the mind's beams.[36]
    Of what matter stars and sky are made
may He tell us who did spread it around
like a small veil, or like light smoke   170
He did fix it, and He made it consistent
and more firm than ice-formed crystal
getting glossy among steep mounts;
more than metal petrifying, condensing[37]
and, like a mirror, returning one's image.
With a like matter the eternal Father
made therefore a pure crystal sky,
provided earthly things may be similar
to heavenly ones; and He made it
turn around the starry spheres as the   180
extreme border of the sensible cosmos,[38]
and He keeps the other waters above.
What waters, O God, did You put above
the stars and sun?[39] And why, or when,

---

[33] "Ma che?" A lively exclamation, not to be mistaken for *macché!*, "not at all!"

[34] From Dante, *Paradiso* 2: 56-57, but Tasso replaces the common word "ali" (wings) with the learned term "vanni." In stressing the limits of human reason, Dante half lies; Tasso doesn't.

[35] Probably respectively: earthly objects, fire, and water. What about air? To be listed together with fire or water?

[36] Especially in poetry, the eyes were called "lumi" or "rai" (= "raggi"), i.e. lights, lamps, beams, since sight was interestingly conceived as an *active* process, projecting rays onto objects. See Heisenberg's principle.

[37] Cf. in Catholic Bibles, the Hymn to Creation in *Ben Sirach* 43, here lines 19-20 (= *Ecclesiastici [liber]* 43: 21-22 in the Latin *Vulgate*).

[38] Both Satan (*Paradise Lost* 3: 540, in descending) and Dante (*Paradiso* 22: 119, in ascending) had the rare opportunity to walk on this outer limit of the universe.

did You retain or pour them as You please?
Are they the spiritual, quick substances[40]
by whom Your glorious, eternal Name
is sung with the most bright praises?
What, alas?[41] Do frost and fire praise You?
Are those waters perhaps the unformed[42] matter?   190
Do You from the beginning draw[43] and shape it?
Are heavy waters there, where the lighter air
cannot reach, flying below the sky, no higher?
Have laws been changed[44] for Nature in the sky?
But You opened the obscure doors of a disturbed
sky to the waters, and poured them onto the earth,
covering it and the highest mountains, when
—the world having been submerged by the Flood—[45]
on the Armenian mounts the seed of mortals
was barely saved in a frail wood-ship.   200
So, the waters up there in the sky are
eternal ministers of pain and terror
to the wretched mortals—or, are they
a relief and escape against the fire,[46]
so that the world may live in various fashions?
Fire is necessary to the usage and art
of our living, a natural friend of ours;
so are the waters, and from different seats
both elements guard against each other.
In comparison to the water, Earth[47] has   210
a small place and circle, the Ancient Mother;
that's why in the womb of dark abysses

---

[39] The questions Dante asks Virgil, Beatrix, or other personages simply aimed at prompting answers. In Tasso, and sometimes Milton, questions are often rhetorical.

[40] The angels, who, according to this hypothesis, would be symbolized by the upper waters.

[41] Again "ma che?" Also translates as "What of that?" or "What then?"

[42] Without the *forma* (*morphe* in Greek), the inner ontological and "morpho-logical" principle, the Aristotelian "act" shaping it. A pure abstraction, anyway, as any *actual* material already possesses "form."

[43] In the sense of drawing as art, as it is implied in the Italian technical verb *fingere*.

[44] Decontextualized quotation from Dante, *Purgatorio* 1: 46. This witty way of paying tribute to Dante by twisting his words was almost the rule in Ludovico Ariosto; but seldom in Tasso.

[45] Another reference to Biblical history. They appear occasionally in the poem as scattered cameos.

[46] Both in *Gerusalemme Liberata* and in *Gerusalemme Conquistata*, the Crusaders happen to be saved from enemies and from thirst by a sudden shower sent by God.

[47] Cf. *Moby-Dick*: Herman Melville's impression of the oceans, covering two thirds of the Earth's surface, as the "dark side" of the world.

she lay hidden, and now she scarcely
shows parts of her limbs, scarcely raises her
forehead out of foamy arms to the sky.

    Most of the sea yet lies in the depths,
but the waters are not only gathered in a dark
recess hidden inside a perpetual night,[48]
nor do they just run hidden underground,
but they are spread all over the earth's face.   220
Therefore, as we see, swamps and lakes stagnate,
and the clear springs rise murmuring,
and torrents and rivers fill their deep banks.
In the Orient, Hydaspes[49] and Indus run,
so do the Ganges, bigger than any other,
the Caspian, Araxes, Cyrus,[50] and Bactrus.
The Don,[51] whose waves the ice constricts,
flows down to the deep salty marsh,[52]
and from Caucasus the Phasis[53] to the Black Sea.[54]
And again, in the West, Tartessus[55] and Danube:[56]   230
the former flowing into the sea beyond the Pillars,[57]
the latter into Pontus after dividing
the peoples of Europe, and fields, and kingdoms.
Oh, how many from Hyperborean mounts
run swiftly, and from the Pyrenees and Alps,
bordering Germans and Belgians and Celts?
In the South, the Nile first floods Ethiopia,
then fertilizes the fields of green Egypt.
More: Cremetes, Egon, Nisava, "the Black."[58]

---

[48] Tasso thought that there was an underground "storehouse" of all waters, where they converged and were redistributed. He even makes us "visit" it in *Gerusalemme Liberata*, Canto 14, an episode anticipating Jules Verne.

[49] Now called Gilam, in India. For this whole section, BB's footnotes proved fundamental. Tasso found these lists in St. Basil's *Hexaemeron* and in Aristotle's *Meteorology*. In this translation, the names have been updated when they refer to well-known rivers; except when the "outdated" names had an important literary tradition.

[50] Two rivers of Armenia.

[51] Called "Tana" (like here) or "Tanai" in Medieval and Renaissance texts.

[52] The Sea of Azov.

[53] Now Rion.

[54] "Mare Eussino," from the Latin *Pontus Euxinus*.

[55] Guadalquivir.

[56] "Istro" in Old Italian.

[57] Of Hercules, i.e. Gibraltar.

[58] Respectively: the African Sakhiet, the Asian Egon(e), the Serbian Nisava ("Nisio"), the German Schwarzbach, whose name means precisely "Black River"; wrongly spelled "Swarzenbach" in BB.

Some spread and blend in Our Sea,[59]   240
some empty themselves into the Ocean's womb.
And the wavy Ocean, in sight superb,
laps on the humble earth,[60] surrounding it.
And a secret Providence on high,
with many waters and humors, hidden
and known, secured the Earth against
the violence of Fire, her enemy—so that
he, who dominates everything[61] by winning
in his rush and wrath and opposing power,
may not dominate like a tyrant   250
usurping the others'[62] realms and thrones,
at least until that last, frightful day[63]
that Divine Judgment prescribed to him.

A time will surely come, as a sacred,
very old Fame blares with many tongues,[64]
wherein the fire will burn earth and water,
and the whole world, wrapped in one flame,
will fall scattered in ash and sparks.
Then rivers and springs will dry up;
not even the dark abysses will be safe   260
from the victor fire. Our trust, meanwhile,
is in Him who has arranged all things
in a sweet harmony, top to bottom
—He who then divided waters from waters.

Hence, these are the waters; and the starry sphere,
the one including and covering seven circles,[65]

---

[59] The Mediterranean, *mare nostrum*.

[60] A pun in Latin, for *humilis* (humble) comes from *humus* (earth).

[61] With a possible, expanded reference to Satan. In this case, Tasso, the accuser of Gnostics, is not very far from their views. This *was* a theological problem: the 1566 *Catechism* of the Council of Trent tried to give a "softer" explanation of Satan's speech in *Luke* 4: 6 as mere bragging. Moreover, in Tasso's opinion, "he who dominates everything" on earth may also indicate the Pope. Is he covertly trying to state something different from the praises of the Pope he wrote in the official dedication of the poem? "Usurping" (line 251) would recall Dante's invective in *Paradiso* 27: 22.

[62] The other elements.

[63] Cf. the famous Medieval hymn *Dies irae, dies illa*: "A day of wrath, that day..." Tasso follows the days of creation quite loosely, often mixing the contents of one Day with those of another, here the Last One.

[64] Including some Greek philosophers; see especially the Stoics, but BB also mentions Aristotle, Simplicius, Cicero.

[65] The skies rotating around the Earth, that were considered to be seven (the Sun and planets) *plus* one (Firmament, stars) *plus* one (First Mover, the origin of all cosmic motion),

lies under waters. And the eternal Master,
when He made them so beautiful to sight,
did not give them[66] a square shape, firm
and steadfast, nor a sharp conical cone,   270
nor did He want them to look like a pyramid
or cylinder in His ancient craftsmanship,
but He turned one circle within another[67]
so that the most sublime and vastest
encircle the less vast and sublime.
As one who first draws and backgrounds[68]
and prepares the whole in its parts,
then adorns it with colors and gold
and paints ornaments with noble art
and adds images and portraits;   280
so He did adorn the whole universe,
part by part. And He did not yet fill
the supreme sphere[69] with burning stars
in different ways: its marks and signs[70] would
have been impressed by the eternal Master
just when He made the fine starry courts,
on the fourth day, when He shared the then-one
light among the two main lamps,[71] and the rest.
He then made not only Arcturus and Orion
but all the others, embellishing the sky: 290
images exposed to our yearning[72] senses,
and to which futurity would give names.
And that sphere, so easy and ready to rotate,
was by Him fixed to two opposing points,

---

while the tenth, the Empyrean (heaven as God's mind, light, love), was supernatural,
transcendent, beyond space and time; see the structure of Dante's *Paradiso.*

[66] These only theoretical and "impossible" universes come from Aristotle (BB). Twentieth-
century Physics has revalued the cone-shaped pattern, along with non-Euclidean
geometrical hypotheses.

[67] See *Ezekiel* 1: 16, a text much beloved by ancient mystics and thinkers. In the twentieth
century, this Biblical passage was re-interpreted by ufologists as the description of a
spaceship, that—all in all—was already suggested by Milton in *Paradise Lost* 6: 751 and
context.

[68] That is, paints a smooth (gold) layer on the wood surface to be drawn on. Here Tasso,
following St. John Chrysostom (BB), describes the technique still used for sacred icons
especially in East-European Orthodox monasteries. Later, he will describe a typically
(Western) Renaissance procedure, and a Baroque one.

[69] The firmament.

[70] The Zodiac.

[71] The Sun and the Moon.

[72] Another one of the meanings of "vaghi."

the two Poles, still and steady in the sky:
the one[73] always seen ascending above,
the other tending towards the deep Styx
and always keeping hidden underground.[74]
This is what God made; then humankind,
imagining many circles in the sky,   300
split it through thought, and divided it into
five zones, and set as many odd strips[75]
for the opaque Earth below the sky.
The largest circle, dividing the sky in half
into two equal parts, and lying here and there
between the two fixed, opposing Poles,
was called Equator because it equalizes
the day and night, when the Sun reaches it.
The other, that obliquely turns around
up to the two points from which the Sun   310
weaves and reweaves the same route,
would be called the Circle of Animals[76]
or of Life by the people to come.
And the two lesser ones around the point
whence the Sun inverts its twisted path
were called Tropics; and the other two,
created by "poles,"[77] were then named Poles.
And the two imperfect circles[78] also had a name
after the revolutions of the glorious planet.
And the one limiting[79] man's sight   320
with the boundaries of darkness and light
was called Horizon; and after *meridies*[80]
the one reached by the Sun at midday,
ever-changing to varying inhabitants.

---

[73] The cosmic North Pole. For more technical notions than this, once again, I owe much to BB. The main contemporary sources used by Tasso were *Sphera mundi* by G. Sacrobosco, i.e. John Holiwood (1518) and *Della sfera del mondo* by A. Piccolomini (1553); both titles mean "The Sphere of Cosmos." Copernicus' work had already been published, but hadn't become a "case" yet.

[74] A nice poetical simile, coming from Virgil, *Georgics* 1: 242-243 (BB).

[75] The five "horizontal" climatic zones of Earth. According to Aristotle and Sacrobosco, only one of them was fit for humans; Tasso will belie him on the basis of the 15th and 16th century explorations.

[76] Zodiac, from the Greek word *Zoa*, animals.

[77] That is, fulcrums.

[78] The Colures. The Sun was listed among the seven planets, not among the stars.

[79] From the Greek verb *(c)horizo.*

[80] Midday. The Celestial Meridian.

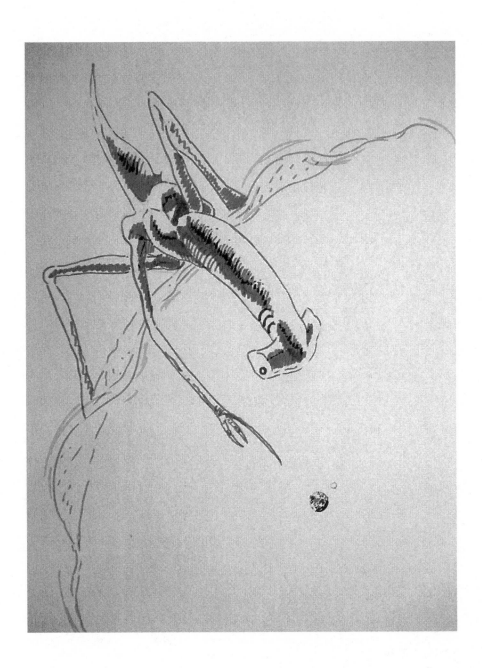

That[81] oblique one—where wandering, turning
lights would follow different paths—
divides the great belt into two like parts
(the cosmos-splitting belt, equaling day and night),
and joins the Tropics on both sides,
it alone being united with three[82] rings.   330
It[83] always shows only one half of itself
with six burning Signs adorned with stars
over the Earth; the other half lying hidden
with the other six remaining below.
Each takes up the same space in the sky
but rises or falls in different times,
either swift or slow; six falling signs
from there above shun the dark night,
and six images of shining stars and gold
see the day, on their turning, once again   340
—as they were imagined by the bold minds
that dark Egypt used to produce;
Greece, too, created monsters for us,
and filling the sky with vain fairy tales,
made it more beautiful with sublime lies.[84]

First, as seen in books and pictures,
without his golden fleece, the carrier[85]
of Phryxus and Helle emits a very dim light,
and after Winter he brings the Spring.
Then, bending one knee, the Bull   350
relaxes his body, and by his bright horns
makes the Earth's humor pregnant with his
fertile light. And the two Twins, together,
spread burning fire out of shining stars.
The flaming Crab almost works as a brake
against the Sun, slowing down its run.
The superb Lion, darting grim looks,

---

[81] The Zodiac, intersecting the Equator.

[82] The Ecliptic, the Colure, the Horizon.

[83] Again the Zodiac.

[84] Once more, Tasso's ambivalent attitude. As we'll immediately see, he "doesn't believe" in astrology, but he devotes a lot of wonderful, refined verses to the subject. And in both his Jerusalem poems, astrology *does* matter.

[85] Aries/Ram; the Golden Fleece was left on earth, in Colchis (the current Western coast of Georgia in the former USSR), then conquered by Jason. To maintain Tasso's lively descriptions, the Signs' names are translated according to their meanings (Bull, Crab, etc.) instead of the astrological terms (Taurus, etc.).

glows and still threatens from the sky.[86]
The Virgin shines next to him, with a golden
Wheat Ear; then light and darkness   360
are balanced on the celestial Scales.
And the heavenly Scorpion usurps more
than its due room; it seems, with its claws,
to form shining scales close to *Astrea*.[87]
The Archer bends the bow in his frightful
hand; and the Capricorn follows him
with a fierce look, like a new obstacle,
over there, to the run of the great Sun,
retaining the lazy and chilly nights.
Behind him, the Trojan lad[88] shines   370
with his glossy amphora. In another star,
a luminous chain, a golden knot is made
by the scaly tails of two wet Fishes.
So did the primeval age depict the burning
signs in the sky, in that oblique circle.

    Then other images on both sides towards
the cold North wind and the cloudy South
were added later and given well-known names.
Close to the Pole, ascending and appearing,
rotating around it in a narrow ring,   380
is the Little Bear,[89] a sign and guide of old
to the bold navigators from Phoenicia.
Further, with seven stars adorning her fur,
the Great Bear makes short, slow rounds:
the Bear who was for the Greeks in the stormy
seas a trustworthy guide, a friendly sign.
Her lazy shepherd Boötes seems to be loudly
shouting behind, and the fierce Dragon
horribly snakes through Ursa, and flaming.[90]
They[91] set Cepheus not far, and Ariadne's   390

---

[86] "Ancor minaccia," from Dante, *Inferno* 31: 43-44, here linked to *Inferno* 1: 46-48.

[87] *Astrea*, the Heavenly, the Starry One, was one of the Latin names of the goddess Justice; here identified with Libra because of the scales (BB). As to the Scorpion, may it be another symbol of the ever-looming Satan, in competition with the Christian God for the domination of the universe? See *Revelation* 9: 10 and 12: 4.

[88] Ganymede/Aquarius.

[89] The Latin name *Ursa*, as well as the Italian "Orsa," means a she-bear.

[90] Again, a monster threatening a female character; see note to line 364.e

[91] The ancient astronomers.

starry crown, and the great Alcides,[92]
and the Lyre and the Swan, and one more
son[93] of the fabled Jove, high in the sky,
whom[94] the North wind's breath from above
lashes; he stretches out his hand to Cassiopeia
and, as a victor, moves his winged feet
upwards, as if flying up from the earth,
all dusty, and quick. And around his left
knee, in a feeble and trembling light,
they set some very, very small stars   400
called "Virgilian"[95] in the ancient times;
a small, little luminous sign in the sky,
but great and famous is its name, instead,
as it lights the very first days of Summer,
inviting industrious mortals to work:
it's now time for the good farmer to entrust
the sowed seeds to the Ancient Mother.
Here they also set a celestial Charioteer
hiding in the chariot his snake-like feet;
and Aesculapius (apparently) portrayed   410
next to the Serpent—and the Arrow, burning
with five stars, and the proud Eagle,
the wriggling Dolphin, and great Pegasus
who carried Bellerophon in his flight.
And the daughter of Cepheus,[96] and Delta nearby
or the image representing and symbolizing
the Island[97] whose three mounts rise on the sea;
the latter lights the dark head of the bare Ram[98]
with its splendor, and in that zone it keeps
closer to the paths of the wandering planets.   420
On the other side, by the Pole[99] against the Bears,
along the crooked route is the fierce monster
exposed to whom, and naked on the shore,

---

[92] Heracles/Hercules, the grandson of Alceus.
[93] Perseus. Tasso will tell the other half of the story, involving Andromeda, in lines 422 ff., but without any reference to Perseus, and vice versa. Tasso deconstructs the myths, and the Christian history of salvation, as if he challenged the readers to re-build them in their minds.
[94] Perseus, as well as "he" in the following line.
[95] The Pleiades. N.B.: Their Latin name comes from the word *ver*, Spring (BB), not from the poet Virgil's name.
[96] Andromeda.
[97] Sicily.
[98] Aries; see note 85.
[99] The cosmic South Pole.

Andromeda had been bound to a hard reef;
and he still seems to be searching for her,
but she's far away now, safe and sound on high,
sheltered from the blowing North wind.[100]
And Orion, all armed with flames and gold
they imagined, who hides late at night
when the Scorpion comes into the world.   430
And the image of a River of eternal fire
also shines there; and a shy Hare, fleeing
the fierce snapping of a fast-running Dog,
was portrayed too. And a lesser Dog burning
with wrath,[101] in being born, saddens the sky
by his unlucky light, and he dries up the fields,
and rising, he appears after the former Dog,
but before it to those[102] who inhabit the torrid
zone beyond Earth's oblique girdle.[103]
The *Argo*,[104] veering in the sky, turns about   440
with its dark prow, and sails backwards;
but its other side is luminous and shining.
Here Hydra, Vase, Crow, and the great Centaur;[105]
here the Wolf and the Altar twinkle.
And another Crown[106] of stars adorns this side
of the sky. And another Fish shines
amid the universe in a farther sector:
the very Fish worshiped in their temples
as their national god by the denizens
of ancient Syria;[107] to whom it did not suffice   450

---

[100] Tasso's sublime version of one of the most successful episodes in his "rival" Ludovico Ariosto's poem *Orlando Furioso*: Ruggiero saving Angelica from the sea Orc, based on the same Greek myth. Cf. also *Revelation* 12: 4, 6. Line 427 has a typo in BB: "e l'aure" (lit. = and the winds) must be corrected into "a l'aura."

[101] Another reference to the "dog days," dramatically described by Tasso in both Jerusalem-poems.

[102] "Commonplace" African peoples.

[103] The Equator.

[104] The ship of the Argonauts. BB interprets "conversa" as "being changed" *into* a constellation, but the simple following words "in ciel[o]" rather suggest "*in* the sky," therefore "conversa" would refer to its veering.

[105] Here Chiron, not Sagittarius (BB).

[106] But meaning Ixion's Wheel.

[107] This half-man half-fish god is none other than Dagon, who will soon play the role of an extra demon in Milton's *Paradise Lost* (1: 462-466) and, especially, will become a protagonist of horror science fiction thanks to H. P. Lovecraft. This fake heavenly glory of Dagon may be an anti-Christ figure (cf. lines 454-455), since the fish is one of the most ancient symbols of Christ—both as God and as a Man: Tasso in fact, who was fascinated by

to make him their god and numen on earth,
but they sketch and worship him in the sky
as if, in the sky, he had attained eternity.

Ha! The old error of raving peoples,
the primeval fraud and badly-nurtured lie,
leading the world astray to ungodly cults![108]
Ha, vain figures of circles and stars
joined together, in vain figured out
against Providence and against Truth!
Ha, vain wisdom, vain intelligence   460
of human nature's pride against God!
Vain thought, vain daring, vain pride,
claiming to number the stars in the sky
and, down here, the smallest grains of sand;
and to measure the measureless fields
of the earth, the sea, the far-reaching sky;
to set limits to the depth and bottom
of endless abysses, and set milestones
upon this uncertain road of life;
and to give an eternal law to the Fates,   470
trying to forcefully enslave Nature
and free will—freely given, unconquerable,
unenforceable by any power or star.
It, on the contrary, dominates and wins;
it can ravish the great heavenly Kingdom
by its strength,[109] by burning with love:
but a holier love, and flames all different
from those[110] by which the old, foolish times,
through mere artificial and false figures,
tried to turn the luminous, pure temple   480
of heaven into a profane, unclean place.

---

sea life, in Day 4 will write time and again, "Man, you are fish!" from different allegorical viewpoints. The term "Syria" in Tasso's works indicates the Holy Land (the Biblical Canaan), or even the whole Middle East, as was common in the Middle Ages and Renaissance; it was often spelled "Sorìa," in addition to "Siria" as it is here.

[108] Tasso obviously had the "new," "heathen" peoples of America in his mind, too. He will briefly describe their religions later on. By saying "primeval fraud," paganism is seen as a consequence of the original sin; cf. Milton, *Paradise Lost* 11: 515 ff. The main N.T. source is Paul's *Letter to the Romans*, see especially 1: 18 ff., 3: 9 ff., 5: 12; as well as *Galatians* 4: 3-8.

[109] Paraphrasing *Matthew* 11: 12. This all-out defense of free will should not, as usual, make us forget the many passages in Tasso's works where the opposite opinion is held; in this very poem, too; see below.

[110] The constellations.

Was it not enough to tell of the furtive love
of the lustful Swan?[111] Or the immoral abduction
by an Eagle[112] no longer carrying lightning
or the fire of wrath, but only pleasures?
Of Ariadne's crown, and a thousand
pleasant[113] tales, and fabulous loves,
that Greece added to the ancient lies
of Babylon and haughty[114] Egypt,
even if the young successor of Alexander   490
the Great had not added Berenice's
cut locks to the other shining stars?[115]
Can earthly mortals allow themselves so much,
not only daring to make, in rough stone
or in some knotty wild wood, such
earthly and proud idols to themselves,
but also violating the eternal natures
and the glory of the celestial spheres?
For the bright light is the stars' own glory,
and every star is like no other in the sky.   500
But those people should not have turned
such pure shapes into means of deceit,
thus falling from pure light into darkness,
headlong down into dark abysses;
ascend to God, indeed, from light to light,
and recognize Him in the sublime works
that are the sparkles and shafts of His radiance.

    God only is the One who can fully number
the water drops in the sea, the stars in the sky.[116]
And God gave a proper name to each,   510
so that, being called, each answers the Lord[117]

---

[111] Zeus/Jove turned into a swan to mate with Leda.

[112] Again Zeus, here kidnapping Ganymede, which suggests lust *plus* homosexuality, provided the Gods have the same genders as humans (Milton was not clear about this, see *Paradise Lost* 1: 422-430 and 10: 888-890). But Tasso condemned homosexuality only in theory, as the love story between Riccardo and Ruperto in *Gerusalemme Conquistata* shows. It is among the new episodes he added—surely not for the sake of "orthodoxy," as it is commonly maintained by scholars who speak of the *Conquistata* without having read it.

[113] "Vaghe."

[114] "Superbo" can also be translated as "superb," but the context suggests a negative nuance.

[115] Queen Berenice whose hair become a constellation; however, she was not the wife of Ptolemy I, Alexander's successor, but of Ptolemy III (BB). Tasso had to remember things by heart; he hadn't all the books he needed handy.

[116] With a pun in Italian: "stille" (drops, from Latin *stillae*) and "stelle" (stars).

[117] These lines recall many Biblical passages praising God the Creator, e.g. *Job* 38: 7, 31-35.

keenly in service to the heavenly empire.
And as trustworthy warriors on guard
in the most dark and shadowy night
go round the city walls, ever vigilant,
so do the burning stars, nocturnal and quick,
surround the other parts of the sky
as were commanded by the supreme Lord.
And He did paint no Bear, no Lion,
no Dragon, no Eagle hung in the sky   520
with eternal lamps and perpetual flames,
nor any other shape was seen in the deep
sea, or a river, or a mountain, or a wood;
only that Cross[118] on which His dead Son
would then triumph over the Styx's kingdom
—*this* He did imprint in the sky, shaping
its pattern with four luminous stars;
at which the past ages could not gaze
under this Pole, where they imagined
Boötes, the Wagon, and the other bright signs,   530
but the current age sees it, high in the sky;
and the other Pole, hidden to our sight,
exalts it in itself[119] to other inhabitants.
This is the eternal sign of assured victory
for the righteous King[120] in his holy war:
the cross that appeared, aflame in the air,
to the glorious, undefeated son of Helen,[121]
he who threw the new Pharaoh[122] into
the Tiber, down from the crumbling bridge,[123]
and freed Rome from the oppressing yoke,   540
and threw the proud idols to the ground.

---

[118] The Southern Cross. An unconscious "prophecy" of it was in Dante, *Purgatorio* 1: 22-27, that Tasso here echoes.

[119] Reworking Dante, *Inferno* 4: 120, who, however, was looking at the "heathen" sages.

[120] Constantine the Great. His victory of 312 AD had been grandly frescoed by Raphael in the Vatican palaces. The synthesis of the Emperor's biography here provided by Tasso is hardly accurate. But—what matters more—neither Ariosto nor Tasso, in the papalist Renaissance, dared repeat Dante's courageous theory that Constantine, by giving earthly power to the Church, had been *the cause of the decadence of Christianity*, even admitting that his personal conversion was sincere. See e.g. *Paradiso* 20: 55-60.

[121] Who would then find a presumed relic of the True Cross in Jerusalem. Her enterprise was frescoed by one of the masters of Renaissance art, Piero Della Francesca, in Arezzo, Tuscany.

[122] Maxentius, Roman Emperor, AD 279-AD 312.

[123] *Pons Milvius*, or the Weak Bridge.

Another cross, then, flashing in mid-air,
manifested itself to an unworthy successor,[124]
and dissolved like inflamed vapors[125]
in those airy and stormy fields.
But this trophy[126] in the sky, with its eternal
and fixed lights, will never fall: the firm sign
(we are entitled to hope) of a lasting empire
and nearly a mark in which the High King
inscribed His laws to victors and vanquished,   550
giving glory to those, salvation to these.
Even Ancient Egypt once realized this,
though in a deep and thick darkness, since
among the other figures, among the signs
of their mysteries, they also engraved a cross.[127]
And the eternal Forger sketched the cross
across the four opposite corners of the world,
so that its shape distinguishes and marks
the East and the West, the North and the South.

These signs of salvation are the signs   551   560
that God imprinted with His eternal art;
nor did He make anything evil or noxious
or causing death or any damage
to wretched mortals. Let the ungodly cease,
let the proud cease to dart and vibrate[128]
their injurious tongues against Heaven!
The serene stars are not malign; they cannot
harm anybody with their fierce aspect,
either by their own choice or by nature.
Not by choice, for they would then   570
have senses and souls,[129] and like animals
they would be moved by feelings like ours.
Not by nature either, if God created them,
because God is the Creator of no evil

---

[124] Julian "the Apostate," who tried *not* to destroy Christianity, but to reinstate religious pluralism.
[125] "Vapori accesi," i.e. falling stars or summer heat flashes, quoting Dante, *Purgatorio* 5: 37.
[126] The Southern Cross.
[127] Tasso knew a recent study *On the Obelisks in Rome* by M. Mercati, 1589 (BB).
[128] Like snakes. "Vibrare" as a technical verb can also refer to hurling a spear.
[129] During the Renaissance, it was not a commonplace to describe the stars as "soulless." The theme of "living" stars was charmingly resumed in modern times by C. S. Lewis in *The Voyage of the Dawn Treader*, ch. 14.

and He never makes any non-good work.
And never could the stars, by shifting place,
become malign after being good,
or good after being evil, lowering their eyes
or changing their figure or countenance
—since, as some say, they look happier   580
and rejoice in the hour of their own birth,
and look sad and sorrowful before falling;
or the other way round, happy before falling,
sad in being born; or getting angry and then
calming down by varying their positions.
If this were the case, human nature
would be less changeable and inconstant
than celestial nature, and in eternal laws
there would be no certainty but vain error.
Nor would it fit Jove's messenger,[130]   590
like that animal[131] which changes its colors
according to the places it approaches,
to receive a thousand and a thousand shades
from its neighbors. In the sky, then, sites
cannot destroy, cannot diminish goodness,
for the sky is all good, and everywhere
Divine Goodness is pleasant and beneficial.[132]

Enough already of lofty stars harboring
celestial hates and celestial loves—unworthy
of Heaven—and their positions:[133]   600
one looks at another across the void;
others stay united; another, turning around
three, or four, or six signs, at last stops
in the middle, gazing at her friendly star,
or maybe enemy… but there is no discord
in the sky, nor any offensive disdain.
In five[134] positions only, and in a different

---

[130] Mercury/Hermes.

[131] The chameleon.

[132] As in the Trent *Catechism*, there is a constant swing between a "Wonderful World" full of the Lord's glory and a decaying world under Satan's power. Already Dante saw, at the very core of the universe, either Lucifer (*Inferno*, esp. Canto 34) or God (*Paradiso*, esp. Canto 28).

[133] The term "aspetti" technically means the distances—in degrees—between stars and planets (BB). The imagery suggests a sort of Baroque dance.

[134] With reference to the five planets having cosmic influences: Mercury, Venus, Mars, Jupiter, Saturn (BB).

manner, could one benign star turn
towards another in a peaceful aspect.
We *do* receive from the sky the signs 610
of what to follow, of what to avoid
in this uncertain span of life, but no star
will ever force or do violence to us:
its omens good or ill, it will always help.
It is good for the pilot to keep the ship
in the harbor when the winds and waves
threaten him with a terrifying storm,
and Orion in arms declares war to him.
It is good for the pilgrim, as he goes,
to skip the annoyance of a sudden rain 620
and take shelter in a solitary inn.[135]
It is good for the ill to observe the days,
the judges of their life and death.
And the good farmer, either in sowing
or in planting, follows in his labors
the rise or fall of the friendly stars[136]
and the most fitting season and time.

What of that? The High Lord forecast[137]
the appearance of terrifying signs
of a world whose ruin will be at hand, 630
in the sun, in the moon, in the stars.
The Moon will deny her light and rays,
and the troubled Sun will turn into blood,[138]
and these will be the horrible signs
of the last collapse. Now, the "ford-passers"[139]
dare assign the causes to man's life;
as if it were wound with a weak thread
to the fatal spindle of a stern Fate,
they subject it to the celestial changes,
praising the genius and art of the Chaldees. 640

---

[135] Solitary inns had a certain importance in the poems of chivalry, for moments of rest and/or unexpected encounters.

[136] The adjective "amico/a" was often used by Tasso in his poems: friendly stars, night, moon, stillness, walls, ...

[137] See *Matthew* 24: 29, though not in every detail.

[138] See *Acts of the Apostles* 2: 20; *Revelation* 6: 12.

[139] "Chi trapassa il guado," explained by BB as "those who assign a function of destiny to the stars"; that fits the context, but is not completely clear from the viewpoint of wording. These "trespassers" (beyond the limits of human reason) probably echo a subtle quotation from Dante, who uses this same unusual word, "guado" (ford), in speaking of God's impenetrable Providence: *Purgatorio* 8: 69.

But, conceding that, written in the sky,
these are not the signs of clouds or storms
or the uncertain changes of the weather,
but of our very life and its destiny:
What will they say? That the wandering stars
and those fixed in the oblique sky belt,
joined together by their entangled knots
and varied figures and varied meetings,
are the causes of a happy, lucky life
to those predestined by the sky?   650
Or rather the causes of a painful doom?
So, to make these doubts clearer, I will
say what others among them say, adducing
their own sayings against one another.
      The inventors of this art[140] would see many
figures in a small room and in a short time,
since they all too swiftly disappeared
before their eyes; so they gathered and enclosed
those shapes within very narrow limits,
almost within one, indivisible dot   660
disappearing in the twinkling of an eye.
So, in those who from maternal shrines[141]
were about to be born into the serene light,[142]
in the first dot, or the one immediately behind,
they[143] noticed a great variety of intellects
and arts and powers and good fortune.
One is born a Cambyses or Cyrus,[144]
or Alexander, or fortunate Augustus,
to the scepter, kingdom, glorious domination,
the honor of triumph and of victory;   670
another, like Irus,[145] to beg door to door

---

[140] Astrology. Tasso's arguments were currency among the Church Fathers. It is interesting to note, however, that Dante *did* believe in astrology, even with reference to himself (Gemini, see *Paradiso* 22: 112-117).

[141] "Chiostri," literally cloisters.

[142] Rather than the "vale of tears," once in a while. Cf. *Luke* 1: 42. But cf. here below, lines 687-688.

[143] The astrologists, as in line 674.

[144] The structure of these verses is based on Dante, *Paradiso* 8: 124 ff. In *MC* Tasso quotes Dante's *Purgatorio* and *Paradiso* much more often than *Inferno*, unlike most poets, students, and scholars. He also offers a reworked version of Dante's *Paradiso* in *Gerusalemme Conquistata*, Canto 20.

[145] BB (and other Italian editions) have "iro," an old form for "(they) went," but it possibly should be written "Iro," capitalized, i.e. Irus, the famous beggar in Homer's *Odyssey*, whose

for what sustains a tiresome life,
in heavy and shameful poverty.
So, they first divided the oblique ring[146]
into twelve parts, and each part into thirty,
the sum of days it takes the Sun to cross one sign
among the twelve Sun-imprinted marks.
They then divided the thirty parts, and again
the sixty into sixty, and by such tiny splinters
they distinguished the degrees and hours   680
to detect the one belonging to the newborn.
They *cannot* be sure about that fleeting point,
since you would see it immediately disappear
and vanish in the sky as time flies by.

    As soon as a naked baby comes into the world,
one looks at the sex, then waits for the little one
to cry—the tearful and painful sign
of human life, the one truly fitting—
the Chaldee finally forecasts their destiny.
How many dots have meanwhile swiftly   690
passed by? Who can descry their figure
in the sky, and which sublime star then
ascends and domineers in that instant,
establishing the fate of the newborn?
Therefore in those varied, vague figures
and in the fleeting hours, a lie does lie.

    Take a newly born baby, sweet-looking,
calm, serious, and gentle, with curly hair:
he's believed to have received his "hour"
from Frixus's beast.[147] *But* he is noble-hearted   700
too, and magnanimous, like the animal
who turns out to be the leader of others:[148]
bold in butting and hitting with his horns,
and then docile while being harmlessly
stripped of his soft and white wool,
with which Nature will then easily cover
and adorn him again.[149] Another, first opening

Greek nickname *Iros* was a mockingly masculine form of Iris, the she-messenger of the Gods. So, Tasso mentions him as a counter-example against Cambyses, etc. Among the people whose destiny was like the Homeric beggar's, Tasso surely included himself—and Dante, see *Paradiso* 17: 55-60. JT uses "Others."

[146] The Zodiac.

[147] Aries, the ram with the Golden Fleece.

[148] Of other sheep only, not the king of animals proper, that would obviously be the lion.

54

his eyes when the Sun dwells in shiny Taurus,
will undergo fatigues with great endurance,
mastering himself in a spirit of service   710
because a bull is used to the heavy yoke.
One, born when Scorpio shines in ascendance,
will disdainfully hit and hurt the others
like the beast of the venomous wounds.
While Libra, equaling things in its scales,
makes a man just, the true friend of Justice.
    Laugh freely! The sign in that crooked path[150]
giving you the celestial beginning of life
—be it the Ram, making nights as long as
the serene days, or the luminous Scales—   720
is just a small, far away point in the sky.
Will you guess and shape the habits of man
on the basis of beasts and filthy flocks?
Is human nature, for you, not only base
but feral?[151] How can you account for bestiality
even in heaven?[152] Should heaven depend
on such filthy and unclean herds?
Will you subject the celestial spheres
to earthly beasts? Ha, such silly, foolish
human wisdom, making man swell   730
with vain pomp and boundless pride!
—like the web of the unhappy Arachne,[153]
who in her texture, with difficulty, catches
the annoying fly by tarring its wings,
but if a heavier thing chances to hit the web,
it cannot stand, and is broken and dissolved.
Oh, may it please Him, who binds us fast
as He likes best, and sometimes unties
the strings of sin and the hard knots by which
Fate[154] traps our souls here below—   740

---

[149] An early example of Tasso's ability in describing living beings; see especially below, Day 6.

[150] Again the Zodiac.

[151] Cf. Dante, *Inferno* 24: 124-126.

[152] Here in the poetical sense of both heaven and sky.

[153] The mythical spinner who gave origin to spiders; see Dante, *Purgatorio* 12: 43-45.

[154] A different point of view suddenly slips in: Fate, as the net of causes, may well exist, but God—who is not the same as Fate, here—is above it, and stronger, and can free us from it. Cf. Dante, *Purgatorio* 16: 73-81. "Entanglement," besides, is the basic meaning of the Hindu and Buddhist concept of *samsara*, and the process of "liberation" would correspond

oh, may it please Him, who sets such a high
value on free will[155]—a celestial gift,
divine indeed, independent of the stars—
to rend the fragile spider webs of all
our woven deceits, adding weight to a word
capable of freeing our unhappy minds.[156]
So—I say—in the continuous run of the seven
wandering planets, some revolve more
quickly around their cores, others slowly;
and in one hour, some look at one   750
another, some hide; and they give rise
to thousands of figures of themselves
among the stars; and from a little
deception, at first, as it keeps on growing,
an infinite error will finally arise.
If, at any instant, the sky alters
and it takes on a thousand shapes a day,
why doesn't each day give us a new king?[157]
And how is the successor of a given king
a son who was born in a different climate,   760
under a different pattern of sky and stars?
Why don't all kings and great emperors wait
for a royal figure and pattern in the sky
when a new son is being born to them?
And what king ever waited for the fittest
time to beget a son, asking the fatal stars
for advice when he longed for an heir?
Was there any royal image in the sky,
made of happy lights, when Gyges was born,
who was a slave and then became a king?   770
Or Servius, who ascended the Roman throne?
Or the Tartar[158] who conquered and crossed Asia?
On the contrary, Croesus was born in the

---

to *moksha, nirvana.* For the "homeomorphic correspondences" (structural parallelisms,
more or less) between religions, see Panikkar.

[155] Cf. Dante, *Paradiso* 5: 19-24.

[156] Cf. New Testament texts like *John* 8: 32.

[157] Tasso is still translating from St. Basil's *Hexaemeron* (BB), but keeping Dante in his
mind at the same time, see *Paradiso* 8: 133 ff. A parallel reflection, since Dante didn't
know Basil's works, except for some scattered quotations he could find in Thomas Aquinas'
Summa Theologiae.

[158] Either Genghis Khan or Tamerlane, BB suggests. The absoluteness of the epithet—*the*
Tartar—seems to indicate the former.

slavish light of a fierce and ominous star.
And Perseus, fierce Jugurtha, and the kings
who adorned the triumph of Unconquered Rome;
as shameful as the unhappy Roman Emperor
caught by the Persian King;[159] or the other
a victim, as well, of barbaric valor.[160]

But may He who transcends all   780
put finally an end to such deep issues.
For useless would then be the sacred laws,
useless the judges, so that virtue is honored
with its reward, vice with penalty and scorn,[161]
if we place elsewhere the grand principles
of just or unjust deeds, rather than
in ourselves. A thief would then be no thief,
he would give no offense with his theft,
nor would the unjust murderer by smiting,
if their sinful hands could not abstain,   790
respectively, from the gold and the blade,
both driven by the force of an adverse doom.
Useless would be the professions, the arts,
as well as our toils; in vain would the good
farmer plow his fields with his plow,
or tame them with a rake or two-pronged fork,
or with a sharpened crescent-shaped scythe,
if the Weather's wrath denied the ripeness
to the crops—or so did Fate's will.
In vain, plowing through the Black Sea, or   800
the Caspian, or the Red, would they labor[162] and trade,
if it is Fate who gathers and squanders wealth.[163]
And the age-old hope of the faithful,
invincibly longing for God's great Kingdom,

---

[159] Valerian, defeated by Shapur I (BB).

[160] Julian "the Apostate," killed during a campaign in Persia. As in his Jerusalem-poems, Tasso never forgets the "equal time rule": a victory of one party is balanced by a victory of the other party, Romans vis-a-vis "barbarians" here, Christians vis-a-vis Muslims there. In other words, the wheel of Fortune never stops turning, that was a deep-rooted concept in Medieval and Renaissance culture.

[161] A widespread philosophical belief; for a more specific literary source, see Dante, *Purgatorio* 16: 70-72.

[162] The verb "travaglia" includes both working (cf. *travailler* in French) and toiling (cf. travail). This reference to international commerce offers a glimpse into the developing European economy, even *over*-seas.

[163] That's precisely what Fortune does, according to Dante, *Inferno* 7: 77 ff. Here—though not everywhere, to be sure—Tasso decides to defend the "worldly values."

could even perish if the reward were not given
for the righteous, punishment for the ungodly.[164]
For, if what dominates and forces us is Fate,
man's dignity and sublime virtue[165] would have
no room left corresponding to such merits.
But we must not fear[166] that Heaven may not keep   810
the final crown and palm for our good deeds.

---

[164] A "commercial" view of religion that, however, is not Tasso's deepest belief. He knew
better than this, and indeed he was possibly afraid that it all could collapse. See line 810.

[165] It may mean virtue in general, praised as a sublime thing, or more specifically free will,
called "the noble virtue" by Dante, through Virgil, in *Purgatorio* 18: 73-74. And in fact, as
Beatrice will confirm, free will is the metaphysical ground of man's dignity, see *Paradiso* 5:
19-24.

[166] *Excusatio non petita, accusatio manifesta.*

Day Three

There are cities[1] proud of their riches
and beauty, and various arts and works,
marvelous, and with the tallest buildings,
or honored because of their ancient glory.
Here, from the dawning of day to sunset,
and, sometimes, as long as the chilly Night
makes her starry chariot turn around,
squares, fields, adorned theaters, arcades
are full of happy and joyful crowds,
who follow after delights and spend   10
the fleeing hours of day, the long and cold
hours of night; and as time flies by, they keep
deceiving themselves of their free will.
Others by the apparent and vain fraud
of a fallacious art, scorning man's senses,
are deluded;[2] and puzzled by conjurings,
marveling, they almost believe falsehood.

Others, in the harmony of varying notes,
or at the sweet sound of a lyre or a harp
—which calms souls, cajoles and softens hearts,   20
keeping them glad or sad by different tones—
forget all worries.[3] Others, in happiness, gaze
at dances and ring-dances of a shameless woman
who in many ways and almost in different
shapes moves and stretches her flexible limbs,
admiring her lustful jumps, styles and art,
alluring, mincing—and they *want* her so much.

---

[1] As BB points out, this section also comes from St. Basil's *Hexaemeron*; but with a strong *contemporaneity* to Tasso, in an epoch in which the splendor and worldly life of Italian Courts reawakened the glory of the Empire of Byzantium. Here Tasso disapproves of the "moral decadence" of Western civilization, but his lively descriptions suggest his deeper sympathies.

[2] "Deluso," in current Italian means being disappointed, but here seems closer to the English sense of the word. The passage refers to the typical Renaissance/Baroque public shows, in which costumes and complex technical devices were employed, designed by great artists and engineers (e.g. Arcimboldo). Plays were often written for special occasions, even by Tasso himself when he was younger (*Aminta*).

[3] Cf. Milton, *Paradise Lost* 2: 546 ff.

Or, where a painted scenery shines with
colors and lamps, and rising arches and *metae,*
and all around sacred temples   30
and high columns, and giants[4] of marble
mourning the fate of Oedipus[5] and Thyestes[6]
(in a fake sky, a fake, darkened sun appears
going backwards from its mid-route);
or, with Davos and Syros,[7] they joyfully laugh
at the false deceits of mocked old men.

Others admire fierce, nimble, fast horses
turning about-face to the right and to the left;
or, behind a closed fence or in an open field,
watch a truthful rendition of a frightful war   40
at the blaring sound of the sharp trumpet,
and the escutcheons and arms of the knights,
whose worth is exalted with merry shouts.[8]

And shall we—whom the King of heaven, maker
of such wonderful works, invites and calls
to admire His divine craftsmanship and art,[9]
and this embellished design of His, this
unified texture of heavenly and earthly
things in so many different modes—
be slow in gazing at it? Will we be lazy   50
in learning how the heavenly Forger made
these sublime marvels by His own hand?
Or wouldn't we rather, looking all around
at this varied and admirable edifice,
each by himself, go back in his mind
to think of that primal time in which
both time and the new[10] world first began?

Like a huge vault, the sky covers
the highest peaks and the starry courts,
so that this serene temple, sacred   60

---

[4] The telamones.

[5] Tasso's own tragedy *Il Re Torrismondo* was based on the myth of Oedipus.

[6] Who was forced to drink the blood of his own son after having raped Europa.

[7] Names of servants in classical comedies (BB).

[8] It is quite unbelievable that Tasso considered jousts a waste of time, as in that very period he was working hard on his 20,000-verse long poem of chivalry *Gerusalemme Conquistata,* that would be published soon, in 1593.

[9] An often repeated Biblical teaching; see Dante, *Purgatorio* 14: 148-150.

[10] Newly created, or more subtly, "new" after the "first world" of heaven, cf. Milton, *Paradise Lost* 2: 347-349.

to God, shines upon us with many lights.
And lying and grounded in itself is
the most heavy, vast, and rough earth.
The wandering air spreads all around,
tender and soft, creating no obstacle
to those moving in it, always giving way
and easily letting all pass through it;
without struggle does it scatter behind,
offering wet nourishment to breathing
beings, and a sweet coolness inside   70
—a true friend to the wandering[11] spirit.
Water also feeds us, being made so useful
to our mortal lives in this unworthy world[12]
by a decree of the eternal Father.
But, unsatisfied with an uncertain seat,
water had its own limits and a fixed place
within certain borders, where it gathered
in obedience and assembled into one
at the command of the divine voice.

    The great God said, "Let the water   80
below the sky gather into one mass,
so that the dry element may appear."
And it was so. Immediately, the water
lying under the turnings of the serene sky
assembled in its own gathering,
so that the dry part could surface;
and the eternal Maker properly called
the dry part "earth," and the tossing waters
"sea"—those contained in the largest pools.
As it happens that a sky-blue curtain   90
hiding a grand theater[13] behind its shadows
withdraws, drawn away from both sides,
and unveils a painted scenery full

---

[11] "Vago," as in line 64 (wandering). The link between air, breath, and soul = biological life is conveyed in several cultures by the terms "spirit," *spiritus* in Latin, *pneuma* in Greek, *nephesh* in Hebrew, etc.

[12] "Mondo immondo," literally, filthy world: an easy pun that has become commonplace in moralistic sermons. But, if the world is filthy, why are the life-giving air and water praised? That, in fact, was the objection of the Church Fathers against Manichean (and Gnostic) thinkers. The most famous Christian hymn to natural elements in Italian literature is St. Francis' *Canticle of the Sun*, of which *Il Mondo Creato* can be seen as an "exploded view" as well as a problematic version.

[13] A key-concept in Tasso. From a historical viewpoint, this is a modern theater; in the Middle Ages, plays were performed in the streets or inside churches.

of arches, statues, pillars, altars, temples;
so, at the gathering of the wet element,
on the dry land did plains and hills appear,
and the high mountains raised their foreheads,
till then hidden, now majestic to see.
Now the rippled, murmuring sea hardly
washed the feet of the Mauritanian Atlas,   100
of the great Taurus,[14] Parnassus, and Athos
which can prolong the brief and frail lives
of weak mortals;[15] of the snowy Apennines,
the sea just lapped against its lower levels.
From the steep valleys of rugged mountains
the rapid torrents then ran downwards,
and with a roaring rumble the muddy waves
went running and rolling in a rush;
downwards did quiet and slow rivers flow,
and so did the glittering brooks.   110
For God by His eternal word ordered
all waters to come running down;[16]
from the very beginning, a hurried pace
was commanded to the wet nature
of the wandering waters: no rest was left
by the holy injunction of God's voice.
Because water grows dull in laziness,
and where it becomes swampy and stagnates,
out of its slothful womb it exhales
heavy, harmful vapors, fierce spirits   120
of evil breezes,[17] thus perturbing the sky
and polluting the air; meanwhile growing
an unhealthy culture[18] in itself, in its
sticky slime, and by this it often infects

---

[14] The Taurus Mountains in current Turkey; Parnassus and Athos are individual mountains in Greece.

[15] An artist wanted to sculpt, Rushmore-like, Alexander the Great's face on Mount Athos, Greece (BB). Athos is now famous for its ultra-orthodox Orthodox community of monks, so it may grant eternity in a more spiritual way.

[16] Tasso will insist on this. At first glance, he simply identifies God's word with the law of gravity, but, in fact, he means the metaphysical *cause* of gravity: Why do particles—the Higgs boson included—act the way they do? See lines 140 ff.

[17] This language may also indirectly refer to *ignis fatuus*, which was believed to be an evil sprite misleading travelers.

[18] Mosquitoes. Unhealthy swamps have existed in Italy up until the first decades of the 20th century. Malaria was possibly the cause of Dante's death, after an embassy in Venice on behalf of the city of Ravenna.

the unlucky neighboring inhabitants.
  While water running quickly downwards,
in any direction it may direct its course,
nurtures the wholesome on its grassy
banks, happily sharing its own treasures:
fish with golden scales and soft silver,   130
or liquid crystals so as to quench
the burning thirst of wretched mortals.
Yet more salutary if, among living rocks
shattering its silver and chilly horns,[19]
facing the Sun who gilds with his rays
its pure silver, it takes ever-better steps[20]
as if it remembered (an obedient servant)
the heavenly sound of the High Voice
who first moved it, making it born to run.
But if water by its intrinsic nature   140
flows downwards and doesn't stop above,
always looking for rest in a lower place,
what was the divine voice needed for?
Its own nature might suffice to make it run;
unnecessary was then the stern command
denying it any rest, in perpetual motion
making it restless, unsettled, and roaming.[21]
No, necessary indeed was the holy command,
for the very sound of the eternal Word,
in creating water, at the same time   150
created the mobile and wandering nature
that preserves it; and by this motion He makes it
almost eternal, in the likeness of heaven.[22]
So that the nature of water is a certain law
of the unchangeable Word, prescribing
a fixed seat for it after running so long.
But, once there, again stirred by the heavenly
spheres, it moves, and flows backwards
ceding the usurped borders, once again,
to the sandy earth. This is why water   160
follows the Sun and the wandering stars,

---

[19] In classical—and Renaissance—poetry and art, rivers were portrayed as horned men.
[20] "I passi in bene avanza," echoing Dante, *Purgatorio* 9: 91. Water purifies, hence the link with purgatory; and the next two verses quote *Luke* 1: 38. The whole passage recalls the ancient sacredness of the liquid element.
[21] A clear symbol of man's life, and, especially, of Tasso.
[22] The "substance" of things *is* movement, as interpreted by Teilhard de Chardin.

and the nearer, white lamp[23] even more,
in their exact shifting and sweet[24] turning;
and it increases, then decreases, every six hours.
For when, above the horizon, the sweet Moon
ascends, on the shore of the resounding sea
the whitish waves grow[25] and victoriously flood
the beach, now covering, now sprinkling
the dry earth, until the cold chariot of
the Moon summits the dome of the sky.   170
Then, when the Moon at the extreme horizon
glides towards her setting, the sea decreases,
gathers in itself, and unveils the beaches
sprinkled with the whitest foam.
But again the sea seethes, and fierce-looking
swells its foamy waves, and covers yards
of the occupied land, when the Moon comes
back to *that* point on the opposite side;
and in the other hemisphere, to others,
she now shines, most high, in mid-sky.   180
Again the sea ebbs, leveling, calming down
the boiling waves to a humble countenance,
seemingly about to flee, forsaking the beach,
when the Moon again reaches the sky ceiling
in her Orient, whence she shows herself to us.[26]

But not every sea follows the selfsame laws,[27]
when waxing, waning, partly varying its orders
and motions, and waving in different ways.
All this much more often occurs in Taormina,[28]
and in Euboea[29]—as one reads—the sea   190
swells and then ebbs even seven times a day:
such a grand marvel that one great mind,[30]

---

[23] The Moon.

[24] "Vago," again (*vaga*, feminine, referring to the Moon; however, here in line 165 because of a syntactical adaptation).

[25] The descriptions of the tides follow Pliny the Elder (BB).

[26] Tasso has been the greatest "landscape painter" among Italian poets, together with Giacomo Leopardi in the early nineteenth century, who, not by chance, admired Tasso deeply in spite of their opposite views on religion. Leopardi was an atheist, and the only one in the "official" history of Italian literature.

[27] Complexity is a fundamental feature of Tasso's worldview.

[28] A beautiful town in Sicily, currently an important tourist destination.

[29] A Greek island.

[30] Aristotle, according to a late legend (BB). Cf. the Wizard of Ascalon in *Gerusalemme Liberata*.

tired and collapsing, reached his death
while looking for the concealed cause of that,
sorry that Nature may keep it hidden from us
in her profound and shadowy womb.
Three times a day are the waves absorbed
and mixed by the stormy, ungodly Charybdis,
not far from the baying of Scylla the horrid.[31]
There are, besides, other seas—they say[32]—   200
that in a period of a full month
will usually raise their foamy waves twice,
and twice lower them down, pressed;[33]
while the sea of sunburnt Ethiopians
has no flux or reflux. And farther still,
under another hemisphere and another Pole
where no lazy Arcturus and no Ursa shine,
the bold seafarer plows through a great sea
of perpetual stillness. And this flood surrounds
the earth all around, murmuring evermore,   210
an untamed Ocean, repels and chases far-
away torrents and rivers through its tides:
so that they seem to be fleeing harbors and
leaving coasts and deserted sands for fear,
and flowing back towards their springs.[34]
So great is the power—repelling and forcing
them—of Ocean, roaring high and superb!
And the Ligurian and the Tuscan seas
(the latter waving by the new Pisa,[35]
that gives prizes to more honorable studies   220
and wreaths to the most learned brows)
hardly have the alternate motion of waves.
     But, if the waters have been first moved
by the clear sound of the divine voice,
why look, either on earth or in mid-sea,

---

[31] Natural phenomena "naturally" drift into mythology.

[32] In his notes, Tasso cites the "Reports from the West Indies," namely G. B. Ramusio's *Navigazioni e Viaggi* (BB), 1550-1606.

[33] Cf. Dante, *Inferno* 21: 21.

[34] Cf. *Psalm* 114: 5.

[35] There was a town called Pisa/Pise in ancient Greece, too, but Tasso here patriotically stresses that the University of the Italian Pisa is more important than the games held in the Greek one. The Italian word *laurea*, university degree, comes from *lauro*, laurel (wreath), which is still used on such occasions. During the Middle Ages, Pisa was one of the four Maritime Republics (together with Amalfi, Genoa, and Venice); then historical changes took place.

for another cause of their perpetual flowing;
or maybe up there, among the starry courts?
That's what many do, whose thoughts waver
like flickering reflections on water.
    Some[36] to the divine motion that turns   230
the most sublime sphere, have seen and assigned
the primal cause; others to the wandering stars,
or rather those with a lesser luminosity,
nearer and therefore exert more power
on the mortal and subjected beings.
Still, according to some, the white ray, oblique
or straight, raises or flattens the waves;
others think the Moon, when full,
fills the sea with stormy surges, and while
waning, causes it to wane; others   240
say that, through Nature's deep *sympathy*,
the sea tacitly imitates the sky's course
—but here they all almost completely agree.
    Others think that, as the wind obliquely blows
and whirls back, it makes the waves reverse their run
as well, shifting their motions both ways.
Others, following an ancient belief,
say that the sea, like a great animal,
as a living limb of the great world,
spouts and then re-gathers the waves,   250
breathing in and out in different modes.
Another thinks in its uncomfortable bed
the Sea cannot have any rest or peace,
so that he continuously shifts and groans,
crying hoarsely; and this unquiet realm
is an ever-perturbed battlefield to him.
And he moves so especially in the Northern
world, facing toward the cool Plow,
where saw-toothed mountains are always
full and laden with an icy humor   260
which, compressed, drips into the sea.
And since the deep, frozen swamp[37]

---

[36] Sources are listed in BB; most of them—Arabian astronomers included—were found by Tasso in Pico Della Mirandola's works. We, however, are more interested in the poetical effects of this phantasmagoria of cosmologies. Readers will decide whether any of them can be updated and reused, in light of Paul Feyerabend's *Against Method*.

[37] The Sea of Azov, East of Crimea; again mentioned in line 269 with an adjective coming from its Latin name *Maeotis*.

congealed, hardened by the North wind,
lies much higher, it afterward falls
into the inhospitable Black Sea—which
then swiftly passes into the Aegean Sea.
But, repelled by a sandy coast, the latter
flows back towards the Black, and thus
back towards the Maeotic swamp.
So, seas always have flux and reflux.   270
    Another,[38] a man of a loftier mind,
likens the sea to unbalanced scales,
therefore raising one part of it upwards,
the other lowering to the sandy bottom.
And out of that old, fabled opening[39]
where Heracles placed the boundary signs
(they say) and out of wavy doors
—provided that Ocean has its own doors—
like a torrent, the sea clears itself away,
basin to basin; and in different ways   280
it represents and unites itself between
curved shores and sandy banks.
It was, indeed, the eternal Master's hand
that in many forms shaped the sea,
making it long, or round, or square,
now like a pyramid, now like a cross
forging it, or even like a fancy bowl: as
there, where the Tyrrhenian Sea laps on
the shores and hills of fair Parthenope,[40]
it fills a huge cup with its foamy humor.   290
    But whatever the sea's shape and motion,
no daily, no nocturnal rest
will it ever find, nor silence in fair
or turbulent weather and horrible times;
although deep silence in friendly nights
is given to the moon. But the cause of this
—I say—is not the sun, not the wandering stars,

---

[38] Aristotle.

[39] The Straits of Gibraltar.

[40] Naples; after the name of a mermaid. More literally, in fact, the text says "the beautiful Parthenope"; and a beautiful mermaid will be Armida in *Gerusalemme Conquistata*—while in the *Liberata* she was a "mere" witch. In the *Conquistata*, inspired descriptions of the coasts and cities of Southern Italy can be found too. The decadence of Naples started much later, with the National Unity of Italy (1861), because of the war strategies of the conquerors (the Savoia House, the Kingdom of Piedmont/Sardinia).

not the oblique or straight moon rays,
nor do I ascribe it to the whirling breath
of the restless winds, or the uneven floor   300
on which the sea is suspended as on scales.
For that primal cause was the high Voice
moving around the sky and the sea at once;
because of which (some[41] say) the waves start
their turns, and turn, and go back home.

    Oh, if it ever happened that, by a living spring
amply spreading water all around,
you sat, tired, and it crossed your mind:
Who is He, who out of the cold womb
of the deep and shadowy Earth   310
sends out the water? Who pushes it ahead,
so that it never ceases, never stops?
From what vessels and underground caves
does it come?[42] And towards what goal
does it hasten its pace? And how come
it does not run out, and the sea isn't filled?
These effects, so hidden from our senses,
do depend on that primal, clear Voice
freeing the waters and making them run.

    You, who used to read the old books   320
and still study the best modern volumes,[43]
remember within yourself the clear
resounding sound of that primal voice:
"Gather, O waters!"—so then raise
your thought to the eternal causes.

    The waters needed running first
to fill their fixed, vast seat completely;
and once in their proper place, they had
to stop in themselves, without hastening
beyond their course and erring endlessly.   330
And this is why each torrent finally
flows into the sea, and the sea isn't filled:
because motion was the waters' lot,
and the sea was circumscribed with limits,

---

[41] St. Ambrose and St. Basil (BB).

[42] Compare Jules Verne; in *Gerusalemme Liberata*, Canto 14, the good Wizard of Ascalon leads two knights through an underground tunnel to the "central water storehouse of the Earth"—an episode that wasn't strictly needed for the plot, showing how much Tasso loved this topic.

[43] Cf. *Matthew* 13: 52, with an obvious autobiographical touch.

as the good Creator-King commanded.
And His command was the primal law,
eternal, common law against which Nature
does not rebel. And within a narrow space
the sea calms its fierce pride down.
Otherwise, spreading and widespread,   340
with an endless flood it would cover
the lower earth it surrounds and divides;
not even the small part of earth appearing
out of the waters would have been
left to the tired and wretched mortals.

When stirred, among thunder and lightning,
by the great fury of the stormy spirits,[44]
aiming at the coasts, and raising towards the sky
high watery mountains, swift and foamy
—as soon as the sea touches the sandy shores,   350
its fury breaks, and into ephemeral foam
it immediately dissolves; broken, scattered,
these mounts collapse, and the sea recedes.
What smaller thing, or humbler, or weaker
than sand could you find? And what
thing more violent and more superb
than the proud sea? And yet the sand
can curb the sea's pride and wrath.[45]

So, shall we not fear that supreme King,
who, with His admirable art, gave the sea   360
the sand as a border? And to make us think
about such skills, He himself stresses this.[46]
What other obstacle or what prohibition,
what earthly power, or law, or strength
could stop the Red Sea, high[47] and swollen,

---

[44] "Spirits" may be something more than simply a synonym for "winds." See the wind/ demons in the Jerusalem-poems, in the wake of Virgil, *Aeneid* 1: 81 ff. This section of *MC* possibly contains the most extensive descriptions of sea landscapes in the history of Italian long poems. Only a saga in verse having Columbus as a hero (like Camões' *Lusiadas* in Portugal, celebrating Vasco Da Gama) could have offered more than this; but, interestingly enough, it has never been written, even though Tasso hoped some poet would do it. Sixteenth-century English prose literature is full of sea travel adventures where landscapes of the sea are prevalent, for example, Haklyut's and Sir Francis Drakes' travels, and many others.

[45] Many of these verses are so enchanting and meaningful—from different viewpoints—that scientific considerations of natural laws seem inapposite. This line, specifically, may sound like a teaching by Confucius.

[46] In *Job* 38: 10, *Jeremiah* 5: 22.

that would otherwise impetuously invade
Egypt, more deeply dug and lower than it,
and submerge it under its vast abyss?
It would have already joined the Indian Sea[48]
effortlessly, without any skills and works   370
of industrious mortals, without the boasts
of proud tyrants either. The great Sesostris,[49]
who kept kings chained to a hard yoke
like horses or oxen, forcefully subjected,
and made them draw his royal chariot
among tamed and subjugated peoples—
this Sesostris, I say, the havoc and terror
of the Northern kingdoms, where he fixed
his seat on high; and rightly does the fabulous
Egypt boast this, by virtue of an old fame—   380
this same Sesostris once tried to unite
the Indian Sea and the Eritrean together
with that of Egypt: but the powerful Pharaoh
had to quit the great enterprise, fearing
that his green lands may be finally flooded
by the sea. And the very same fear would
then hold back King Cyrus' successor.[50]
    The day the waves were left free to run,
cavernous and curved mountains[51] filled
grottoes and the dark, shadowy caves,   390

---

[47] That is, on a higher level than the Egyptian lands, according to Basil, who quotes
Aristotle (BB).

[48] At that time, "Ocean" only referred to the Atlantic.

[49] Egyptian Pharaoh ca, 1950 B.C.E.; here Tasso's source is Herodotus (BB). As mentioned
in the notes to Day 1, in Europe it was during the Renaissance that the mental picture of
Ancient Egypt started to go beyond Biblical stereotypes and regain historical traits: its
Pharaohs, religion, architecture, etc. This information came from the books of classical
authors, not from direct research as would happen with the Napoleonic campaigns. The first
attempts at reading the hieroglyphs were also made, though following criteria that would
hardly look reliable nowadays. The Renaissance also marked the rebirth of esoteric groups
whose doctrines were based on supposed Egyptian wisdom. In the late 19th century, Gustave
Doré will blend all these "Egypts" in his illustrations for Ariosto's *Orlando Furioso*: the
story takes place in the epoch of Charlemagne, it was written in the early 16th century, and
Doré sets some episodes among ruins that are based on drawings by the Napoleonic
archeologists.

[50] Persian king Darius I, who reigned in 522-485 B.C., but was Cambyses' successor (BB).

[51] Liquid mountains, huge bending waves—with a Baroque love for paradoxes and
subtleties (cavernous mountains filling caves!). Here and elsewhere, Tasso shows a deep
interest in geology, which will become a systematic science no sooner than in the 18th
century.

and swampy valleys leaning in different
ways, low among mounts and hills;
almost recalling seas, the vast fields
until then were filled with silvery liquid
—but all together found themselves emptied
at the command of the divine voice,
by which the waters were moved, pushed
away from the four corners of the world,
and then gathered all together into one.
At that same time, indeed, the divine   400
hand shaped the huge basins, and springs,
and rocky urns and the other places
where water flows in and out. There was
not yet—beyond the narrow opening[52]
that divides Abila and Kalpe with its waves,
facing Libya and Europe—the sea of Atlas,
nor the stormy Ocean,[53] the most frightful
to seamen, which all around encompasses
the happy kingdoms once ruled by Geryon,[54]
and England, and the neighboring Ireland;   410
but, at the loud thunder of that Voice,
the shores and seabeds were manufactured,
where the running waters were to gather.

Against truth, let no experience of erring
mortals dare speak boasting words: misleading,
vain experience of man, whose pride
grows on the brief span of a few years.
Yes, I say, if you honestly recall and think
about the number of the flying centuries,
no human experience can fill such expanse.   420
Let no expert[55] who searched the extreme
parts of the Earth raise against our thesis

---

[52] The Straits of Gibraltar; the names in the following lines indicate the two respective promontories.

[53] Apparently Tasso draws a distinction between the Ocean and the Atlantic Sea, but he often used particles like "and," "or," or "nor" simply to add variation to the same theme.

[54] Geryon was a fictional tyrant, a three-headed monster and a serial killer, so his island, off the coast of Spain, had no reasons for being happy. But, in Renaissance maps, the Happy or Fortunate Isles were usually placed somewhere between Gibraltar and the Americas, maybe in the Canaries (see Umberto Eco, *The Book of Legendary Lands*, Rizzoli Ex Libris/International Publications, 2013); Tasso "describes" them in *Gerusalemme Liberata*. Dante's monster Geryon, except for the name, has little to do with the classical personage referred to here (see *Dante Was a Fantasy Writer*, op. cit.)

[55] Renaissance explorer.

the trenches, muddy ponds, low and swampy
lakes[56] in which the laziest humors gather,
which God deemed unworthy of the name
"seas." For He only called so[57] the vast, grand
assemblies of waters—only such, indeed,
the biggest and most perfect, in which
the liquid element collects in its own seat.

    As fire, when split and divided   430
into most tiny fragments, shines here
in green wood or dry tinder, for our use,
in the shape of a burning lump of coal,
or a bright flame, or a smoking one,
so that it spreads in cinder and sparkles,
but below the lowest and smallest sky[58]
it all gathers in a concave space;
or as the air, that expands and breathes
in different places, and passes through
the hidden womb of water, bubbling, foamy,   440
and penetrates grottoes and cavernous
mountains, and the innermost veins
of the deep and shadowy earth,
but, all together, fills its own locus;
so does the water gather and spread
in varying beds, within narrow limits,
but then, collected in a vast, empty place,
the salty element fills its own site.[59]
The other waters, gathering anywhere
in the likeness of this, received therefore   450
the famous, illustrious name of "Seas."
There, see, where the cold North wind
forever pours down hoarfrost and ice,
freezing vast fields and rugged mounts
that turn hoary with perpetual snow:

---

[56] The vast lakes in Latin America that were called "seas," as Tasso will explain below.

[57] On the basis of *Genesis* 1: 9-10.

[58] In the "sphere of fire" that—following Aristotle's cosmology—was believed to lie below the "sky of the Moon," the lowest among the skies revolving around the Earth. The flames supposedly stretched upwards because they tended towards their natural "home." In a wonderful flash of poetry, Dante describes passing through the sphere of fire in *Paradiso* 1: 58-63.

[59] The so-to-speak underground "sphere of water" didn't belong to Aristotle's cosmology. BB indicates Theophile of Antioch as a source; but, as it has already been pointed out, Tasso had a personal enthusiasm for this topic.

there, as Fame divulges even to us,[60]
are immense ponds and—in deep beds
among superb, frightful banks—abysmal
swamps aiming at emulating the sea.
Turning into ice, hardened, thickened   460
into a shining adamantine enamel,
they can sustain the course and the weight
of the quick wheels of big, ponderous carts
drawn by animals unknown to our eyes,[61]
whose high and proud-looking foreheads
are armed with long, branching antlers;
ever they move the heavy peasant carts
where caulked ships used to travel.
  Bigger than any other, a snowy lake[62]
there, below the icy Seven Oxen,[63]   470
shines white, and like the Caspian Sea,
round its freezing banks it hosts many cities,
provinces, kingdoms, unknown folk,
barbarian peoples. And they go shooting
along the shores, since the flying birds,
either on the waves or[64] under the waves,
look for wet prey, or for that food[65]
loved by both scaly and winged beings.
Botnia,[66] a country full of fish, quite close
to the *Biarms*[67] at the very world's end,   480

---

[60] One of Tasso's favorite authors, Olaus Magnus, i.e. Olof Månsson, who wrote *Historia de Gentibus Septentrionalibus*, "History of the Nordic Peoples," published in 1555. The very copy read by Tasso, with his handwritten notes, is currently kept in Saint Petersburg, Russia (BB). Olaus was the main source of inspiration for Tasso's Shakespearean and Sophoclean tragedy *Il Re Torrismondo*, set in the same area and, more or less, the same epoch as *Beowulf*; it is a unique work in Italian literature because of its setting and gloomy Shakespearean atmospheres. But *Gerusalemme Conquistata* itself shows the "marks" of Nordic epic, with its muscular, gory battles that remind us of Conan the Barbarian much more than the refined Ariostesque duels in *Gerusalemme Liberata*. In fact, many battles in the *Conquistata* are translations from Homer and Virgil, but "Viking-ized," so to speak.
[61] Reindeer. Tasso's verses, here and in *Il Re Torrismondo*, represent possibly the first occurrences of reindeer in Italian poetry.
[62] The Vänern Lake in SW Sweden, which is actually a large one, but smaller than what these verses might lead one to imagine. BB's notes are the source for geographic references noted in this section.
[63] The Big Bear stars (BB), *Septem Triones* in Latin, from which "Settentrione" in Italian comes, i.e. the North Pole.
[64] The "e" (= and) in BB must be edited into "o."
[65] Weeds, etc. Foreshadowing Tasso's keen interest in the behavior of animals, see Days Five and Six.
[66] An area between Sweden and Finland.

among its icy, saw-toothed mountains
includes several quasi-seas, and it feeds
all neighboring people on those fish,
and could feed half the world's people.
Nor elsewhere lies the Lake of Venus,[68]
spreading far and wide below the Bears
and in its spacious, vast womb receiving
through twenty-four doors the rivers,
its tributaries. But it leaves only one
open way out to the precipitating waters,   490
that through a stony path run towards
the roaring sea, deafening the inhabitants.
In its liquid womb, the lake hosts many
islands and temples of the Heavenly King,
where He is worshiped with a devout cult.[69]
Here the *Melce*[70] Lake stagnates between the
kingdom of the Swedes and that of the Goths.[71]
And nearby the Vättern[72] also undulates,
sounding like the thunder of lightning, or
of metals that imitate the lightning   500
with the thunder of its waters, from above
precipitating; one might often think
an iron device[73] is thundering and striking,
and as it rumbles, knocks down the walls.
Both lakes are, in fact, rich in metals,

---

[67] The inhabitants of Kola Island.

[68] Again the Vänern, or "il lago di Venere." Was Tasso inspired by its sound, in calling Venus into question? Or by its great "sex" appeal (see lines 487-488)?

[69] Tasso's source, Olaus Magnus, was a Catholic bishop: this idyllic religious situation apparently does not fit in with the fact that Luther's Reformation was taking root in Sweden too. But in Roman Catholic milieus, they often thought Protestantism would prove just a temporary phenomenon. In his long poems, Tasso will directly, and polemically, refer to Luther just once in the *Conquistata*. A more interesting connection with Olaus is found in *Il Re Torrismondo*, set in Scandinavia in the seventh century A.D., where it is not very clear—as it is also the case with *Beowulf*—if the protagonists are already Christians or still pagans. Surely, no "Christian hope" permeates its pages, rather recalling *Richard III* or *Macbeth*. The stories written by the Catholic J. R. R. Tolkien are not much more optimistic, for that matter. Interestingly enough, Tolkien's *Tale of the Children of Húrin* is a gloomy saga based on the myth of Oedipus, as is the *Torrismondo*.

[70] Mälar, in SE Sweden.

[71] Norway, Sweden, and *Gothia* (Southern Scandinavia) are the three Kingdoms involved in the *Torrismondo*.

[72] In this case the Italian form, *Vetere*, agrees with the original name. Tasso here cites from the then recent book *L'universale fabrica del mondo, overo Cosmografia*, "The Whole Building of the World, or Cosmography" by G. L. D'Anania, 1582 (BB).

[73] A cannon.

since their fortunate banks abound
in long-drawn veins of silver and iron.
The Kingdom of Norway has a lake
nourishing in its bosom a prodigy—
a horrible, frightful, ungodly snake.[74]   510
Ireland has one, where a weak, sick man cannot,
however tired, exhale his spirit and soul,
unless pulled out. Among the Britons
there is a lake[75] that has alternate tides
following the opposite rhythm of the sea:
when the latter lowers, the former floods,
but it gathers its waves and turns back
when the superb Ocean raises itself.
Scotland has the Tay famous for its cry
as well as the wonderful, deep swamp   520
that, when the sky is all serene and pure
and no wind or breeze blows in the air,
swells—who knows why?—and lifts its waves.
Many are in Germany, France; and the famous
lake[76] from which the Rhone reaches the sea.
From the *Lugean* swamp, a source of pride
to noble Carnia,[77] no length of time
could lessen its honor and its fame.
Here they fish, at first; when it becomes
completely dry, they sow the seeds in it   530
and harvest, then; and among the green trees
the people catch the unwary birds.
So it happens that, in various times,
it works as swamp and field and wood.
Well known, as well, are the marvels
of Thrace and Arcadia. And on the other side
of the world,[78] where the sun scorches and dries
the earth, there lie, in that sunburnt soil,
swamps and ponds of amazing powers,

---

[74] A "cryptid," like the Loch Ness Monster, or the *Manipogo* in Canada. Water monsters belong to Nordic imagery, see *Beowulf*. A snake like this, though a terrestrial variety, appears in Tasso's Jerusalem-poems.

[75] Windermere.

[76] The Lake of Geneva, but Tasso mixes up the data from his sources (BB).

[77] A pleasant strip of land between Italy and Austria.

[78] Latin America. Tasso's source, as it has already been mentioned, is Ramusio (see note 32). The Enriquillo Lake, in the current Dominican Republic, had been called "Caspian Sea" by the Spaniards (BB).

to which the name "seas" was not denied. 540
    In Judea, a miracle we are still being shown
is the lake[79] into which, from a sky aflame,
a just fire fell; and the other, nearby,
from which the Jordan River first flows.
Between Palestine and green Egypt
a wide lake lies in the Arabian desert,
called *Semhovitë*.[80] But why should I speak
of stagnant waters in Arabia and Syria,
if even the land of Ethiopia and India,[81]
much more subject to the sun, is watered 550
by its famous lakes? And the story goes
that drinking from them, a man quickly becomes
foolish and crazy; then heavy with sleep,
he lies, overwhelmed by deadly lethargy.[82]
Beyond Heracles' boundary rocks,[83]
between the Tropic of Cancer and the wide
belt[84] dividing and wrapping the main sphere,
in Kingdoms unknown so far, a lake[85] ripples
which does not ebb and flow hourly
nor day by day, nor does it move 560
season by season, or year after year;
but like an earthly man late in reaching
his perfect state, and late as well
in declining in size as he grows old,
this lake keeps filling up for fifty years,
then in fifty more it decreases and empties.
    But why, Italy, O Beauty, am I omitting
your lakes, described in endless books,
most clear[86] in their fame and waves?

---

[79] The Dead Sea. In the Jerusalem-poems, the castle of the witch Armida stands in this area.

[80] *Sic!* Actually the "Serbonis" Lake, mentioned in St. Basil's *Hexaemeron* (BB).

[81] As seen in Renaissance maps, they were basically *one* land, supposing that SE Africa swerved eastward a lot. See especially the legendary Kingdom of the "Priest John," that was set in India and/or Ethiopia (cf. Umberto Eco, *op. cit.*). A funny, witty reworking of that long-lasting myth is offered by Ariosto in *Orlando Furioso*.

[82] Waters with wonderful effects can be found in both Ariosto's and Tasso's poems; as well as in C. S. Lewis' Narnian, neo-Renaissance novel *The Voyage of the Dawn Treader* (cf. Salwa Khoddam, *Mythopoeic Narnia*, Winged Lion Press, 2013, especially ch. 8).

[83] Once again the Straits of Gibraltar.

[84] The Equator.

[85] The "Temistitan," a lake in Mexico in the Kingdom of Montezuma (BB).

[86] With a pun that, more or less, works in both languages: the superlative form "chiarissimi" in literary Italian also means "renown, celebrated."

Who ignores Trasimeno?[87] Or the one   570
hosting Mantua within its sweet basin?
Or the grandest *Lario*, or the grand *Benaco*, too,[88]
resembling the sea in its pride and waves?
And many others so happily washing you?[89]
Why am I silent about the old marvels
of the ponds of Rieti, where they could see
the slight islets, ripples round them, as if swimming?
Or, in the lake of Tarquinia, shady woods
crossing over the waves, often changing
their shapes and figures, now as a circle,   580
now a triangle with an acute angle?[90]

    But... who diverts me from God's works
making me instead tell about Nature's effects,[91]
both old and new? Thus to fill my pages,
consecrated to the Supreme King's majesty,
with different glories, stories, and names,
or with rare, lofty marvels, but other
than His own? Or, are perhaps Nature's
works divine works themselves?
—and Nature's craftsmanship is the art   590
of the First Maker, of whom the Great Mother
Nature is a creature and daughter.[92] In her we
honor, in her we can recognize and admire
the all-surpassing mind and power[93]
of the High King, her Maker and Father.
He gave the seas their figure and name,
and the swelling with stormy surges
to the gathered waters. They were many,
but He made one sea by His eminent art,

---

[87] In Umbria, central Italy.

[88] The Lakes of Como and Garda in Northern Italy, respectively. Tasso exaggerates a bit.

[89] Italy.

[90] The two latter "phenomena" had been "reported" by Pliny the Elder (BB). For a modern, enchanting description of Living—and dancing—Trees, see Lewis' *Chronicles of Narnia*.

[91] As we will immediately see, the distinction between God's and/or Nature's works is not obvious in Tasso.

[92] Cf. Dante, *Inferno* 11: 97-105, human activity as "God's granddaughter" because it follows Nature that is God's daughter. But even more than that, here Nature as the Great Mother is likened to the Virgin Mary, "the daughter of her Son," Dante, *Paradiso* 33: 1. See what Tasso adds next.

[93] Cf. Dante, *Paradiso* 33: 19-21 (Mary), and also 18: 109-111 (God's power and its "reflected" effects). See, besides, the classic theological locus by St. Paul in *Romans* 1: 19-20.

though partly hidden[94] to our erring senses: 600
one out of the waters' widespread element.
To which, between the heavy, steady earth
and the light and wandering air, He fixed
its proper seat and place, thus on both sides
establishing almost[95] eternal borders to the sea.
    One, therefore, is the wholly gathered sea,
of endless waters and endless deeps,
as those men[96] reported, who—like the sun—
sailed[97] along the earth or circled it: pilgrims
wandering from the West to the East,   610
from Southern to Northern kingdoms.
Though somebody thinks the Caspian Sea
is detached and cut off from any other sea,
as being encircled by coasts on all sides;
human senses do agree, but wrongly so,
as the age-old mistake clearly showed
of those who thought that, in the same way,
the Red Sea had no direct link with
the Indian Sea. But no sense, nor "certain"
experience of ingenious mortals   620
can demonstrate that the Caspian waves
are united to other seas, though separate
and surrounded by such a long strip of land.
Only the rare,[98] high mind of a Pilgrim knows:
by ascending to heaven and passing through

---

[94] Referring to the "one sea," not to God's art; as the grammatical genders in Italian show. Here Tasso again makes reference to his theory of an underground sea as the "main storehouse" of all the waters of the Earth.

[95] The universe's solidity is always in jeopardy in Tasso's worldview. He thought, or rather wished, that the End was close at hand: see his prayer in the final verses of the poem.

[96] Again, the Renaissance navigators. After blaming himself for exalting the works of Nature instead of those of God, Tasso glorifies the enterprises of Man.

[97] Here a technical verb is used: *lustrare*, nowadays meaning "to polish, to shine," but in Renaissance sea parlance it meant to sail, and more precisely to sail along, to coast. "Survey" or "explore" are possible alternatives.

[98] Dante? Tasso plays on the two meanings of "peregrino," i.e. rare, precious, or pilgrim. It would probably be the first time in history that the author of *Paradiso* is described as an astronaut, or an artificial satellite providing readers with a sort of Google Maps. Or, maybe, venturing an extreme conjecture: Tasso here refers to the "spirit" who sometimes talked to him. His friend, Giovanni Battista Manso tried to convince him that the spirit was only the fruit of his imagination. Tasso replied that it was not possible, because the spirit knew many more things than he himself: wonderful, unheard-of things (see Fabio Pittorru, *Torquato Tasso*, Bompiani, 1982, pp. 350-351). Cf. the *Erdengeist* who appears to Goethe's Faust much before Mephistopheles.

the starry cloisters from star to star, beyond
the borders and narrow spaces of Cosmos
(those exposed to senses), in eternal peace
uniting with the pure, eternal minds.[99]
That genius can search the beds and bottoms   630
of the wavy seas; then, underground, spy
on the most hidden, most inner parts,
which Nature keeps in her secret depths.
About the Caspian Sea, *he* dared affirm
that it joined, underground, the other seas,
precisely as we can read of Alpheus[100]
and Tigris, as well as all other rivers.
God, in fact—like the ancient founder
of a noble city, or an eminent architect who,
to the city's benefit, makes long, deep   640
roads underground[101] for the hidden course
of wandering waters, conducting them
from elsewhere, spring or river or swamp—
likewise drilled hidden sea channels
in the cold and tenebrous earth.
From their springs, He (or, the Divine
Daedalus, I dare say) turned the waters
so that not only is the African sea linked
to that of Cadiz and that of Sardinia,
and the Ligurian Sea to the Thyrrenian,   650
and the Adriatic, and Ionian, and Aegean
with its many islands and many harbors,
and the neighboring *Myrthoum*,[102] and the Pontus
with its Hellespont[103] and the bitter swamp[104]
—but the wide gulfs of Arabia, and Persia,
and sunburnt India are joined to the deep
Ocean, and much more wonderfully so.
The Caspian Sea, which encloses and covers itself
over a large area and appears isolated
from all others like a solitary pilgrim,[105]   660

---

[99] The angels. See, e.g., *Paradiso* 28: 52-54.

[100] A river in the Peloponnesus, Southern Greece.

[101] Aqueducts; with a typical Renaissance interest in science and technology, in spite of all mysticism.

[102] The Western Aegean Sea (BB).

[103] Here the latter term strictly indicates the Black Sea; the former, in a broader sense, the surrounding area.

[104] The Sea of Azov.

hides its deep union and its grand source.

God did not then say, "Let the earth surface,"
but, "Let the dryness appear," thus calling
the earth "dryness," showing by such a name
that it was dry before there was any sun,[106]
even before a newly-born sun in the sky
may dry it by its rays; the Ancient Mother
would present herself with dry limbs.
In fact, at the sound of the divine voice,
all waters immediately ran downwards,   670
so that the land was left muddy, mixed
with stagnant waters, an unadorned sight;
but its first and primal quality was
dryness nonetheless, this the old feature
proper to it, fulfilling its substance.[107]

As coldness belongs to water, warmth
to fire, and a humid nature to air,
so dryness characterizes the earth.
And as the bull is recognized by its bellow
and the fierce lion by its roar of pride,   680
and the horse by its whinny, so the earth
is "in-formed"[108] and distinguished by dryness.

But about the primal, unmixed elements,
no more than this can the sage understand
through contemplating eternal objects,
since what is *now* subject to our senses are
solely the great principles of ever-changing,
perishable things, so that a perpetual war
is waged below the revolving cold Moon.
Nothing pure or sincere can now be seen   690
in all of them, nothing simple or solitary:
they are mixed up, the primal qualities
currently pairing the one with the other.
So the earth has become both cold and dry;
the water, cold and damp; damp and warm,
the air; and above it, and closer to the sky,
the fire is both warm and dry by nature.

---

[105] With a slight hint at Dante, *Paradiso* 17: 55-69, and/or himself.
[106] It will be created "tomorrow," on the Fourth Day.
[107] Its *quidditas* (what is what) in Aristotelian and Medieval Scholastic parlance.
[108] The Aristotelian *morphe*/Scholastic *forma* is the principle making everything what it is (*quo quid est*).

Thus the qualities have been connected,
pair by pair, in the first natural bodies,
whereby they are mixed with one another,   700
briefly in peace. As it happens in a ball,[109]
that one in the middle is bound by two hands
and binds with two hands, and both ways,
in a wide circle, the entwined dancers go
back to the starting point after their rounds:
so the choir and dance of the elements
circle around and return to their places.
Water in fact is here linked by coldness
with (say) one of her hands to the icy terrain
of the cold Earth; on the other side,   710
with her other hand, (say) her damp hand,
she touches Air, who, between Water and Fire,
is linked to Water by her own dampness,
and she joins Fire by virtue of her warmth.
The struggle and wrath of two conflicting
and fighting natures[110] both divides them
and unites them in an alloy,[111] nonetheless.

    Oh, the wonderful world-chain, all joined
in varied ways with strong knots into one,
indissoluble, much more resistant   720
than solid iron or brilliant adamant,
thanks to the art of the Supreme Smith![112]
Oh, the ever-changing and perishable things,
but with a firm, steady, nearly eternal order!
In your endless varying, World, you follow
uncorrupted, universal, ancient laws

---

[109] Dante too had described the dances of his times, see *Purgatorio* 28: 52-54; 29: 127-129;
Paradiso 12: 5-6; 14: 19-21. A Renaissance dance like this can be seen in Andrea
Mantegna's painting *Parnassus* (in Paris, Louvre).

[110] Echoing Dante, *Inferno* 25: 100-102 (in the context of the whole Canto), and lending the
passage a more ominous character. The mixing of heterogeneous bodies, together with the
splitting of the psyche in the case of human beings, is the climax of horror, as it had been
described by Tasso—there also on the basis of *Inferno* 25—in *Gerusalemme Liberata*, when
Armida, as a new Circe, turns her prisoners into beasts (fish). See a fine illustration of the
episode by Eva "Nivalis" Nieri in the anthology *Emanations: Third Eye* (International
Authors, 2013), p. 195. "…Into a beast, and mixed with bestial slime, / This essence to
incarnate and imbrute," as Milton would powerfully put it in *Paradise Lost* 9: 165-166. A
modern masterpiece dealing with metamorphosis is John Carpenter's 1982 film *The Thing*.

[111] "Lega" means either alloy or league. "Alloy" has been chosen because it conveys
something "stronger."

[112] There may be a reminiscence of the indestructible net forged by Hephaestus in Homer's
Iliad, also mentioned in Ariosto's *Orlando Furioso*, but in a humorous episode.

which are known from sun-burnt Ethiopia
to icy Schythia;[113] partly resembling,
though with vicissitudes and uncertain motions,
the certain, divine laws higher than the sky.   730
    After the vast masses of running waters
had been gathered in their deep site,
God saw that the new sea was beautiful[114]
—not by any eyes, but in His eternal mind,
in which He admires the noble work
He himself made, and His own creatures.
    Happy sight, and joyful, and sweet[115]
is that of the sea, when, tranquil and flat,
it murmurs lying whitish by the shore.
And beautiful, when its back is spurred   740
by a pleasant breeze rippling its waves;
when the sea shines cerulean or purple
to the watcher, not angrily hitting
the neighboring land with violence,
but sweetly spreading friendly arms
around the coast, embracing it to its breast.
But not so beautiful or dear was
the sea's first sight to the heavenly King;
not here did the senses judge its beauty,
but the *logos*[116] of this amazing work   750
is pleasant and lovely in God's own mind.
    Surrounding the wide earth, the sea is the
first and perpetual source of all humors.
Through dark and shadowy passages
under the cavernous and hollow earth,
the sea divides and shares itself
as across very deep, hidden mines;

---

[113] The belief that the main ideas were common to the whole of humanity took a long time to die out. Among the first Western thinkers who foresaw the cultural shock that would be caused by the discovery of completely different worldviews was Arthur Schopenhauer, see his collection of essays *On the Will in Nature*, 1854 (1st ed. 1836), ch. 7.

[114] One of the meanings of the Hebrew word *tov*, usually translated as "good."

[115] BB notes that this description translates St. Basil's prose into verse, but the Neapolitan Tasso surely *felt* as if he himself had written the whole thing.

[116] Here the word "ragion[e]" used by Tasso is more than "reason"; it includes the deep cosmic, philosophical, and theological meanings of the Greek word *logos*. It would be interesting, by the way, to learn how Tasso and/or Basil could know about God's tastes; but even more interesting is that Tasso, here and elsewhere, adopts a non-anthropocentric viewpoint. The whole poem, on the other hand, has no human protagonist: that makes it unique.

and after it finds itself shut up below,
it swerves upwards with crooked courses.
Finally, pushed by the spirit[117] that moves it,   760
and breaking through the earth's hard womb,[118]
it comes out; and by purifying its humors,
it sweetens its terrestrial bitterness.[119]
Meanwhile, from metals the sea takes on
a much hotter quality, so that it often
burns and boils with foaming waters
round islands bathed by the surrounding sea,
or also in areas closer to the salty shores,
and even, sometimes, far away inland.[120]

    So, beautiful is the sea in God's mind   770
because it has a bed deep underground.
Beautiful, because in its wide salty bosom
it gathers all rivers from every side,
and restrains itself within its limits.
Beautiful, because it is the primary source
of the rain, and of every humor being poured
by the air, condensed in frost, snow, or ice;
or warmed by the sun's burning beams,
the sea exhales its lighter parts upwards,
which arrive later at the coldest heights   780
where no heat reaches, since the sun's rays
get twisted there. And there they condense
because of the cold surrounding them,
and finally fall as a heavy, thick humor.
So the Rain impregnates the dry womb[121]
of the Earth, who then conceives and bears
so many, varied, and pleasant shapes
of plants, and beasts, and flowers and herbs.[122]

---

[117] "Spirit" as pressure or the like; but a "spirit moving" a body seems to recall the concept of soul.

[118] Sort of a caesarean birth.

[119] This explanation comes from Aristotle (BB). Fresh water in Italian is *acqua dolce*, literally sweet water.

[120] Geysers.

[121] It is not the first time that copulation is described in Italian literature; see Dante, *Purgatorio* 25: 43-45. The ancient Phoenicians called the rain "[god's] Baal's sperm."

[122] This line echoes St. Francis of Assisi's *Canticle of the Sun*, more properly "Canticle of the Creatures." Even more closely, it seems to cite the *Catechism* of the Council of Trent, published in 1566, often rendering theology in a poetical fashion: *Deinde [Deus] non solum arboribus, omnique herbarum, et florum varietate [terram] convestivit, atque ornavit; sed*

Who could deny the truth of what I say,[123]
envisioning how on a burning fire a pot   790
boils and fumes, when full of water,
so that, the latter exhaling its lighter parts
in the air, the pot empties itself of half?
And often the very water of the sea,
picked up with sponges and boiled,
will meet the needs of thirsty, tired
navigators, comforting them in part.
But most beautiful is the sea in the eyes
of the divine, unchangeable mind
because, with its curved foamy arms,   800
it gathers and clasps so many islands;
and because it connects the faraway,
diverse parts of the Earth and the shores
divided by Nature, offering a wide, easy way
to helmsmen, who can thus sail across it,
shipping valuable and precious goods
coast to coast, so as to fill the want
of the one people, and ease the other
by diminishing what abounds too much.[124]
With such goods, of more hidden things,   810
indeed of odd, unknown wonders they report
modern stories and fascinating news.[125]
But from what high, projecting cliff,
from what sky-scraping rock, or what
sublime, steep mountain range
towering above the sea on both sides
will I be able to see its beauty so clearly
as it then unfolded before its Maker?[126]
But so beautiful and praiseworthy
the wavy sea may be before Divinity,   820
much more beautiful is the thick, rejoicing
crowd of His faithful gathered and mixed,
that wave before the doors and inside the temple
and offer their vows, and devoutly effuse

---

innumerabilibus animantium generibus… (Part I, ch. 2, the paragraphs about the words *creatorem coeli et terrae* in the *Credo*).
[123] A fictional "I" since the example is taken from St. Basil (BB).
[124] This description of trade between America and Europe is a bit biased, to say the least.
[125] That was probably the "import good" Tasso was most interested in, among the things listed in the "reports" from the New Lands.
[126] Caspar David Friedrich's paintings come to mind.

their prayers[127] to Heaven—you hear a sound
as when the sea breaks against the shore.[128]

So, may the great Clement[129] forever keep
that merciful and happy-looking face and
his still, serene peace in the magnificent,
sacred ceremonies. May he spread   830
the true worship throughout the world,
opening heaven and its eternal treasures,
and sharing and giving its graces to all;[130]
may he not judge me unworthy of seeing him.[131]

Then God said, "Let the Earth germinate
her green grass and her fertile wood
yielding its own fruit, both[132] according
to the respective seeds she hides within."
So did He say. The great Ancient Mother,
who had shaken off the waters' weight,   840
already breathed, and did look relieved,[133]
in part, after giving birth to her newborn.
For the voice of the supreme command
was a constant, certain, unchangeable
law of Nature; and nowhere does Nature
vary according to the varying of time,
but it stays identical age after age.
So, the pregnant[134] and burdened Earth
has the green germ as her firstborn;
which later, slowly raising from   850
her cold, damp womb, first turns into grass,

---

[127] Cf. *Revelation* 5: 8.

[128] Such solemn celebrations were a "modern"—Renaissance, then Baroque—phenomenon, also meant as a counterattack against the sobered Protestant liturgy. There are no descriptions like this in the *Divine Comedy*.

[129] Pope Clement VIII. Lines 827-830 have been here reassembled for syntactical reasons: in a Latinizing structure, the subject, Clement, appears three lines below its direct objects.

[130] A good wish for the Jubilee (Holy Year) of the year 1600, which would be actually held under Clement VIII, though Tasso wouldn't be there to see it. Jubilees, with the selling of indulgences, had been the *casus belli* for Luther's Reformation, but the Roman Catholic Church basically did not change its course.

[131] The Pope and his family were Tasso's sponsors during the last years of his troubled life.

[132] Grass and trees.

[133] In past times, childbirth could be even more painful than now. For literary sources, cf. *John* 16: 21, and Dante, *Paradiso* 15: 133. In Tasso's tragedy *Il Re Torrismondo* (2. 4. 1241-1245), Princess Rosmonda, though not a nun, wants neither to have any children, nor to become a slave to family rules; surely a bold choice at that time.

[134] Here "pregnante" has the same meaning as in English. In current Italian, it means poignant.

90

then gains strength and firmness,
until it looks like straw[135] or another
full-formed plant; and by growing older,
each gets its green, grassy features.
So, as though they were sisters[136] or twins,
they do not look identical, nor exceedingly
different, but indeed similar to one another.
Without anybody's help[137] the Ancient Mother
produced these, needing no alien   860
power in addition to God's decision.

Some[138] thought the sun was the sublime
cause of what clings[139] to her or is born of her,
warming her by means of its burning rays
and attracting upwards her inner powers
from her depths with its life-giving heat;
but they go astray in the wake of Reason,
because Mother Earth is more ancient,
born before the sun was born in the sky.
Let therefore no vain error perplex them: 870
may they stop worshiping the Sun's light[140]
as if it were the eternal cause of life.
Enough of the old and new oddities,[141]
enough of such prayers, sacrifices,[142] vows!
Enough of not only high marble Colossi
but of altars, idols, and temples also!
And away with every false, ungodly cult,
that yet makes the rough, silly peoples[143]

---

[135] Cf. *Mark* 4: 28.

[136] "Erbe" and "piante" (the latter being implied in the original text) are feminine words.

[137] Again an anthropomorphism, referring to midwives. It may also aim at strengthening the parallel between Sacred Nature and the Virgin Mary. Midwives helping Mary in Bethlehem were often portrayed by artists, but this detail came from apocryphal texts, that the Catholic Church—officially, at least—didn't accept and—formally—condemned. In lines 1230 ff., Tasso will mention some plants as symbols of the Mother of God.

[138] Aristotle, Philo of Alexandria (BB).

[139] The puzzling verb "s'appiglia" may come from *Inferno* 25: 51, where a strong physical "link" is described, including a simile with a plant, ivy (line 58).

[140] With an updated reference to American pre-Columbian religions, see below. Tasso recalls the religions of ancient Egyptians and Persians, as well as "old and new oddities." Lines 875-876 mention the temples of the Egyptian solar cult.

[141] Here "maraviglie," usually meaning "wonders, marvels," has a negative sense.

[142] Including human sacrifices—as the Spanish *Conquistadores* reported? Only in one brief passage—in *Gerusalemme Conquistata*, not here—will Tasso justify the forced conversion of natives.

living beyond the Pillars of Hercules
—unknown land below an unknown sky,[144]   880
that the Ocean deeply divides from us—
worship the Sun, consecrating their lying[145]
idols to him as to a most high god.
May they learn, following a holy voice[146]
telling the marvels of the newborn world
to them, and the activity and the work
and the art of the heavenly Forger—
may they learn, I say, provided no deceit
or doubt is left in those simple souls—
may they learn that the shining Sun   890
illuminates the whole world with its light,
running across it all and surrounding it;
that golden source of serene light, that
great eye in the sky, that sublime father
of our mortal life, that highest guide
leading and accompanying us by its beams,[147]
is newer and younger than hay and grass,
to *them* yielding the honor of seniority!
What then! Before the Sun was, for woolly
flocks and horned herds God did prepare   900
the green grassy food!—when human food
was still uncared for by Providence.
May that very Lord (who to slow, lazy
oxen and to swiftly running horses
prearranged such easy nourishment)
prepare sweet and dear food for you too,
letting you rejoice in laying a rich table.[148]
He himself, who feeds your livestock
fattening the herds on grassy fields,
upon big plates of silver and fine gold,   910
spices the dishes; He feeds and benefits you,

---

[143] Political correctness was not his strong point. The interesting cultural datum, however, is that Native Americans are no longer "general savages," nor literally "Indians," but peoples with an identity of their own. It was the first time that so many materials from the reports from America were inserted in an Italian long poem.

[144] Cf. Dante, *Inferno* 26: 127, in Ulysses' bold/crazy voyage beyond the Pillars of Hercules.

[145] A "topical" adjective from Dante, *Inferno* 1: 72.

[146] Tasso's, with this very poem? Was America his intended audience?

[147] Tasso ironically piles up commonplace. Among billions of sources, cf. Dante, *Purgatorio* 13: 16-21.

[148] The poet is literally using the carrot and the stick.

and tickles your taste with those flavors.[149]

  Yes, the sprouting of the sown seed
is nothing less than preparing, in advance,
that which will keep and save your life.
Nourishment for humans are the herbs
and other plants the fertile soil yields,
somehow classified between the herbs
and the leafy trees, of uncertain breed.
But not always is the grassy soil   920
a matrix to the germinating seeds:
not the spear grass, giving glorious crowns
to good Romans in the ancient times;
nor the reed, whose sweet sound often
tempers the rough loves of lazy shepherds;
nor the mint, the saffron, as in thousands
are they produced and created with no seed
by the wet-faced and fertile Earth.[150]
In fact, either in the root or the bottom
there is a seed-like power. That is why   930
the empty reed, after a whole year's
growth, dressed in its green bark,
out of its root sends and sticks out
who-knows-what, yet having the seed's
strength and principle, instead of a seed.
No olive has ever come out of a reed,
but a reed is always born of a reed,
and olive of olive; so that they fulfill
God's orders to them in the beginning.[151]
That which, in that first, ancient birth,   940
was earth-generated and projected outside
from the gloomy shadows to the bright light,
season after season and age after age,
is born again and renewed in its likeness,
and in its generations is nearly eternal.

  Ha, think! At the sound of few words
of brief command, all of a sudden

---

[149] Unlike the stern Dante (see *Purgatorio* 22: 145 ff.), the Renaissance courtier Tasso praises the pleasures of the table.
[150] Cf. *Purgatorio* 28: 112 ff., but Dante admitted the existence of "seed-less born" plants only as an exception. In this section Tasso depends on Basil, Pliny the Elder and Aristotle, or rather an author now called Pseudo-Aristotle (BB).
[151] *Genesis* 1: 11. Again, it is not a matter of genetics, but the metaphysical principle of genetics.

94

the once cold and dry and barren Earth
felt the sorrow and pain of bearing.
Being moved to beget her dear fruits, she   950
opened the green shrines[152] of her closed womb.
As a woman,[153] recently ill and grieved,
now puts away her black dress and veil,
wears rich clothes and golden embroidery,
adorned with an unusually precious art;
so too the Earth, who looked then sorrowful,
squalid in countenance, presently
with herbs and flowers and happy, leafy
newborn plants, to her embellished limbs
wove a verdant and richest gown,   960
braiding gay garlands for her long hair.[154]

Ha, think to yourself, in every detail,
how many marvels God made in creating;
and to make His sublime miracle affixed
to your heart's depths, wherever you turn
your eyes and heart to the created works,
may you always remember Him, the Source.
For no plant is so low and rough,
no ignored herb so small in the soil,
that could not renew in your heart the image   970
and the memory of the eternal Maker,
calling us wretched mortals to Him.

Before the hay were seen flowers and grass;
but think to yourself that just like the hay,
human flesh fades[155] and loses its
native hue and gets dry to sight,[156]
and the "green"[157] mortal glory, once mown,
suddenly falls. Today, a graceful lover[158]
in the most green and serene Spring

---

[152] Literally "cloisters."

[153] A widow. At that time, a new wedding was often celebrated in a few weeks since women were not economically independent.

[154] Poetical commonplace, but see in Dante, *Purgatorio* 27: 102, a dream introducing paradise.

[155] Cf. *Isaiah* 40: 6-8.

[156] Exactly as it happened to the formerly handsome Tasso after the seven years (1579-86) in a "political" asylum. See the documented history of Tasso's alleged "insanity" in Fabio Pittorru, *op. cit.*

[157] The pun is even more fitting in Italian: *in erba* literally means "in [a condition like green] grass."

[158] A male one. Another autobiographical hint, since Tasso was bisexual.

95

of his happy and joyful existence   980
—feeding on sweet, gentle thoughts,
self-confident with juvenile hopes,
adorned with purple and golden frills,
his face, hair, scenting with Arabian smells,
strong in his youth[159]—exhibits here and there
an imposing horse, riding him full gallop;
or in an alien pomp, in a fake appearance,
wearing a false mask, shows up to witness
and breaks heavy lances in a fenced field.[160]
Tomorrow he will be deathly pale, though;   990
his eyes dark and hollow in his forehead,[161]
or with limbs worn-out and trembling, he
will lie on an odious bed;[162] feverish, weak,
with his broken words hardly understood.

    Another[163]—proud of his old and new wealth
gathered by him or by illustrious ancestors,
and proud of his own fame and honor,
followed by a thick and humble crowd,
indeed, by the numerous and long herd
of his servants and chosen ministers,   1000
or of flattering and false friends[164] perhaps—
comes out of his high, golden palace,
then comes back in a superb splendor;
and in coming and going, he triggers envy
and disdain in those he meets first and last;
from all around he sees people rushing
towards him; all are led and attracted
by grace, money, favors, rewards, food.
And to wealth add a widespread power,
and ruling a free city, and being in charge   1010
of armed troops, and the honor and power
granted him by unconquered kings,[165]

---

[159] With slight Biblical references, e.g. *Psalm* 133: 2, *Song of Songs* 3: 6-8.
[160] Masked balls and jousts (where the "mask" is the helm) were very frequent in the Este Court in Ferrara, the city of the poet's Rise and Fall. See F. Pittorru, *op. cit.*
[161] Tasso knows this all too well, but, in describing it, he echoes Dante, *Purgatorio* 23: 31 ff.
[162] "Piume," literally feathers.
[163] BB indicates St. Basil as the source; but once again, Tasso simply follows somebody else's phrasing to voice his own experience. He himself had belonged to both groups: the courtiers and the beggars. In different periods, he had asked the Este family and others for *all* the things listed in line 1008.
[164] This was an obsession for Tasso.

and a rare Guard with gleaming weapons,
fierce and feared, in outdated garb.
Thence the fear of a burdensome exile,[166]
of a stripped-down and naked poverty,
of the dark, forbidding shadows in a jail
in heavy shackles,[167] or of horrible death,
upsets and torments both mob and knights.
Even worse! In the space of a brief night,   1020
a strong, burning fever attacks and tames
his sides and stomach,[168] and from this happy state,
from such a height, from the world indeed,
snatches away the unlucky Lord by force,[169]
suddenly pulling away from him
the painted scene[170] of this existence.
And you see his majesty blurred, vanishing
as quickly as dreams and shadows flee.
So, the glory of mortals is like a low,
languishing flower; lofty and superb one   1030
minute, Fortune's toy and laughingstock the next.
    And among the things in which the weak
mortals would find their food and life,
the murdering poison[171] was also made.
Born together with the wheat, the hemlock,
and, among the edible plants, suddenly
appeared the hellebore, black and white.
Well-known to cruel stepmothers,[172] here is

---

[165] In mid-Renaissance, the "granter" was often Emperor Charles V.

[166] See again Dante, *Paradiso* 17: 58 ff.

[167] During his first months in St. Anne Hospital, Tasso was chained *as*—or rather, *like*—a raving madman.

[168] Another of Tasso's chronic health problems, probably an ulcer; see F. Pittorru, *op. cit.*

[169] Like a river in a flood, an image appearing in the very last letter the poet wrote before dying; see Pittorru, *op. cit.*

[170] Tasso had used this simile in describing the city of Ferrara, then an important Court in northern Italy, the first time he went there; see Pittorru, *op. cit.*

[171] Being poisoned was a frequent cause of death in Renaissance Courts, probably including Tasso's mother, by her own brothers (see Pittorru once again). The poet himself was often afraid it would happen to him as well. Of theological interest here is that venom and "bad" elements in general were present in Nature even before the Fall, against the opinion of many authors. Later on, however, Tasso will express the opposite opinion (lines 1166 and 1173). The list of plants follows Basil's (BB).

[172] Herb she-healers, here identified with witches, whom Tasso—unlike Ariosto—tends to see in a negative light. We are now in the atmosphere of Catholic Counter-Reformation; the Trent *Catechism* clearly distinguishes between traditional = "demonic" medicine and "scientific" = good medicine.

the aconite, nor did the mandrake remain
hidden in earth, nor did the poppy flower,   1040
yielding a juice which dulls the mind.
Shall we then blame the eternal hand
that made the world, producing on earth
what might infect and corrupt our life?
But must we think that everything exists
for our greedy belly, to fill up the sack,[173]
or titillate our taste buds with sweetness?[174]
For each food prepared for us as bait
offers itself well-known, useful, and ready;
and each has its purpose and way   1050
to be useful to us. If a bull's blood
proved poisonous to you, famous Chief[175]
—who first routed the Persian king, then
did not disdain, you and your ancient
homeland, to be a subject of his—
should, because of this, that robust beast
destined to the yoke and plow, so useful
to man in a thousand ways, have never
been born? Or born bloodless, perhaps?[176]
Isn't this a good reason to avoid   1060
what injures you, and choose what avails?

   The meek and simple-minded sheep,
as well as the goats, the upper inhabitants
of steep mountains and desolate rocks, can
avoid what is detrimental to their health,
distinguishing by their senses. To your senses
reason has been added, a gift from Heaven,
together with experience and skill.[177]
And even from injuries something useful
can be drawn, turning to one's benefit,   1070
and often things prove advantageous to one
while damaging to another. In this way,
Evil and Good mix and balance, so that
nothing has been created by God in vain.[178]

---

[173] From Dante, *Inferno* 28: 26-27, but in the following line Tasso sugars the pill. Cf. also *I Corinthians* 6: 13.

[174] In BB, the line ends with a question mark; here deleted to accommodate the syntax.

[175] Themistocles (BB).

[176] Again a non-anthropocentric view. Against most "classic" Christian authors, Tasso doesn't think that *all* creatures have been made for the sake of Man; see below.

[177] Literally "art" in its medieval sense; here medicine.

The hemlock is a favorite food of starlings;
nor, however cold, does it harm the hot[179] body
of the small bird; while the partridges look
for the white hellebore, and feed on it.
So the right dose does prevent damages.[180]
Mandrake and opium bring on sleep,   1080
but they could strengthen the languishing
famous women and the heroes whom
illness defeated, though no arms could.
The old cure from the good hellebore
is in the philosophical family[181]
still praised, for it prods and awakens
the mind most versed in deep issues—as
Praetus' daughters[182] already discovered,
and the enraged[183] Heracles, and that famous
teacher and guide[184] of good Pericles.   1090
The hemlock flings back and represses
one's furious hunger.[185] So, change your
accusations into thanksgivings! Praise God
who so quickly draws good from evil,[186]
He who even drew Life from death.
Do not think that, trespassing the command
of His voice, a disdaining Earth may
ever beget any forbidden creatures,
although foolish Antiquity pictures her
as the mother of fierce monsters and giants.[187]   1100
However, the unlucky and unfortunate fern,
never producing any flower or fruit,
and the barren rye-grass came out

---

[178] These two verses might be used as a summary of Tasso's worldview—or rather, of *one* of his worldviews.

[179] "Cold" and "hot" not in their common sense, but as principles or general characteristics that were applied to natural things, midway between (what we would now call) medicine and magic.

[180] The Renaissance roots of homeopathic medicine: *Sola dosis facit venenum* (Paracelsus), "only a wrong dose turns a natural substance into a venom," otherwise it can be healthy.

[181] Dante, *Inferno* 4: 132.

[182] Whom Dionysus/Bacchus drove crazy.

[183] "Forsennato," i.e. raving madman; and the technical term they had used for interning Tasso.

[184] The philosopher Zeno (BB).

[185] Dante, *Inferno* 1: 47. With a juicy semantic shift; in fact, BB informs us that in St. Basil's source text the reference was to sex.

[186] It is a key concept in Milton's *Paradise Lost*, see e.g. 2: 382-386.

[187] This is not Tasso's last word on this topic that fascinated Renaissance thinkers.

of their own inner principle, not otherwise
corrupted or changed into new forms.
And they were in the likeness of those[188]
whose words and teachings would
fruitlessly germinate in the old, holy
Scriptures and, being mixed with truth,
make it, in part, less sincere and pure: 1110
as it happens when an illustrious lineage
is mixed with illegitimate children.[189]
The Lord himself likens His perfect
followers, having a firm faith in Him,
to the young seed that keeps growing until
it finally yields its full-ripe fruit.[190]
   So, in order to fulfill the eternal law
of the Lord's voice and His command,
in one instant had the Ancient Mother
ripened the dear seeds in her womb;   1120
already fertile were the grassy meadows,
and looking like a stormy sea, green
fields waved with ears of wheat.
Each herb, each shoot, each shrub,
each humble plant, or tall-trunked tree,
the leafiest and loftiest, and all
those that to feed us germinate and grow
  —or are otherwise useful to mortal life—
were already born, and green on top,
they wholly filled the fertile womb   1130
of the wide Earth. No untimely rain
was feared, nor any sudden twister,
nor any noisy and cloudy storm.
In fact, no inexperienced and lazy
farmer, lingering in his indolence
or arrogance; and no ill-compounded,

---

[188] Tasso translates from ancient sources (BB: Epiphanius), but he obviously has con-
temporary Lutherans in his mind. In 1577, in an outburst of rage, he had even accused
himself before the Inquisition in Ferrara to justify the "forbidden books" he owned,
meanwhile pointing out the shameful ideas and lifestyle of several people in the Este Court,
including a Cardinal, Luigi. That was the beginning of all his troubles. Anyway, Tasso was
no bigot: he hardly ever accepted the corrections to his main poem that were suggested by
conformist editors. See Pittorru, *op. cit.* And, in addition, *Gerusalemme Conquistata* (1593)
is still more daring than the *Liberata* (1581).
[189] Possibly a jibe at the Este family, since Duke Alphonse II couldn't have children.
[190] *Matthew* 13: 23, etc.

impure air; no lightning, no tempest[191]
or any other sign of heavenly wrath
could harm the sweet ripe fruits
or damage the waving wheat.   1140
The great prohibition in God's bitter verdict
did not prevent the Earth's abundance yet:[192]
the manifold fruits were in fact older
than our sin and our ancient fault,
because of which we have been damned
to such a hard, toilsome tilling for food,
our faces now dripping with sweat.
    At that sound of the supreme voice, all
forests shone green, densely bristling[193]
with thick trees and tangled branches,[194]   1150
together with those raising green heads
to the sky for a more sublime height:
sweet-smelling cedars, conifers, palms
given to winners as a sign; and cypresses
which imitate the old *metae* of Greece.[195]
The lowly ones, like junipers, willows,
also unfolded their green leaves by then;
all the while the plants later used to plait
a noble crown for honored foreheads
—roses, sacred laurels, myrtles, I say—   1160
suddenly leafed in sprouting together:
each different in its own distinct virtues
that, like manifold marks, God's eternal
hand inscribed on them as their features.[196]

---

[191] The typical climatic features of Eden; see Dante, *Purgatorio* 21: 43 ff.; Milton, *Paradise Lost* 4: 153 ff., etc.

[192] A most literal translation would read: "the great prohibition of [= coming from] the bitter verdict." The general meaning seems to be that the whole Earth was then luxuriant because humankind had not begun to till and transform it, as would happen after the original sin when man was chased away from paradise, never to return. In this case, against all then current theology, Tasso would express a surprising early ecological awareness, seeing (fallen) man not as the "perfecter" but as the destroyer—or, at least, the "reducer"—of Nature. This is the first time that Adam and original sin are mentioned in the poem; Tasso shows a very personal way of dealing with the topic. Notice, meanwhile, that he says "our sin": all times are one, and this is our own story.

[193] *Orrore* not as "horror" (Eng.) but in one of the senses of the Latin word *horror*.

[194] Dante's dark forest (*Inferno* 1: 5) changed here into an evocative landscape.

[195] Sort of conic columns used as "goals"—*mete* in current Italian—during sport games (BB).

[196] Once in a while, BB's explanations are so tortuous that they make the text more obscure. It seems obvious that Tasso is simply echoing a very typical Renaissance concept: the

And only then, in those primordial times,
without any sharp and stinging thorns
did the deep-red rose unfold its petals.
To this sweetest flower's beauty the hard,
pointed thorn was afterward added
so that pain may meet our joys,[197]   1170
and we may remember our ancient sin,
because of which the Earth was justly
condemned to beget nettles and thorns.
But how come, at the divine command,
many plants, as if resisting and rebelling,
disobeyed the order of yielding fruits
and did not germinate out of seeds?[198]
The tree[199] with which, as old fame tells,
strong Heracles adorned his unkempt hair,
can display either a white or a black bark,   1180
but neither type will ever yield a fruit.
Barren are the willow and elm as well,
though both have their characteristic seeds,
if you carefully look and recall that
under the leaves lies a small bead
called *moskon*[200] by the industrious Greeks,
who devoted much study and much care
to creating made-up, imaginary names.[201]
This bead has the same hidden-seed power
as the other plants have, that normally   1190
germinate out of roots. But God gave that
law[202] just to the worthiest, well-known kinds,

---

outward shape of a plant hints at its—usually healing—virtues. Namely, Paracelsus'
signaturae; the word "note" in line 1163 means precisely "signs, marks."

[197] The first reason is more existential than theological. Roses and thorns were ubiquitous in
Baroque religious imagery; in his last years, Tasso also worked on two poems treating the
sorrows of the Virgin Mary and Jesus.

[198] We may smile at this, but it is an example of the growing awareness, in the Renaissance,
that Nature and History were more complex than "expected," and a literal interpretation of
the Bible was no longer sufficient. The Discovery of America and the Copernican
revolution are just the most macroscopic cases. In Day 6, Tasso will reflect doubtfully on
the existence of "monsters," i.e. genetic malformations.

[199] The poplar (BB).

[200] Tasso draws this notion from St. Basil (BB).

[201] In the Jerusalem-poems we find a much more serious accusation against the Greeks:
cowardice. During the Middle Ages and Renaissance, in the West, the admiration for the
Ancient Greeks went with the contempt for their successors (in a broad sense, including all
of Byzantium's lands): *Graeculi*, the "petty Greeks."

[202] Of having seeds and fruits.

whose memory He meant to glorify;
see the vine and the peaceful olive tree,
the former as it produces sweet wine,
the latter, oil: wine, the comfort and joy
of the most painfully suffering hearts;[203]
oil making our faces shiny and happy.[204]
But whose speech may ever be able to list[205]
so many, so different secret virtues,   1200
so many features, and species transplanted
from strange lands, rare and wonderful,
or our own, those either growing beneath
our sky or on some wild, uncanny[206] soil,
or within the walls of one's home,[207]
making such a long and famous history?
The vine alone suffices—which stretches out her
twisted arms, and with her leafy turnings
twines herself around the friendly elm—
the vine suffices to make us wise   1210
about our lives: as a natural example
it's been given us, indeed a worthier image
than any natural or heavenly sign.
So humbly glorious, she reminds us of
the eternal Father of Mother Nature,
the heavenly Father; or the eternal Son,
who gave himself the name of vine[208]
while calling his Father the viticulturist,
and we, grafted[209] onto the Church by faith,
have gracefully been called the shoots.   1220
In fact it is our duty, just like a fertile vine,
yes, it is our duty, like a fecund olive tree,
to produce our sweet fruits plentifully,
without ever dropping—by time or chance—
the green leaves of unearthly hope;[210]

---

[203] Tasso himself was a *connoisseur*, and used to drink a lot. See Pittorru, *op. cit.*

[204] Cosmetics (BB). Translating *Psalm* 133: 2 in an abridged form.

[205] Cf. Dante, *Inferno* 28: 1. Canto 28 of *Inferno* is the most "Tassean" section in the *Divine Comedy*, with gory descriptions in the style of the future battles of *Gerusalemme Conquistata*.

[206] Again "orrido."

[207] Tasso loved buildings with gardens, monasteries included. See Pittorru, *op. cit.*

[208] *John* 15: 1 ff., while the vine/Father correspondence was based on Basil's *Hexaemeron* (BB).

[209] Here *John* is mixed with Paul, *Romans* 11: 17, dealing with an olive tree. See line 1222.

but with a joyful, blooming countenance,[211]
let us always be luxuriant with good deeds,
leaving to God all glory and merit,[212]
to Him, the divine tiller of pure minds.

Closer to these, in their dignity,   1230
are those happy and fortunate plants[213]
almost made in the likeness of His Mother.
She is mirrored in the cypress as well
as in the palm; the sweet-smelling cedars
and plane trees are not disdained by her,
nor are the features and name of myrrh.[214]
But all these plants, and many others still,
are useful to the craftsmanship and arts
of our life, nearly[215] created for this
by Nature, indeed by the eternal   1240
Forger through Nature in those early times.
Some seem to be born to make buildings,
and some to frame either ships or carts,
others to make lances, arrows, and bows,
(dread weapons feared in horrible wars)[216]
and others destined to light our fires,
others to shade the wandering pilgrims
at midday, or to cover the sweet springs
with their branching arms all around,
or to shade the tables set for the rich.[217]   1250
But what belongs to each, and by which

---

[210] Cf. Dante, *Purgatorio* 3: 135, where an excommunicated sinner is nonetheless saved by God.

[211] *Not* a very autobiographical hint.

[212] Tasso was suspected to be a bit "Lutheran," see Pittorru. He was not; but moreover the fierce clash between Catholics and Protestants can be seen as an issue of power rather than theology, in spite of official declarations. Good Catholics knew and know that the merit of one's merits belongs to God only. "To God all glory" echoes the Jesuit motto, *Ad maiorem Dei gloriam.*

[213] He found the following allegories in a devotional book, *Theotocodia sive Parthenodia* (Greek neologisms: "In Praise of the Mother of God; or, In Praise of the Virgin") by a certain Father Martinengo, 1583 (BB).

[214] If we mentally capitalize *mirra*, so as to read "di Mirra," it may be a wittingly reversed citation from Dante, *Inferno* 30: 25-27, 38.

[215] "Quasi" is often a filler, and the Latin *quasi* rather meant "(in one's role) as"; but its position here looks significant. Immediately below, the uncertainty about God and Nature—are they the same thing, or not?—returns.

[216] Arquebuses and cannons were already used, but Tasso may have his own poems in mind.

[217] The two environments he loved most: Nature and the Courts. And his needs as a restless traveler.

traits they are different from one another,
or, under their rough, coarse rinds, what
secret loves and hidden hates may lie—
it is perhaps a pastime for lazy minds.
And to study which extend their roots
into the deep womb of the wide earth,
which cling strongly to the upper lands,
which start straight up, over firm trunks
happily growing, reaching for the sky,   1260
and which stretch out their distorted arms
dividing themselves into many branches,
and which, humbly snaking, lower their green
leaves down to earth, not daring to rise
without a support to which they may stick—
this is the idle interest of a vain mind.[218]
Those trees that divide themselves and split
through the air with many branches all around,
usually have, as well, roots penetrating
deep down, spreading wide, entwined in circles,   1270
for Nature stabilizes and grounds the
burdensome weight of the upper parts
against the North and the South winds.
A great diversity emerges among the natural,
untilled[219] barks. Some are rough, coarse,
some less hard, some softer and smoother;
others appear content with one rind,
still others clothe themselves with many.
But what will truly marvel you is that,
by looking carefully, you will find   1280
in them the various traits and examples
of either human youth or old age,
for the still tender and green plants
display a smooth, almost tight bark,
but if they happen to grow very old,
they wind up with wrinkles, and corrugate.
Some, after having been cut, succeed
in germinating again; to others, the ax

---

[218] That doesn't prevent Tasso from delving into it, as BB ironically stresses.

[219] An interesting specification, all the more so if it is linked with lines 1306, 1321, 1348.
Charles Darwin will start to work on his theory precisely by studying the species selected
and modified by man. Milton, who didn't like the excesses of artificial cultivation, in
Paradise Lost promoted that type of natural-looking garden that in Italy, in fact, would be
called *all'inglese*, "after the English manner."

causes almost inexorable death.
Another, which a violent whirlwind   1290
had uprooted by its roots, was afterward
able to rise again, and cling anew to
the hard bosom of the Ancient Mother,
as it occurred not less than twice
in the fields of Pharsalia;[220] and elsewhere,
not only—as they[221] write and tell—did a tree
cling back to the same soil as before,
but it even happened that a cut and burnt
pine tree passed from forest to forest,
then flourished again among strong oaks: 1300
a great, rare, natural wonder, if Nature
the Life-Giver[222] can work miracles too.

    And whoever watches how a good farmer
takes care of the diseases of sickly trees,
corrects the defects of their weakened
nature, making them evolve for the best,
may here learn the way to cure himself.
The fine African apple[223]—under a soft rind
hiding and covering purple and white
gems, then opening and sharing them   1310
so as to quench man's thirst, in part—
will often change its sour flavor into
sweet juice. And the bitter almond becomes
sweet, losing its malignant bitterness,
if an opening is drilled in its tree
by the roots, and through the hole a wedge
is driven, covered with pitch, into
the tree's fat pith.[224] Barley also works
as a medicine for the leafy trees, making
them beautiful beyond measure and happy;   1320

---

[220] Tasso quotes from Theophrastus' *De Causis Plantarum*, but the place was Philippi (BB).

[221] St. Basil (BB).

[222] "Alma," from Latin *alere*, to feed, a word used only in poetry, see e.g. Dante, *Inferno* 2: 20. A "wonder-full" tree (in this case because of an enchantment) plays a key role in both Jerusalem-poems, when Rinaldo/Riccardo finds himself in front of the Dryad-like spirit of Armida. The place, being a "dark forest" near Jerusalem, is precisely where Dante's voyage fictionally began: Tasso's hero goes and verifies the spot.

[223] The pomegranate, whose linguistic root *pom[o]* means apple, or a round fruit in general. Cf. *pomme* in French and, in Italian, *pomodoro* = *pomo d'oro* = "gold apple" = tomato. These verses on the pomegranate are very beautiful in their imagery and sound, in the original version at least.

[224] Tasso learned this "country trick" from Basil's *Hexaemeron* (BB).

that much can the art of a skilled tiller achieve.
But, if he is slothful, lazy in his work,
because of his careless agricultural art
the trees will fall from bad to worse.

Other species change color and shape
without the help of a friendly hand.
The white poplar dyes its pale leaves
black, while the flax often turns
into rye grass, and water mint[225] into
plain mint, if exceedingly tilled.[226]   1330
Similarly the soul,[227] if no study or care
of his stains cleans and polishes it,
loses its native innocence[228] and blackens;
or, formerly a great soul, it gets small,
formerly high, then low, falling by itself;
but being cultivated, it rises, and joyfully
tends to heaven, thus surpassing itself.[229]
So, let mortals learn to cultivate the human
minds, and heal the various diseases
of weakened, languishing souls.   1340

Now, whose speech may ever be able to list[230]
the various fruits, and show the differences
in colors, flavors, and the specific effects
and virtues, hardly known by taste?
Not only a thousand types and forms
of trees make fruits in a thousand ways,
but in one single species and in one terrain
a great variety can be seen and studied:
colors, and shapes, and even sex.

---

[225] "Sisimbrio," *Mentha aquatica* (BB).

[226] According to Theophrastus (BB).

[227] "Così l'animo ancor," from Dante, *Inferno* 1: 25. But here *ancòr[a]* means "too, as well," rather than "still."

[228] "Candore" means both whiteness and innocence, not precisely candor. A "Pelagian" viewpoint, but immediately counterbalanced (line 1340) by an "Augustinian" teaching. Dante also oscillated like this.

[229] Again Dantean wordings or concepts. See e.g. *Paradiso* 18, 58-60 (virtue that *avanza*, becoming more perfect; Tasso changes it into *se medesmo avanza*, surpassing oneself) and 27: 121-148 (with metaphors from agriculture). Incidentally, *Paradiso* 18 is the Canto in which Dante mentions personages who will become Tassean par excellence: Godfrey of Bouillon—*Godfrey* was the title of the first draft of *Jerusalem Delivered*—and Robert Guiscard, the Norman warrior inspiring the main hero in *Gerusalemme Conquistata*, Richard.

[230] Identical with line 1199, except for the first word.

For example, among the palms, some   1350
can distinguish male and female trees
because she, being moved and pushed
by an inner love, spreads out her arms
and longs for her husband's embrace.[231]
The same happens between fig and fig
when a wild tree plants itself close
to one growing among well-closed
and guarded walls, or they bind fruit
to fruit with each other; and that's how
illness is cured, for it is believed   1360
that the trees will not decay and fall.
What does this natural enigma mean?
Nature perhaps shows and teaches us
that by uniting foreigners to our strength,
virtue is gained for good deeds and firm
constancy. So, let Italy have a look
—the still weak Italy, still in her illness
in a lazy peace even more than in war,
unable to see or feel her inner evil—
have a look at the mountains, and there   1370
search for those dreadful, savage peoples;
and hence make her languishing tenderness,
indeed her softness, firmer and harder
by forming a league, or by learning, at least.[232]
But in no worse and more saddening way
does a strong tree degenerate, losing
its vigor and its primordial strength,
than when—as it has so often occurred—
it changes from a male into a female.[233]

---

[231] Such classic(al) examples of vegetable loves are also mentioned in a book by an author who could be dubbed "the last Renaissance man": Salvador Dali's *50 Secrets of Magic Craftsmanship*.

[232] "Mountains" means the Alps, the country's Northern borders. These verses are coined after Dante's "Apostrophe to Italy" in *Purgatorio* 6, 76 ff., that have become a "must" in Italian official culture after the Wars of Independence in the mid-nineteenth century, when all speeches and songs attacked "the Foreigner" (*lo stranièr*, in the singular, like one dark entity). Actually, these verses simply show that Dante did not have a very clear perception of the political problems of his times, let alone of later periods. Here Tasso expressly states the contrary: Italians should look for foreign allies, and learn and absorb vitality from them, less refined as they may seem. The triumph of Nordic vigor in action is obviously seen in *Gerusalemme Conquistata*.

Therefore let man mind, lest his   1380
tough heart (Nature's gift), like a woman,
be softened, among leisure and luxury,
by idleness, pleasure or blandishments.[234]
    Among some plants of different species,
a friendly Nature creates love and peace;
though enmity and wrath among others.[235]
The beautiful gem-apple[236] and the green myrtle,
as well as the myrtle and the bountiful olive
are naturally friends: they can be planted
close to each other, no injury follows.   1390
But the sweet vine and the sweet fig
are hostile beyond measure and obnoxious.
Quite unbelievable, eh? You teach, O Nature,
that disdain and war can split good people.[237]
But vine and fig can get merrily married,[238]
as when between Kingdom and Kingdom
a wedding stops their hateful war.[239]
Then, if anyone uproots the husband,
the wife will in a short time droop and die:
a noble example of human love,   1400
of a lasting and firm marital fidelity.[240]
And the cabbage, approaching the vine,
tempers the latter's great, generous spirit,
so that the wine flares up and foams,
and benefits the drunkards by appeasing
their inner flame, fervent and fuming.
But the highest honor of innocence is owed
to the fine pomegranate[241] and sweet apple,

---

[233] Against homosexuality? Not at all, as the following lines make clear. The "saddening" detail is male chauvinism (line 1381), but the heart of the Tassean she-warrior Clorinda is as brave as the heart of the strongest male heroes.

[234] As it is the case with the knight Ruggiero, seduced by the witch Alcina in Ariosto's *Orlando Furioso*, and with Rinaldo/Riccardo (Richard) seduced by Armida in the parallel episode in Tasso's Jerusalem-poems.

[235] Sources: the usual Pliny, Theophrastus, etc. (BB)

[236] Pomegranate.

[237] Again with autobiographical references.

[238] "Vite" is a feminine noun, "fico" masculine.

[239] Common praxis during the Renaissance; Tasso often wrote the poems for such occasions. And an attempt at "peace through wedding" is the starting point of his tragedy *Il Re Torrismondo*.

[240] That, among the upper classes, was absolutely not the rule.

[241] The third form to indicate this fruit, and the most similar to the current one: "pomo granato." This verse seems to imply that the forbidden fruit in paradise was either an apple

never harming or injuring any type of plant.
Innocently the pine[242] rises and spreads   1410
his leaves to the sky, shading several yards
with his broad "hair" and open arms
while occupying little room with his roots
underground; and in his friendly shade
the myrtle and laurel[243] lie green and safe.
In the shade of such a powerful king,
who never proves greedy for treasures
or lands, who does not occupy and usurp
his neighbor's soil by using force,
many often grow happily in peace,   1420
and scholarship flourishes, and the arts
of eloquence, and the deserved honors.
There also are plants of uncertain nature
and double life, in the water and on earth.
Among them, the tamarisk,[244] often luxuriant
in the most solitary and deserted sites
or also born in lakes and ponds:
similar to those who very often change
their residence, following Fortune from
place to place, from Lord to Lord,   1430
always uneasy[245] by nature and habit.
But shall I leave out the plants' weeping?
Who can leave out their tears dripping
from rough rinds, and the living humors,
clear, transparent, gathered into one?
Out of its strong, elastic wood, the mastic
tree sheds its tears; and a sweet juice
of odorous tears is poured out by
the balsam, a small, precious plant
in the Jewish lands.[246] Green Egypt   1440

---

or a pomegranate. Hypotheses are not lacking. Just keeping within the limits of Renaissance, Michelangelo, e.g., in the Sistine Chapel pictured it as a fig. Which species may be referred to by Milton with the general term "apple" is a controversial issue.

[242] The Mediterranean cluster-pine.

[243] Two plants classically associated with love and poetry. The following hint at the—not always achieved—ideal of the perfect Renaissance Lord is all too transparent.

[244] Providing an autobiography of Tasso in brief, who also had a sexual "double life," or "double knots," as his enemies liked to divulge; and wept (line 1432) when he was most discomforted. See Pittorru, *op. cit.*

[245] "Maligni" here does not mean "evil" but a plant that very seldom takes root.

and sandy Africa also know about
the weeping ferula. The clear *élektron*[247]
is a rare, dripping humor falling from
a dark[248] tree, turning into fine petrified tears.
 But, alas, words flow and grow too much,[249]
and in the open and measureless fields
of the earth and sea they find no limit
or restraint to their run; so, lost, wandering,
they would go astray among the minutia
in which great and powerful God   1450
appears, the Creator of sublime things, too.[250]
Thus, I will have to stop writing, compelled
by an inflexible and inexorable necessity,
before the brief day of this fleeting life
of mine may fail and leave the toil behind.
 O you, who observe[251] the different plants
in the gardens, or forests, or mountains,
as well as those in swamps and ponds,
or in the red womb of the Eritrean Sea,
and admire the green trunks and branches   1460
and their leafy tops blooming with flowers,
recognize the *more* in the *less*, and
to these few, brief words,[252] in your minds
you will be able to add great marvels

---

[246] Literally, "Kingdom of the Jews," but of course it is only a poetical expression. Quite interestingly, in *Gerusalemme Liberata* no present-day Jew is mentioned, while some will appear in the *Conquistata*.

[247] The Greek name of amber. The modern term "electricity" came from natural phenomena involving amber.

[248] BB's note was essential so as not to misinterpret "fumosa," literally "smoking." On second thought, a—later—image of the same kind applies to a dark gray color called *fumo di Londra*, London smoke.

[249] Cf. Dante, *Purgatorio* 29: 97-99 and 33: 136-141, but from a more tragic viewpoint in Tasso. He is just one third of the way into the poem, and he is already afraid—and not without good reason—that he may be unable to finish it, though he is less than 50 years old. On the other hand, it seems that Dante himself, at basically the same age, also had the same doubt about his work, since in *Purgatorio* 15-18 he is already anticipating many major ideas of *Paradiso*.

[250] The underlying poetics of the whole poem. He lamented that, because of deprivation and illness, his prodigious memory had failed, and this might be true relative to former times, but it remained exceptional nonetheless.

[251] "Voi che mirate…," with an interesting shift of genre, as these words recall the graves or monuments of people who had a tragic life and/or death. Cf. in the Bible, *Lamentations* 1: 12.

[252] He is not joking. His contemporary poem *Gerusalemme Conquistata* is one-and-a-half times the length of the *Divine Comedy*.

thinking of the Lord who made the world,
wonderful for craftsmanship and art,[253]
He who said, "Let the Earth germinate
the wood, producing its sweet fruits
on earth." So, by virtue of the high voice,
like an iron-cored spinning top[254]   1470
rotating after having been first hit
and returning to itself with many turns,
so the Earth goes around[255] and circles its own
seasons, so that she strips and dresses again,
yielding and keeping her dear fruits.
For, being driven on by the divine voice
of Him who commands Nature and sky,
she turns year after year in regular circles
as in the beginning. Until she stops,
when time and the world finally end;   1480
then not only she will enjoy quiet and peace,
but the skies themselves, eternal rest.[256]

---

[253] Like the sword Godfrey of Bouillon gives the ambassador Argantes in *Gerusalemme Liberata* 2: 93, and other clothes and weapons described in Tasso's poems: (a) precious materials (b) being skillfully manufactured.

[254] The toy with the noblest poetical pedigree. Cf. e.g. Dante, *Paradiso* 18: 42. That the Earth has an iron core makes the comparison with this top seem prescient.

[255] He is not saying that the Earth itself turns around the sun. It simply spins. And yet, these lines may imply some hidden sympathy for the new heliocentric theory. Tasso even held a chair of Astronomy (see Pittorru, *op. cit.*).

[256] Cf. Day 7, lines 1086 ff., the very last lines of the poem.

Day Four

T hose who watch the matches and skills
   of wrestlers, or of athletes nimbly hurrying
their naked limbs to race on a solemn day,[1]
or the various enterprises and arms of knights
in an ample field or within a closed fence,
clashing in tournaments and jousts,[2]
feel an inner stirring within themselves
that moves and excites them together with
those fighting hard against each other;
and their feelings lean more and more   10
towards one competitor, hoping, longing
for his victory, and they often raise their
voices and shout so as to encourage him.
Hence, those who gaze at the marvels
of eternal heavenly objects
and the great immeasurable things, or hear
that which surpasses each estimation
in works of ineffable Wisdom and Art,
must create for—or rather in—themselves
inner bursts, living ardors, and fervent   20
zeal, turning with eyes fixed to admire
so many great things being made in a few
days by the sound of the divine voice.[3]
By gathering all of their inner strength,
as partners or trustworthy friends,
they must join the fight and help,
so that the Truth may not be hidden or
concealed, and, with no conceits or lies,
may shine, and out of its light enlighten hearts.
But what am I saying? Speaking to whom?[4]   30
While in such a tiring and just enterprise

---

[1] Christian metaphors taken from sports were first used by St. Paul in his letters. In 20th century Italian poetry the praise of modern athletes, together with descriptions of spectators reacting, can be found in Guido Gozzano (boxing) and Umberto Saba (soccer).

[2] Cf. Dante, *Inferno* 22: 1-6.

[3] Tasso stresses the purpose of his poem. See the following lines. *But* see also lines 30 ff.

[4] An interesting example of "meta-narrative." See lines 44-46. The opposite of Dante, *Paradiso* 17: 116 ff.

I almost dare place the skies on a scale
and weigh the universe in the pans,[5]
telling the first works and the first days
and the world's birth; its first, sublime
principles not seeking at random
among the lies of Ancient Greece,[6]
where others voluntarily blind themselves
and lose the right light in philosophizing,
or even in the Academy or the Lyceum,[7]   40
or else among the errors of dark Egypt;
but from[8] Him[9] who freed us from there, and led
His faithful people amid the roaring sea,
may He pull me to the shore, safe and sound,
out of this very turbulent and deep sea[10]
of human ignorance and human pride.

    You,[11] indeed, High Father, resembling Moses
in renewing that primal, holy example;
you, who are like him, are also like the King
of heaven, of whom was Moses a quasi-image,   50
but hidden among the horrors and shadows
of old times; you now are the new, true,
breathing image and noble simulacrum[12]
of His ever-un-darkenable glory, so that
you gleam and shine with His rays.
Please, impart to my troubled mind:
share a part of that holy, pure light that,
instilled by you, may guide and lead

---

[5] Cf. *Isaiah* 40: 12.

[6] As usual, this is not all of Tasso's opinion about Ancient Greece, to be sure.

[7] The schools of Plato and Aristotle, respectively.

[8] To be linked to "seeking" in line 35.

[9] Moses, according to BB. The theological context, see especially line 44, rather indicates God. But, on the other hand, lines 47 ff. clearly refer to Moses, creating a tangled coherence among the latter, the Pope, and God. The translation will expressly add the name of Moses for the sake of clarity.

[10] Cf. Dante, *Inferno* 1: 22-24. Perhaps not only a quote but actually a key to those verses, interpreting the dark forest as something more precise that "sin" in general. For Dante's trees meaning ignorance and mental sloth, see Giovanni Pascoli's poem on the *Divine Comedy* published at the beginning of the twentieth century. According to Dante's son Jacopo, the dark forest meant the "man of the masses": Dante (and Tasso) tried to avoid being such.

[11] Pope Clement VIII. Moses is the "main hero" in the monument to another Renaissance Pontiff: Michelangelo's sculpture for Julius II, currently in the church of *San Pietro in Vincoli* in Rome, but it was meant for the Basilica.

[12] Protestants accusing Catholics of "Papolatry" can find here a convincing ground.

gentle souls and spirits on pilgrimage.[13]
If they ever turn their eyes upward,   60
under a beautiful, shining nocturnal sky,
to the immortal beauty of the golden stars,[14]
thus to ponder the eternal Maker's works:
"Who is the One who embellished the sky so,
and varied it all by painting it, as it were,
with such different flowers of light and gold?
How, in the things exposed to our senses,
does pleasure exceed necessity so?"[15]
And if, through this admiration, they learn
the sublime marvels of the Most High,   70
and from that which the eyes can see,
they know then the other, invisible forms,[16]
they can well fill the seats, all around,
of this theater sacred to God, and the stands
in which His glory is told and sung.[17]
Oh, if I may[18]—as an escort and guide
leading an unknown pilgrim all about,
showing and pointing to the buildings
and masterpieces of a famous city—
be able to so lead the pilgrim minds   80
of the ever-erring mortals down here
to the sublime though hidden wonders
of this vast city, I mean the heavenly
city, that is the ancient home of us all,
of us children of Adam, the high palace
where the King assigns eternal rewards.
But we were then driven into sorrowful
exile by the proud, murderous[19] demon,

---

[13] "Pellegrini" also suggests something rare, noble; but in 1: 77 the target of the poem was just the opposite—the sinners.

[14] Such landscapes are Tasso's trump card.

[15] Along with BB, and with Schopenhauer in mind, these lines may be interpreted as follows: the deep joy felt in admiring Nature "as is" cancels any interest in its "practical" side, with its laws, needs, and so on.

[16] Literally translating from St. Paul's *Letter to the Romans* 1: 20.

[17] Cf. Dante "mystical rose," an amphitheater of light in heaven (*Paradiso* 30: 100 ff., then 31: 1 ff.).

[18] Another long section (lines 76-123) reflecting on the purpose and scope of the poem. Tasso plays the role Virgil assumes towards Dante in *Inferno* and *Purgatorio*; even more clearly so in Salvador Dali's illustrations for the *Divine Comedy*, in which the two protagonists look like tourists in a surreal world.

who first sweetly lures us then kills us
with an eternal death, enslaving us   90
by tying us in the hard bonds of sin
with knots of the strongest adamant.[20]
Once there, men will clearly and surely see
the high principle and heavenly origin
of our immortal and noble soul;
and, suddenly then attacking us,
horrid, frightful, fierce Death, she
who is the sorrowful daughter[21] of Sin
—Sin, who is the fist-born son
of the proud devil rebelling against God,   100
the prince of evil and the very[22] source
of all evil thrown and spread over us.
There they can also know themselves,[23]
as they are naturally earthly and frail,
but a work made, as well, by the divine
and holy hand of the eternal Lord.
By knowing themselves, then they ascend[24]
to know God,[25] He who made the Whole,
and to worship the world's Creator;
serving the Lord, glorifying the Father,   110
loving Him who feeds and keeps us,
praising Him who shares His benefits,
He, the Prince of this and the other life,
transient and immortal, earthly and heavenly
—this they may learn, never sated, never

---

[19] *John* 8: 44. A "Miltonian" cameo, in which Satan explicitly appears for the first time. Satan's grand speech in *Gerusalemme Liberata*, Canto 4, then in *Gerusalemme Conquistata*, Canto 5, with significant changes, is echoed in Milton's *Paradise Lost*, 1: 622 ff.; see it in the website *tassonomia.blogspot.it* (in English). Also noteworthy is the fact that in this passage Tasso seems to consider Man's original homeland, paradise, as synonymous with heaven, advancing a nearly Gnostic interpretation of the Fall.

[20] Cf. Milton, *Paradise Lost* 1: 46-48.

[21] Literally "daughter," as *morte* (death) is a feminine noun, while *peccato* (sin) is masculine. Echo of *Romans* 7: 11 and *James* 1: 15. Cf. Satan's daughter (Sin), and their son (Death), in *Paradise Lost* 2.

[22] In old Italian, *quasi* often had a quite different meaning than it does today, i.e. almost, nearly. Closer to Latin, it meant "(in the quality, role) as." It is not always easy to decide which translation is the most fitting.

[23] The well-known *gnothi seauton* of the Delphic Oracle, here in a Christian key.

[24] To be linked to "learn" in line 115.

[25] Echoing St. Augustine's famous *noverim te, noverim me*, which actually means, "If I may know you [God], I will be able to know myself," but it has often been interpreted the other way around.

tired of exalting Him more and more: for he
by His gifts enriching and enlightening[26]
and gladdening the weak mortals here below,
again confirms His ancient promises
of heavenly treasures and of an eternal   120
divine Kingdom, which He calls us to join,
thus lifting and feeding human hope
that, by itself, would snake on the ground.[27]

  But if things subjected here below
to varying time are so many and great,
what about the eternal things in heaven?
And if the visible things are so dear
to our eyes, what would the invisible
objects be to our noble minds, at the end?
If the sky's expanse surpasses   130
any measure of the human intellect,
who shall comprehend eternal and
measureless nature? And if the Sun is
so beautiful, and so big, and so swift,
so orderly in its oblique turns, so Earth-
friendly, and so shining, eye-like,
adorning, illuminating the world;[28]
if the Sun, in leaving, never leaves us
sated with its serene and clear sight
—though it also is subject to death,   140
whenever it may be[29]—what eternal beauty
will we see in the great Sun of justice?[30]
If not seeing it in the sky is a punishment,[31]
what a punishment indeed to the ungrateful
sinner devoid of the true, eternal light!

  Already made by now were the primal sky
and the earth, and so was the light;

---

[26] Cf. *Letter of James* 1: 17.

[27] The pun "snake on the ground" works in English as well as in Italian ("a terra serpe"). In the several allusions to original sin that Tasso will make, there will be no direct reference to the Serpent, except this pun. See Dante, *Purgatorio* 8: 100, where the poet meets the very Serpent of Eden. Cf. Milton, *Paradise Lost* 9: 408, 497.

[28] Remembering that sight was conceived as a sheaf of rays.

[29] This vision of a—however slowly—dying universe was alien to Dante.

[30] For the link between God, Sun, and Justice, see Salwa Khoddam, *Mythopoeic Narnia*, op. cit., ch. 2.

[31] Giving a more universal meaning to the condition of the souls in Dante's Limbo, cf. *Inferno* 4: 41-42. Tasso, who spent seven years in isolation in prison, knew it all too well. The word *pena* means both pain and punishment.

already distinct were night and day;
and that further sky[32] already existed
borrowing its name from firmness,   150
the extreme border of the sensible world.
The dry land, so far hidden and deep
in water, was no longer covered, in part,
by the waving humor, and the waters
were already gathered in their own place.
The Earth had now her womb pregnant
with her offspring, painted and strewn
with fecund seeds of grass and flowers;
the trees, above shadowy feet, spread
their green leaves. Yet, there was not   160
any sun or moon; the former was not
hailed as the perennial father of light,
and father, almost forger, of all things
—those things, I say, produced and fed
by the Mother Earth. The vain, false error
of mortals led and deceived by their own
senses as by an alluring and lying escort,
had not made a god of it. But God was
finished with the noble works of Day Three
and happily began with Day Four.   170
    "Let the two great lamps,"[33] He said, "be made
in the steady sky, and let both shine
over the earth, clearly distinguishing
Day on the one side, and on the other—
the half belonging to dark—cold Night."
So did He speak, and two lamps He made.
But, who spoke? Who made? Can't you see
the double Person?[34] A great, hidden,
ineffable Mystery, infusing and strewing[35]
the Holy History with deep wisdom,   180

---

[32] The firmament.
[33] The Sun and the Moon.
[34] Following St. Basil (BB), Tasso here inserts a theological consideration of the Father and the Son in the creation starting from two roles: the Speaker, the Maker. This is only two-thirds of the story, however, as the third Person, the Holy Spirit, surely did not play a minor role. The "Old Fathers" are the Biblical writers, especially Moses, by tradition the author of *Genesis*, and King David for his many *Psalms* dealing with the creation. But the phrase "*double* person"—not *two* persons—is also meaningful from a psychological viewpoint because Tasso often held "inner dialogues" with an "elf" on the mysteries of the cosmos.
[35] BB's "infuso e sparso" (masculine, seemingly referring to *mistero*, mystery) must be edited into "infusa e sparsa" (feminine, referring to *sacra istoria*).

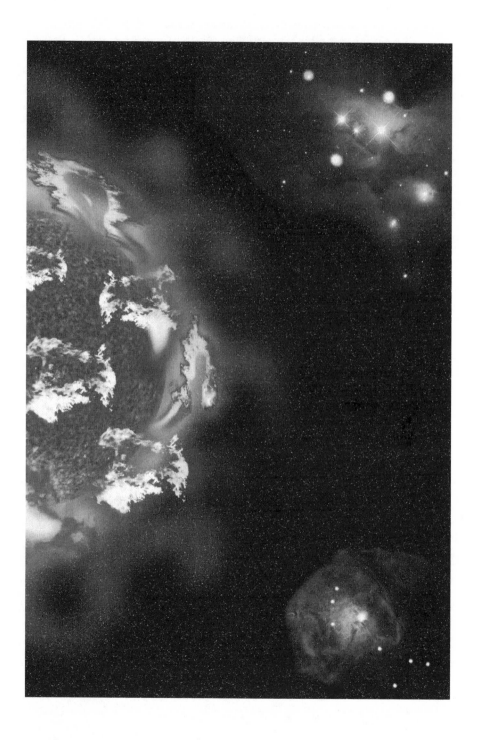

revealed by grace to Old Fathers, which
in the ancient books still shines as through
a cloud, and partly veils itself to us?
Can't you see how useful to mortals the holy
command of His sublime voice is?

   "Let them shine," He said, "above the Earth
to illumine her, and warm her frozen
limbs with their vital, temperate fire."
So did He speak; and *ab aeterno* ordered
the Sun to pour its rays unto the righteous   190
and the unrighteous,[36] since these also He
wanted to benefit, He who teaches to benefit.
Even unto the wicked He strews and pours
his goods, and his graces that fill the sky
and are transmitted by the Sun and stars.[37]
Not that, in his spoken words or works,
the eternal Father contradicted himself
since He first created the beautiful light
and later the Sun. Without any sun the clear
light existed; with no sun or stars yet   200
was in the beginning. As body to soul,
as chariot to charioteer, so were the two
great lamps then given the primal
light that showed shining through them.[38]
For Light *per se* first shines to the lofty
intellects and to the purest minds:[39]
an intellectual, almost eternal offspring.
Then, on its double chariots, to our senses
it gleams by day and by shadowy night,
never tired nor slackening its pace   210
along the oblique, crooked paths there.
Thus, there was pure light before the day,
which the ray-adorned Sun would then split.
God indeed decided to distinguish
and utterly divide light from darkness,

---

[36] *Matthew* 5: 45. A well-known Gospel teaching, but Dante didn't stress this as much.

[37] Here Tasso seems to believe in astrology, in spite of himself.

[38] Tasso possibly suggested this kind of primal light/sunlight relationship to Milton (*Paradise Lost* 7: 355 ff.), but the latter would rework it a bit grossly, honestly, describing the light rays as sort of appendages. The image of the charioteer may rather recall the origin of the Sun and Moon in J. R. R. Tolkien's *Silmarillion.*

[39] The angels. For this hymn to Light in its different facets, cf. Milton, *Paradise Lost* 3: 1 ff., here sublime. Cf. also Dante, *Paradiso* 13: 52 ff. and elsewhere.

but He commanded that the Sun part
the clear day from the dark of night:
for, to the noble mind, He distinguishes
pure objects, and later commands the Sun
to show them divided to the errant senses,[40]   220
as He commands the white Moon, the servant
of the Sun's splendor; and He wants both
to equally divide the time and hours.
Let us therefore, without deceit or fear
in our sublime, brave thought at least,
dare to separate the sun from its light,
as in fire one can distinguish between
the effects of burning and of illumining.
And it was already wonderfully split
by God when He gave rubies a fire   230
—a shiny one—from its splendor splitting
the other power proper, that of burning,
which remains idle, then conceals itself:
such is the power of the divine voice,
capable of cutting flames from fire.[41]
When indeed He allots eternal rewards
and pains, then the very nature of fire
will be distinct and divided in the end:
the light will be destined to the just,
for them to enjoy; the burning force   240
to punish the ungodly in blind hell.[42]

The changes of the inconstant Moon
show and tell us the same thing[43]
via her different and varying shapes.
While waning and losing her light, she
does not wholly consume her pale face,
for she takes on or leaves the white
crown of her rays and varies her image,
displaying how very different is her

---

[40] An obvious Neoplatonic idea: things exist in their "pure forms" earlier than in their material appearance.

[41] In this section, Tasso depends on the *Hexaemeron* not by the "usual" Basil but by St. Gregory of Nyssa (BB).

[42] The phrase "blind hell" comes from Dante. This curious doctrine about light and flame has significant consequences not so much on our perception of the afterlife but of this world, the only one we actually know, in which the two phenomena are linked: the world as an inextricable mix of contraries, "angels" (light) and "devils" (flames).

[43] The fact that there was a primal light then "given" to the celestial bodies.

body from the one lighting her.   250
That's what happened to the Sun, too,
but his light, though drawn from elsewhere
after having once adorned and dressed him,
never leaves. The Moon is often cloaked
by the light of him, and often humbly
casts it off, alternating her places.
This way God ordered the two grand lamps
to distinguish between the middle point
of clear day and the middle of night,
so that they may not be blended and mixed,   260
nor any fellowship or friendship may ever
rise between Light and Darkness on earth.[44]
But as shadows exist in the light of day,
so across the space of the dark night,
in the then murky and horrid Nature,
the outlines of opaque, thick bodies yield
to the brilliance of their shining contraries;[45]
and in the morning they stretch westward,
and towards the east they tend in the evening,
and at midday they shorten and narrow,   270
hardly unfolding towards the Bears.
Night, by turning to the opposite side,
yields to the shining rays; in its nature
there is nothing more than cold, dark shadow,
coming from the opaque Earth's womb;
and always before the brilliance of day it
flees to the opposite side and vanishes.

    This is the way the eternal Father imposed
the measures of day to the bright Sun
and made the white Moon, when she fills   280
her whole ring with silver and splendor,
the Princess of cold, dark night.[46]
The two beautiful sky lamps were then
nearly by right facing each other[47]—and

---

[44] Cf. *II Corinthians* 6: 14. But, on several occasions, Tasso describes a world where contraries cohabit. See, in this very Day, lines 190-191.

[45] Moon and stars.

[46] In some religious cosmologies, see e.g. William Blake's *Jerusalem*, the Moon is a negative, demonic symbol. Not so in Tasso.

[47] In the Middle Ages and Renaissance they often tried to calculate the year, season, and even day of the world's creation. The year usually fell about 4400 B.C. (cf. e.g. Dante, *Paradiso* 26: 119, where the figure is supplied by Adam in person); the season was "surely"

as soon as the Sun rises, the noble Moon's
round image darkens and disappears;
and when the Sun precipitously sets,
she, vice versa, appears in the East
rising and showing her adorned face.
But in her other figures and shapes   290
she does not disappear together with night;
indeed, in her whole, perfect state, when
her beautiful circle is filled with light,
she, crowned with her white rays,
is the Queen of night, excelling all
the golden stars in her light and beauty,
illuminating the earth in the Sun's stead.
The Sun: the king of the luminous day,
who, like a bridegroom,[48] out of the sky's halls
comes adorned with rays and gold,   300
with a much bigger and brighter crown
encircling his noble, flaming forehead;
and like a tall, superb[49] giant, he crosses
the sky and dominates all around, so great
is he, burning with such a powerful light.
And ample is the less warm Moon also,
but how much so?—either with reference
to the stars, which look much smaller;
or in being inscribed and self-enclosed
by her contour within her pure ring,   310
the way the sea and sky look so mighty;
or because her serene splendor suffices
to illumine the measureless fields
of the earth, of the sea, of the deep sky.
Her size in fact does not change, when
she is full to Ethiopians and Indians,[50]
to cold Scythians, unknown Hyperboreans,
either in dark sunset or burnished rising

Spring (Dante, *Inferno* 1: 37-40; Milton, *Paradise Lost* 10: 329); the day, possibly the beginning of that season. Regardless, since before the original sin it was "perpetual Spring" (Dante, *Purgatorio* 28: 76-102; Milton, *Paradise Lost* 12: 678-679), the month didn't make a great difference.

[48] Here and in line 303, paraphrasing *Psalm* 18 [19]: 6, see especially the LXX version.

[49] And/or proud (*superbo* in Italian). A superb, proud, imposing giant is the character *Solimano*, Solyman, in Tasso's Jerusalem-poems, introduced as an ancestor of Saladin. Does his name start with *Sol* just by chance?

[50] Who were basically considered to make up one people; see above, 3: 549 and footnote.

or when she tarries at the sky's top.
But her size does not decrease or increase   320
because of the Earth's wide bosom (or back)
making her look smaller in the distance
or else bigger when she comes nearer,
as it occurs with all objects on earth.
Nor from the Sun is anyone ever farther
or closer, but the same distance is kept
by all inhabitants of opposite climates.
   Recall, if ever from the loftiest range[51]
of a craggy mountain, looking down you saw
in a humble field or valley, how the   330
yokes of the oxen appear in sight,
and the size of the plowmen themselves!
They surely looked like minute ants,
their limbs shortening and withdrawing
into their bodies in most narrow sizes.[52]
So much does the uncertain perception
of mortal sight submerge and vanish
amid such a vast and deep space that
it hardly visits such far-away things!
Again, if ever from a peak or high rock   340
you fixed your gaze at the sea below,
how many islands scattered across it
could you make out? Or perhaps a black ship
loaded with fine and precious goods
—look!—aloft unfurling her white sails,
like wings, from her steadfast mast,
on the sea's sky-blue and foaming back?
Surely, smaller than a snow-white dove
that tiny image appeared to your eyes,
so much in the void and in the expanses   350
does human sight weaken and grow lost.
Already you thought lofty mountains
and deep valleys were even and round,
since no caves there could be made out,

---

[51] After Dante, *Purgatorio* 17: 1. Here a quite long section with landscape descriptions begins, often drawing on St. Basil's *Hexaemeron* (BB).

[52] An optical effect due to distance, but this metamorphosis physically occurred in *Gerusalemme Liberata* 10, stanza 66, when the Circe-like witch Armida changed her guests—not into pigs, but fish. The classical source for these kinds of descriptions is Ovid, but more directly, with a Christian hellish shade, see Dante, *Inferno* 25: 112 (in its wider context), which also inspired Milton, *Paradise Lost* 11: 512.

nor any uneven, rugged rocky formation;
but hollows and cavities are hidden
because of distance, and with a plain deceit
every unevenness seems to be leveled.
And you would say towers are round,
in spite of having four edges and faces,   360
facing respectively North and South
and, opposite, the other world quarters.
So, without harboring doubts, believe
that with distance every faraway image
gets blurred, and our senses are deceived
in many ways. Grand therefore is the Sun,
but the most certain mark[53] of its size
is that, endless as stars may be in the sky,
by each of them the light spreads,
nevertheless the sum of them all   370
will not expel the night's horror and sadness.
Only the Sun, ascending on the horizon,
indeed, while still awaited, before rising
above the earth and radiating its beams,
already dispels darkness and overcomes
the golden stars by its light; the thick air,
condensed into frost by nocturnal chill,
is melted and freed; and clear liquid[54] sky
is most sweetly illumined and warmed.
Then scented breezes murmuring blow   380
before the day, and meanwhile a dewy,
crystalline humor rains down in showers.
Here learn the divine art of the eternal
Master, who placed the Sun thus far,
and tempered its heat in such a way
that it does not, too strong, burn the soil,
nor, too weak, freeze it; nor leave it all
faint and sad and barren of life.

As for the white Moon, now understand
and think something similar to this.   390
In fact—as I said—its body is large
and, except for the fine, bright Sun,
the Moon exceeds all lamps in the sky,

---

[53] For witty and ironic use of such "scientific evidence" from the Middle Ages to the Baroque era, see Umberto Eco's novels *Baudolino* and *The Island of the Day Before*.
[54] The word "gas" was not used then.

129

but it is not always seen, and does not
shine in the same way at any time,
but it sometimes fills its empty ring,
sometimes appears partly diminished.
And as it ascends, it becomes dark
on the one side; in falling, the other side
darkens. Yes, the eternal, wise Forger's   400
craftsmanship and art is beyond words:
He who, in the sky, set a clear example[55]
—through the changes in the inconstant Moon—
of human inconstancy, of the uncertainty
of our unsteady and wandering life,
which is unable to maintain one purpose,
to keep and last in one firm state.
But it first augments and advances
until it reaches its maximum size,
then it declines, wastes away, falls,   410
and finally dies out into nothingness.[56]
Let nobody therefore parade his glory[57]
or show off pride and magnificence
in all his treasures, or be confident
in his power, boasting beyond measure;[58]
nor for ancient crown and gold scepter
walk imperiously and gravely in public.
Let him rather despise his own perishable,
frail part, and only esteem the inward good
and his immortal, inextinguishable soul;   420
may he often think about the uncertain
turns of human things, and keep his mind
fixed on the eternal as its center.
And if a pale, diminished Moon makes
him sad with its darkened aspect,
may he rather be sorry for his soul,
which gains virtue—the treasure and precious
gift of Heaven—and so it first advances,

---

[55] Cf. Paracelsus' doctrine of the "correspondences" between earth and sky, as reflections in a mirror.

[56] Cf. the devotional pictures of the "double stairs of human life," first growing, then declining.

[57] The Italian wording (*in vista altero*) echoes Dante, *Purgatorio* 12: 70 (*col viso altero*).

[58] A "due" specification. As Nietzsche pointed out, Renaissance heroism was at the antipodes of Franciscan humility, and the German philosopher sided with the former. Tasso tried to achieve a difficult balance, especially in *Gerusalemme Conquistata*.

then however loses it and does not preserve
its honor of old and its dignity.   430
Truly, the various, long wanderings of
the unstable planet[59] the foolish[60] man
recalls in his ravings; and in many ways,
like the Moon, he changes and varies.[61]
    One author,[62] since our human mind
possesses two powers or two joined parts,[63]
one fitted for action, the other for passivity,[64]
likens the illuminating part to the Sun;
the other, illuminated and lighting
what is dark and black, is likened   440
to the Moon, finding its glimmer elsewhere
and shining with a borrowed splendor.
In fact, the part of us subject to death
—provided any part of intellect ever dies—[65]
through the other's light adorns and illumines
a thousand fine, clear shapes in itself.
But the one sharing its rays with others
cannot fear the tough fate of death;
to the extent it was believed to be God
by the philosophical schools of old.[66]   450
Some[67] disagree: "Not God, but a creature,
God's offspring, to whom is granted
the name *Sun* because of its noble light."
Let the bold reason of clever men stand

---

[59] The Moon was considered a planet, the first revolving around the Earth.

[60] Tasso uses two words: *folle* (etymologically close to "fool," and meaning mad or madman) and *stolto* (fool proper, stupid). The Madman/Foolish Man was a frequent personage in Medieval and Renaissance allegories, both in literature and art; cf. also the Tarot. Tasso often baroquely employs two synonyms to convey one concept; in this translation, they are often reduced to one word for reasons of poetry and/or language.

[61] Possibly with a hint at Dante, *Inferno* 25: 143, adding a touch of horror to the human predicament.

[62] Unnamed "recent philosopher[s]"; Tasso found this reference in Pico Della Mirandola's *Heptaplus* (BB).

[63] The so-called active (thought) and passive intellect (the mind's storage).

[64] From Dante, *Purgatorio* 25: 47, where sexual intercourse is described. A fine example of Tasso's wit.

[65] Deism and "natural philosophy" were constant "temptations" for Tasso; see Luigi Firpo (ed.), *Torquato Tasso. Tre Scritti Politici*, Turin: UTET, 1980, *passim*. For Averroes' doctrine of passive intellect, cf. Dante, *Purgatorio* 25: 62-66. Tasso was obviously fascinated by Canto 25 of *Purgatorio*, Dante's brief handbook on biology.

[66] Especially, again, Averroes.

[67] Alexander of Aphrodisia and his followers (BB).

aside; let it surrender before that which
ancient belief[68] most clearly affirms;
bold nonetheless, as in God it does know
truth better than any primal intellect does.[69]

Now let us show how the wandering Moon
helps by its varying—augmenting   460
the things that the Earth bears in her womb or
that the sea's liquid, salty bosom feeds;
for by rising, the Moon fills up all bodies
with humors, and empties them by falling
almost completely; so harmoniously does it
unite and stir the dampness and the heat.
In fact, not cold at all is the white Moon,[70]
as someone thinks: it only seems chilly
if compared to the Sun that warms it.
And so, in her full circle, when she[71]   470
shows her whole body high in the sky,
a beautiful "emulator" of her brother[72]
and nearly—so to speak—a nocturnal Sun,
then nights become warmer and more
serene than usual, when she has the shape
of a hooked sickle, or with silver horns
she turns before or else behind the Sun;
and green trees germinate much more
with leaves and branches, and their damp
medullas fatten inside their barks;   480
and undersea, the hard shells are fuller

---

[68] The Bible; Christianity.

[69] If directly united with God, man's mind even surpasses the angels' minds. That's easier said than done; see Dante, *Paradiso* 33: 139. Cf. also *Letter to the Hebrews* 1: 4-14 (since the Christians' condition is supposed to become the same as Christ, namely, *theosis*; cf. e.g. S. Khoddam, *op. cit.*, ch. 10). Typical of Renaissance religiosity is this paradoxical need to be, at the same time, humble because of our present condition *and* bold because of God's promises. For an updated re-proposal of this twofold attitude, see C. S. Lewis, *Mere Christianity*, Part III, ch. 8 and 12.

[70] This interesting remark dates back to no less than St. Basil (BB) or possibly some even more ancient author.

[71] A major problem with translating is the issue of grammatical genders. *Luna* (Moon) is feminine in Italian, but to always render it as "she" would not have fitted astronomical descriptions. So, as a rule, "Moon" has been dealt with as "it" in scientific contexts, and "she" in mythological ones, but things tend to blend in this poem, especially in the current section. In the lines above, "she" was the Earth and "it" the Moon; here however the latter must be "feminized."

[72] Artemis/Diana was the sister of Apollo, who became the solar god, though originally there was another god of the sun, Helios.

of savory food; and it may also happen that
someone, sleeping in the open air, winds up
with his head heavy with humors.[73]
Here I will not tell how the Moon moves the
air and the winds, stirring and calming the sea.
Suffice it, at this point, to have hinted at
its size and the many effects by which
it proves useful. Let not the human senses
dare ever try to measure the Moon, since   490
here their judgment is uncertain and false:
so grand is it that it illuminates[74]
all inhabitants and cities separated
by the most vast sea, by the wide earth
—may they live where the Sun sets, or in
the kingdoms of the beautiful Aurora,
or under the Bears in the chilliest zone,
or in the arid, hot climatic band[75] that
encircles and divides the Earth in two;
it lights them all (I say) in basically   500
the same way, not some with oblique rays,
some with straight ones. And *this* does show
how big it is, and in vain the senses or false
reason, saying falsehoods, will oppose;
no room is left to the sophists' niceties.[76]
But may He, who gave us the dearest gift
of our immortal minds,[77] also teach us
how to know truth. That eternal wisdom
of His, by which He made the world,
proves great in the smallest things,   510
and greater in the greatest appears to us,
such as the Sun and the round Moon.
Even though they may be partly likened
or compared to their eternal Maker,

---

[73] On Medieval and Renaissance medicine linking a person's health with the influences of the whole cosmos, see e.g. the *Divine Comedy* with medical-historical notes by Dr. Donatella Lippi, 3 volumes (Fidenza, IT: Mattioli1885, 2009-2010). This verse may partly hint at lycanthropy too.

[74] "Cotanto è grande..." echoes Dante, *Paradiso* 33: 13, with reference to the Virgin Mary, of whom the Moon is a symbol in Catholic art, especially from the Renaissance/Baroque period on.

[75] The Equatorial area.

[76] The verse almost literally quotes Dante, *Paradiso* 24: 81.

[77] *Mens* (mind) was often a synonym of soul, especially its "apex" (*apex mentis*) directly in touch with God.

before Him who gathers all greatness
in himself, and like a tiny toy, holds
and grips the universe in his fist,
the Sun and Moon will physically look
like greedy fleas, like busy ants.[78]

He simultaneously made the stars,   520
He who had already made the firmament
in Day Two, but not fully adorned yet.
The name "stars" is even given by some
not to the sublime, heavenly and nearly
eternal lights, fixed in their own turns,
but to comets and other flaming figures
that we see burn in various shapes, high
in the atmosphere or in that lofty fire[79]
which, gathering under the Moon's circle,
turns with it in perpetual motion.   530
But these cannot have any firm seat,
nor any constant size or shape or order
on high; and after a quite brief time
they usually disappear from our sight
and vanish, dispersing through the air, as
phenomena having their fuel and tinder
in the smoking bosom of the earth.[80]
Or maybe Mother Earth stops giving them
their dry food, quickly becoming burned,
and they can no longer live, and shortly   540
their lives come definitively to an end;
sometimes not one day passes, and the
instant they light up, they do die out.
So, that tiny beast born along the banks
of the roaring *Ipani*,[81] experiencing only

---

[78] For this image, Tasso could resort to the Bible, e.g. *Isaiah* 40: 12, since Dante didn't use this metaphor of a partly threatening hand—fist, indeed—let alone Ariosto. The comparison with fleas and ants is a Baroque touch. On the whole, these lines recall the vivid imagery of Counter-Reformation preaching.

[79] The "sphere of fire" between the Earth and the Moon. Comets were a phenomenon that fascinated Renaissance people in general, and Tasso in particular; see lines 577 ff.

[80] According to Aristotle's theory of comets originating from earthly exhalations (BB). That is one of the explanations suggested by scholars for the event occurring in Dante, *Inferno* 3: 130-134, though it could instead be interpreted on the basis of the phenomena concomitant with Christ's resurrection.

[81] The Bug River, flowing into the Black Sea (BB). The insect is the mayfly, in Italian *effimera* from Greek *eph' hemera*, "[all] in one day." The pun with "bug" is an amusing coincidence.

one Sun swiftly rising at one dawn
and reaching its final fate in the evening—
that beast (I say) whose nature and fortune[82]
were meaner and sparer than any other's,
is born on earth with a far better fate   550
than those flaming shapes in the sky.
Yet, some call and define them "stars"
or "falling stars." So that, many times,
the erring masses gaze and wonder[83]
whether stars can die, or perhaps fall,
which should, by dignity, be eternal
or almost eternal, and keep living across
the long course of the flying aeons.
Such is the way of addressing the senses
of the weak plebs, adapting one's speech.   560
But among those figures lighted and nearly
printed in the sky, branded with their marks,
some have such a fixed and certain seat
and such a long and firm existence
that they can be deemed not only a part
of the sky, but a dear and beautiful one:
see that shining and whitish Way[84]
adding to a milky whiteness the lights
of many fixed stars scattered there.
That is the way leading to the lofty   570
palace of the fabled gods, and the path
also is open to the human soul, the passage
by which to descend into its bodily
dwelling and then return, soaring high,
each to its pure and destined star.
So did they[85] believe. So did old Fame say.

But a comet,[86] so powerful in its appearance,
which, flaming, kills purple-clad tyrants and

---

[82] "Cielo," literally sky/heaven.

[83] A similar scene and mood in Dante, *Paradiso* 18: 100-102.

[84] The Milky Way was not considered as a mass of stars, but no theory prevailed as to what it might be. See Dante, *Paradiso* 14: 99 (who calls it "the Galaxy," but not in our modern sense; the Greek term *galaktikos* simply means "Milky").

[85] Macrobius and Platonic thinkers (BB). Tasso loved classical culture so much that, at times, he pocketed his Christian beliefs and let imagination run.

[86] A much talked-about one had appeared in 1585 (BB). In that very year, Tasso had written a perspicacious essay on the Civil War then going on in France; the whole text is included in Luigi Firpo, *op. cit.*

unconquered kings, and changes kingdoms,
has a brief lifespan for all its power,   580
and within two years comes to its end;
and so, as quickly as man's early childhood,
that fearful light grows old and dies,
after frightening us wretched mortals.
Never do comets appear between Capricorn
and Cancer, or but very rarely will they
show there, and before they flare up in all
of their strength, the Sun dissolves them.
Beyond that oblique, crooked route[87]
along which the planets eternally turn,   590
they light up, shining between it and the Bears;
then, unfolding their burning manes[88]
or their beards burning and strewn with
blood-red flames, with frightful faces
they threaten us by announcing death.[89]
These, however harmful and fierce,
were given the glorious name of "stars,"
unfitting their so malign appearance,
unable to boast of any harmless light
—though someone[90] said that one appeared   600
harmless to Nero, but he just flattered,
since it harmed the whole world by sparing
the Emperor's life; it proved more harmful
and ungodly in saving such a ruthless
monster than in murdering anyone else.[91]
    One of these was perhaps that pure, beautiful
and holy light, the dear, trustworthy guide
of the Eastern Kings[92] on pilgrimage:
He only knows, who by his eternal hand

---

[87] The ecliptic (BB).

[88] Comas, but a literal translation better highlights the link with the following line. The dismal light of comets was associated with Satan's eyes by Tasso in *Gerusalemme Liberata* 4, stanza 7, and with Satan's attitude by Milton, *Paradise Lost* 2: 708-711.

[89] Partly echoing Dante, *Inferno* 13: 12.

[90] The philosopher Seneca (BB).

[91] Tasso follows the standard Christian historiography. Ariosto, more revolutionary, said that Nero would be considered a great personage if he had had more favorable PR (*Orlando Furioso* 35, stanza 26).

[92] The three Wise Men, then traditionally considered to be kings, though *Matthew*, ch. 2, doesn't say so. The "star" guiding them was interpreted either as an extraordinary natural phenomenon or as an angel. According to some scholars, the "star" painted by Giotto in his *Nativity of Jesus* is Halley's Comet, which had impressed Medieval observers.

first shaped it, and gave it light and motion   610
that might then appear endowed with will,
as if it had its own intellect and soul;
an unprecedented work, anyway, of the
divine hand for a transcendent purpose.
    The others,[93] in Day Four, had already
been created (we guess), and given mind
and life by the eternal heavenly Forger
—life not feeding and not drawing energy
from food,[94] or weakening from starvation,
looking, by shifting, for nourishment   620
from the earth and the ever-exhaling sea,
as some ancient authors[95] did affirm
who unjustly had the fame of wise men;
but a joyful, glorious, pure life that,
gazing at God, in Him makes itself eternal,
nurtured by the knowledge and love of Him.
    These divine and glorious intelligences had
been created by God in Day One, before
the Sun and the beautiful starry circles;
then, on Day Four, they were split among   630
their proper places, as a wise captain
divides his loyal soldiers into squads
and places them on duty, entrusting them
with a strong, elevated city or high tower.[96]
Some of them were sent to run[97] in a ring,
without toiling at all, without being forced,

---

[93] The other "heavenly lights," the angels. The Italian phrasing is quite awkward; it might be translated as "the other ones [also] were created in Day 4," but line 628 will make all this clear. Consistent with his inconsistency, Tasso, in the wake of most Church Fathers, thinks that the angels had been created in Day 1 when God said, "Let there be light!" but he deals with them here in Day 4: a very interesting "Treatise of Angelology," extending up to line 760.

[94] Anticipating the fascinating, science fiction Angelology of Milton.

[95] In his notes, Tasso indicates Anaxagoras (BB).

[96] Godfrey of Bouillon does carefully so in both Jerusalem-poems, in fact. In the *Divine Comedy*, angels were ethereal creatures; in Ariosto, they were mockingly militarized; with Tasso, and then Milton, their regimentation is complete. Here Tasso diverges from Dante in other respects too. According to the latter (*Paradiso* 29: 37-45), angels were immediately given their roles. Also, while Dante put all angels in the nine circles governing the universe, Tasso sees this as their secondary function (see "part" in line 635), the main one being the praise of God. And here he agrees with Milton; see Uriel, the solitary "regent"—not strictly the mover—of the Sun; or rather, just a bit more than a Foreign Minister on holiday (*Paradise Lost* 3: 629, 654-658, 690).

[97] Transitive, referring to the cosmic circles (line 637). The pun works in both languages.

139

those sublime and shining circles of His.
Others, from their very origin in eternity,
had the defense of humankind as their
destiny from that supreme King;   640
later, as flying messengers, they would
make His decrees manifest on earth,
carrying to-and-fro graces and prayers:
divine graces always swift and ready,
human prayers often slow and late.[98]
Still others, forever intent on His service,
stay as loyal ministers nearby and around,
almost like innumerable children.
From the day in which our father Adam[99]
opened his eyes to the serene light,   650
not as many tired and wretched mortals
have been produced of his corrupt,
unclean seed to labor in this world,
as those divine and winged spirits,
who were destined to that eternal peace,
to that joy without end, out of time,
making them always care-free[100] and happy
with an eternal leisure, with no duties at all,
without having unease about earthly cares.
Those[101] who bind angels to the heavy duty   660
of turning the skies ceaselessly by force,
almost like beasts tied to a marble stone,
or after the fashion of suffering Ixion,
forever bound, forever turning:
they are wrong, blinded by their own lies.
    Even the great Master of those who know,[102]
he whose doctrines are worldwide taught,
did err by following motion and sense
(untrustworthy guides), but less seriously so,
when he philosophically attempted   670

---

[98] Italian scholars who describe the late works by Tasso as dull expressions of Counter-Reformation ideology lack appreciation for the beauty—and existential truth—of verses like these. A little below, see the contrast between "serene light" and "wretched mortals."
[99] Distant echoes of Dante, *Paradiso* 7: 112-113.
[100] "Neghittosi," literally: idle. It is nearly always used in a negative sense, but here, quite surprisingly, we find it referring to angels. See also "ozio" in line 658, corresponding to its original Latin meaning (*otium*).
[101] Epicurus and Cicero, in Tasso's notes (BB). He probably didn't dare list Dante also.
[102] Aristotle; from Dante, *Inferno* 4: 131.

to compute those eternal, divine minds,
and to a small figure[103] he strictly limited
the citizens of the heavenly kingdom.
In fact, following the various motions
by which the sky is variously moved,
he assigns movers to the celestial spheres,
but does not worship or propitiate
or recognize in the divine empire
further functions, or deities, or gods.
Without any purpose or duty,[104]   680
he thought, no idle Intelligences could
exist, living lazily and in vain;
so, in his erring opinion, only as
many could exist as necessary for
the heavenly circles; the others he deemed
supernumerary, worshiped in vain,
false gods from Greece or Egypt. His mind,
however singular, did not understand
that to the glorious, eternal Court
other functions and duties belong,   690
besides making the eternal spheres
turn in their many, differing motions.
He did not want to see—or pretended so—
that a higher, worthier, and nobler end
than that befitted the eternal minds,
without which he considers divine natures
supernumerary and somewhat useless.
But keeping the starry wheels in motion
is a mechanical end, sticking to bodies
and occupied with them: a low duty,   700
contrary to the most sublime spirits
who stand by and around the supreme God.
Thus, another purpose, higher and nobler,
another worthier and more honored end,
another holier and more sacred ministry
demands and requires a far greater number

---

[103] That is, one "motion-giving intelligence" per sky. Dante, not altogether successfully, tried to reconcile the two conceptions. In *Paradiso*, while exploring the heavens, he refers each time to one angel "in charge" there, but in the final, overall vision the angels are numberless, all making the universe turn. Tasso's "lazy" angelic multitudes also hint at his non-anthropocentric worldview—which was the "spirit," if not the "letter," of the Copernican revolution.

[104] A stance against utilitarianism, not only with regard to angels.

of immortal minds. The Lord of Lords,
the King of Kings cannot reign solitary
in a solitary palace and in
an empty kingdom, while filling the lower   710
world with inhabitants, as if to increase
the pride and pomp of the earthly empire.[105]
Nor could God give to glorious Emperors
and others, down here, crowns and scepters,
and so many peoples, arms and squads,
and so many armies, in so many ways
gathering and scattering on earth and at sea,
while possessing no phalanx for Himself,
though He suffices. Ha, too unworthy
of His glory that would be! And so, too,   720
limited are the measures linked to matter!
Too scanty are the numbers used to count
all that's contained in the bosoms of the earth
and sea, or the sky exposed to the senses.
There is a number[106] that does not increase
by adding further fractions, superior
to all other figures. Now, who will presume
to compute the pure, eternal minds?
Oh, don't you see how many rays are
projected by this corporeal, unsteady Sun,   730
which is like one ray of the Sun supreme?[107]
Or, in how many shining rays, how many
flames, how many ardors on high will
the eternal, primal Source of light spread?[108]
Neither can thought comprehend, nor tongue

---

[105] Tasso capsizes a venerable theological conception developed by the Church Fathers, and continued by St. Anselm and Milton, i.e., that God created humankind precisely in order to restock the number of His faithful after the devils' rebellion. Tasso, on the contrary, starts from the earthly numbers, and infers that the heavenly inhabitants cannot be less numerous. But in so doing, he doesn't see that, by describing God as *needing* a Renaissance-like Court, he demotes Him. Cf. Dante, *Paradiso* 29: 13-15, though the third line is not very clear. It is also interesting to note that, in both Jerusalem-poems, Satan decides to intervene in the Crusade, obviously against the Christians, because he would not like to reign in an empty kingdom (*GL* 4: 14 and par.).

[106] A noteworthy foray into infinitesimal calculus; but the source indicated by Tasso in his notes is, surprisingly enough, St. Thomas Aquinas. Cf. Dante, *Paradiso* 28: 92-93.

[107] In the Metaphysics of Light (Robert Grosseteste, Dante, Milton) it is not completely clear if "light" is a metaphor or a true substance analogically common to both God and His creatures.

[108] Cf. Dante, *Paradiso* 19: 52-54, who also includes man's mind among God's rays.

express it:[109] what is calculated above the sky
appears numberless to human senses.
    Surely, high reason and eternal will[110]
moved[111] the supreme Lord, the world-shaper,
to make the more perfect more numerous,   740
as He does not multiply imperfect things.[112]
This is the reason why fierce carnivores
live, few and rare, in solitary forests
or in wild, secluded mountains; whereas
below great herds graze in the fields[113]
and the humble sheep in large numbers
follow the shepherd, the trustworthy guide.
But the widespread seed of the sons of Adam
fill Europe, and occupy the other parts
of the Earth, that is narrow and low   750
in comparison with the vast, lofty sky.
And heaven's[114] highest parts are full of
glorious inhabitants, more than of stars;
but, not content with its primal, ancient
and nearly eternal celestial inhabitants,
heaven welcomes mortal pilgrims, those
who are born on earth from earthly mud.
And for these foreign crowds the high seats
are prepared: they are accompanied, united
with the angelic teams nearly as equals.   760
Indeed, the malconceived children of Adam
are not foreign whatsoever to the wide heaven

---

[109] Cf. *I Corinthians* 2: 9. With a significant shift: Tasso doesn't refer to the Mystery of salvation and the ineffability of eschatological bliss, but to mathematical speculation about angels. As we will see in Day 5, he can rework St. Paul's texts in much more unexpected ways than this.

[110] Literally: judgment.

[111] Cf. Dante, *Inferno* 3: 4-6, at the opposite end of the cosmic order.

[112] According to widespread religious beliefs (see e.g. Raimon Panikkar's interreligious essays on this topic), that which is perfect—especially saints—is *less* numerous. But Tasso already has in mind his ideas on ecosystems that he explains here below.

[113] This remark—based on St. Basil (BB)—will find a parallel in the evolutionary theory by Alfred R. Wallace, Charles Darwin's often forgotten *Doppelgänger*. The strange thing is that big cats, wolves, etc., are associated with the "imperfect" part of Nature, perhaps because they kill, against *Isaiah* 11: 6-7. This would fit in with other half-Gnostic (or something more than "half") statements from Tasso, who elsewhere praises *any* creature, however.

[114] Tasso continuously shifts from one meaning to the other of the Italian word *cielo* (sky, heaven). Much more indirectly, these lines may be read in a science fiction key, cf. Milton, *Paradise Lost* 3: 565 ff.

since heavenly is the fine, sublime origin
of the human soul; and happy it returns
there as to its true home and ancient land
—from this shadowy cloister of earth[115]
where it dwelt as a wandering pilgrim.
Man, wrapped in corporeal limbs, was
born from Adam, who was generated out
of muddy earth, but he is re-born   770
in God, regenerated by water and Spirit,[116]
and as the heir of his Father's kingdom,
he longs for a sublime, heavenly crown.

    But—where am I dragged, before due time,[117]
by humanity's love, so sweetly grafted onto
us by our nature?[118] Let's follow the wonderful
course of the sky and the wandering stars,
to whom, as their movers, the eternal Father
assigned those pure, sublime minds,
not as "forms" embedded[119] in their matter,   780
but rather as a charioteer to a fast chariot.
That was when the sky's motions began,[120]
the one from the right side towards the left,
the other from the left towards the right
—by the "right" meaning the luminous East,
whence the First Sphere moves turning,
pushing and dragging all the others,[121]
nearly removing them from their route;
by the "left" part meaning the West, whence
the others move, and the same Sun   790
which shows itself to us from the East

---

[115] Less tragic than Dante's "small yard that makes us so fierce" (*Paradiso* 22: 151).

[116] *John* 3: 5.

[117] A clever expression of the poem's anti-structural development.

[118] As we'll see later, Tasso has a tendency to think of behavior as determined by genes ("nature").

[119] "Immerse," editing the BB reading "immense." With reference to the Aristotelian *morphai*.

[120] Sources: Thomas Aquinas' commentary to *De Caelo*; A. Piccolomini; G. Fracastoro (BB).

[121] The *Primum Mobile*, rather than the starry firmament, as explained by BB. Cf. Dante, *Paradiso* 27: 99-108, where, however, the celestial motions were much simpler (Dante knew the more complex astronomical patterns, see his *Convivio*, but in the *Divine Comedy* he simplified them for the sake of poetry). The astronomers followed by Tasso thought, e.g., that the natural motion of the Sun was from the West, but it was mostly "dragged" by the First Mover in the opposite direction. This "confliction" explains the aberrations in its course.

by means of another's thrust, in one day
is led back there whence it had left.
In fact, in one day—including light and dark
in itself—a perfect turn is performed
by the First Sphere, while the others variously
in their motions follow the opposite path,
like a tiny ant or small caterpillar
being dragged all around by a fast wheel,
meanwhile to the opposite side   800
moves on its own, but much more slowly.

    In thirty years he makes a whole turn, that
one who seems lazy to us, Saturn, but
swifter than the others, running faster;
and in two times six, placid Jupiter,
and in a couple of years fierce Mars
(the planet so known and called by the plebs
on Earth), and in only one the Sun,
and in a little less that charming star[122]
which happily rises earlier than dawn,   810
then called Lucifer,[123] and reappearing as
Hesperus, named so when the Sun sets.
In nearly the same time does that once-
believed flying messenger[124] go back home.
And again, in twenty-seven days
the slower Moon completes its route,
which looks faster, and this happens
because it turns in a smaller circle,
and sooner returns whence it first moved.
The Moon was man's ancient master   820
of the year's division, that into twelve months
the old Numa[125] made for his Romans,
because so many times does the Moon
reach the Sun in restarting its own course.
Earlier, Greeks and the older Hebrews
had divided one year in the same manner.
Romulus then, less skilled in celestial
motions than in war, and quite ignorant
about divine things, had divided it

---

[122] Venus.
[123] In its original meaning: light-bearer.
[124] Hermes/Mercury.
[125] King Numa Pompilius (BB).

into ten: this mistake was rectified 830
by the wise, white-bearded Sabine King.[126]
This is how the two glorious planets,[127] with
their turns, were destined to mark the year by those[128]
who escort them in their perpetual paths.
"Year" means the return of the running Sun
from one Sign to the very same Sign
it started from; or rather, to a fixed point
in that Sign as to an unvarying end,
since simply going back to the same star
whence it started, the Sun would find 840
it quite far now, abducted by the First Sky
with its quick movement in its own circle.
Who leads them to make summer and winter?
Italy and all Europe call them
by the names of lying and false gods;[129]
but *angels* they are, they are pure minds,
in the sky, the servants of high Providence,
who along an oblique path set the seven
wandering planets—among them the Sun,
so that it may vary our seasons and times; 850
and by this, it may cause in our world
either birth or death, and may transform
life into death, death into life alternately.[130]

Accordingly, as the Sun lies far away,
on the side whence the cloudy South wind blows,[131]
our places darken with the longest nights,
and the air gets cold, and the earth is upset
all around, and in a thick rain, condensed
vapors fall, as well as broad layers
of snow, which then, shrinking into ice, 860
cloak the backs of the high mountains
and, braking the great rivers in their flow,

---

[126] Again, Numa Pompilius.

[127] Sun and Moon; cf. *Genesis* 1: 16.

[128] The angels. The words "gli scorge nel" might also mean "those who watch them," i.e. the astronomers, but the occurrence of the same verb in line 843 resolves all ambiguity. Cf. in English "to see [someone home]."

[129] From Dante, *Inferno* 1: 72, but inverting the two adjectives.

[130] The vicissitudes of the ever-fleeting world were a basic feature of Primary Epic (Homer, *Beowulf*), see C. S. Lewis, *A Prologue to Paradise Lost*, ch. 5. In Renaissance poems, this theme mixed and clashed with Christian Providence.

[131] That is, in winter, when the Sun is in the farthest cosmic South.

slow them down, and almost into solid glass
change the swamps and the lazy ponds.
But when the Sun comes back from the South,
almost in the middle of its circling way,[132]
it divides night and day into equal parts
and warms up the air in a soft balance.
Then Zephyr blows, then Spring returns
all dressed up in green, and joyful   870
with herbs and flowers, her sweet family;[133]
and the pregnant Earth gently opens
her fertile womb, so far closed by snow
and ice, for the new births to come.
The shadowy plants germinate and bloom,
animals are born on earth and in water
and the perpetual birthing goes on,[134]
as long as the Sun, as much as it can, draws
near to the snowy kingdom of the North.
And when it stays in Cancer, stopping   880
its run—it then makes the days longer,
and with slower pace passes now vertically
ranging into the space above our heads,
while it warms the air all around us—
it dries the earth and the sown seeds
and fully ripens the fruits of trees.
During this month, the Sun is aflame
more than ever, and from high unfolds
less oblique rays to illuminate the Earth.
Very long are therefore the summer days,   890
and very short the shadows; while vice versa
in the shortest days any opaque body
casts its longest shadows away from sunlight.[135]

    This happens to us, the inhabitants of lands
between the circle whence Apollo returns,[136]
and the other named after the Bears, those
posited not far from the seven icy Oxen.[137]

---

[132] "In mezzo . . . del cam[m]in," jokingly from the first verse of the *Divine Comedy*.
[133] This line blends various expressions from Dante. Conjecture: there may also be a reference to Sandro Botticelli's celebrated painting customarily known as *La Primavera* ("Spring"), though its actual subject is disputed.
[134] Anticipating *Genesis* 1: 22, Day 5.
[135] As usual, natural phenomena—and all the more so light and shadow—are symbols of the alternating, ambiguous human condition. Cf. *John* 12: 35, and the note to line 853.
[136] The Tropic of Cancer (BB).

We always[138] cast our shadows on the right
in the direction of Boreas and the Plow;
others live in hotter climatic zones,   900
who, one or two whole days every year,
don't have any shadow when the Sun turns
in the Southern circle, and the other parts
it illuminates and warms with straight rays.
And it then occurs, in those zones, that
through their small mouths, hollow wells
are illumined down to their bottoms,
like in Syene as well as in Berenice,[139]
and farther on, in the honored palace
built between two branches of the Nile,   910
in the city that from Cambyses' dead sister
got its name and her famous grave.[140]
But beyond the sunny and spicy land
of the happy Arabians,[141] strange people
cast their shadows (this gives them their name)[142]
on both sides, both north- and southward.
This happens when the Sun passes close
to the cold kingdoms of the North,
and already joyful Fall welcomes us,[143]
rich in fruits and sparkling wines,   920
but still green with crowns of vine leaves.
Then Time tempers the summer Sun's rays,[144]
diminishes its heat, increases the friendly shadows,
makes nights and days equal in the Scales,[145]
and harmlessly leads us towards Winter,
when the Sun again moves away from us
and gets nearer Arabians and Indians.
These are the Sun's motions and course,

---

[137] The *septem Triones*, see note to 3: 470.
[138] At midday.
[139] In Ancient Egypt (BB).
[140] The place's name is Meroe, some 200 kilometers north of Karthoum. Tasso found this piece of information in Strabo, but the grave belonged to another personage, the Egyptian queen Amanishakadeto (BB).
[141] The inhabitants of the *Arabia Felix*.
[142] The legendary *amphiskioi*, i.e. "double-shadowed"; again from Strabo, and other ancient writers (BB).
[143] Tasso overturns two clichés: Fall is not a sad season, and it welcomes us, not vice versa.
[144] With an odd syntactical structure, literally: "[it] tempers the rays...," where "Time" is just logically implied, but it will be mentioned pointedly in line 929.
[145] In both senses: balanced and in Libra.

149

these are Time's turns and vicissitudes
through which here human life is ruled.   930
And so wonder worthy is the art of the
eternal Maker, his noble and sublime
Providence, establishing the limits to
the oblique paths of the Wandering Seven[146]
and a much narrower[147] way to the Sun.
In fact, only the latter never leaves
the curved path[148] that divides and splits
the Ring of Life[149] into equal parts;
the other planets do swerve, here or there,
more or less, and the fecund Moon   940
boldly wanders throughout that circle.
Venus goes off that same circle too, even
bolder than the Moon and more fecund;
therefore[150] in uncultivated deserts there
lie both sandy Africa and torrid India,
the mother and nurse of such varied beasts.
Let no one blame eternal Providence
if to the world's order, to the very top
of all things being produced in it
fierce and strange creatures[151] add   950
marvel and beauty, as do cruel monsters.
    Now, as the Sun, revolving on high,
never goes off the established route, this
clear, enlightening example shows
to earthly monarchs the narrow path
fixed to them by virtue and by law.
When the Sun sees straight before himself
the round Moon (she tramps on the proud
Dragon's head[152] or else depresses its tail),

---

[146] Planets.

[147] Insofar as more regular, less "swerving." A plain circumference is shorter than a roundish zigzagging line.

[148] The Ecliptic.

[149] The Zodiac. These descriptions come from such authors as Ptolemy, Pliny, Martianus Capella, Fracastoro (BB).

[150] Because of Venus' aberrant influence (BB). Venus' love for India is one of the main threads in Camões' *Lusiad.*

[151] Cf. *Inferno* 6: 13 for this detail; but the paradoxical, upsetting conception of the cosmos depicted here belongs wholly to the Renaissance, not to Dante.

[152] Not the constellation but the irregular, serpentine line drawn by the Moon's course (BB). Additionally, a clear reference to Catholic imagery of the Virgin Mary: an admixture of *Genesis* 3: 15 and *Revelation* 12: 1-3.

he denies his sweet rays and bright light   960
to her, and the dry Earth shifts in between,
so that the Moon grows dim and darkens.[153]
But if the beautiful Moon meets the Sun
(as actually happens twice in Gemini),
the latter partly veils himself to our eyes.
From all this learn that, if celestial light
above can darken, weaken, and wane,
there is no mortal light on this base world,
nor splendor of fortune—so often dazzling
to the weak sight of the errant throng—   970
which may not get blurred and vanish.
So, lift your thoughts to the high, primal,
holy divine Light, the eternal Light
never subject to any sunset or dawn,[154]
nor to any defect, forever undiminished.
But, when Light himself took on humanity,
He made the very Sun eclipse with him
unexpectedly, to the astonishment and shame
of a tearful and dolorous Nature,[155]
and no man's mind understands how.[156]   980
    But as to how the Sun goes to and fro,
so that the inconstant Moon always rises
in the evening, and hides in the morning;
why Saturn, Jupiter, and fierce Mars
follow the opposite order, all rising
before dawn, falling in the late hours;
and as to so many different effects
appearing above, sphere after sphere,
various reasons were adduced as proofs
by various schools of differing perceptions.[157]   990

---

[153] The lunar eclipse. A description of the solar eclipse follows.

[154] Quoting Dante, *Purgatorio* 30: 2.

[155] Cf. Milton, *Paradise Lost* 10: 782-783 and 1000-1003, with reference to the original sin, that is a "parallel" event to Jesus' death on the cross.

[156] There was much arguing about the natural and/or supernatural reason of the eclipse in *Matthew* 27: 45; see Dante, *Paradiso* 29: 97-102, who dared counter no less than his beloved Thomas Aquinas. Tasso's fascinating suggestion is that the death of Light (*John* 1: 9 and 8: 12) affected natural light.

[157] "In contemplar discordi." A subtle methodological insight: not only did they model differently, *a posteriori*, the things they had seen, but they actually saw different things. We perceive what we expect to. For the very technical notions in the following section, BB's notes proved indispensable. Anyway, what interests us here is the overall effect created by

Some,[158] observing the two contrary motions
in the skies—the primal one diverting and dragging
the lower ones against their own routes—
said that the true center of each sky was
the Earth's same center, around which their
spheres turned in full, perfect circles.
Above the starry courts they did not place
any other body, any further sky, but set
below the stars these Wandering Seven
that create a supreme harmony   1000
as with a fine celestial lyre; to each
planet giving several rotating spheres,
like different wheels, or many chariots
belonging to a Lord for different purposes,
one to take him away, another to
bring him back along a contrary path.
And on such turning and re-turning globes,
more or less, their theories abounded.
Three shining, wandering carrier spheres were
first given the Sun by old Eudoxus;   1010
three, similarly, to the ever-shifting Moon;
four to the other planets, one to each[159]
in order to carry it back—except for
the Moon, that does not need any of them
to be brought back to the farthest point.
Two more "carriers" did Callippus add
to the Sun, and he added two spheres
at the service of the nocturnal lamp;
in the end, all in all, fifty-five were
computed by those classical thinkers.   1020
So many chariots, strewn with stars and gold,
so many frantic wheels and devices,
so many and different motions and turns
obey the vast, supreme, eternal mass[160]

---

these cosmic "dances." From a historical viewpoint, we note that there was not just *one* geocentric pattern of the universe, as popularizations often imply.

[158] Pre-Aristotelian thinkers offering the model of homocentric spheres, originally with 27 of them, then adding more (BB).

[159] Each "planet" was moved by four spheres, except the Moon who had only three of them, so that the sum is $(6 \times 4) + 3 = 27$. The text, however, is badly twisted; Tasso says "un meno assegna / fuor che...," that literally makes no sense ("he gives one less, except...") and must be reinterpreted by keeping in mind Eudoxus' theory.

[160] "Mole," i.e. an imposing mass; the *Primum Mobile*.

which turns on itself and around itself.
The great master of those who know,[161]
the one being taught worldwide in schools,
followed them—in his high soaring
maybe erring twice—when he increased
the bodies, but reduced pure minds.[162]   1030
    Now the modern era[163] upsets the old order
more and more, adding spheres to spheres,
motions to motions; the sky is now imagined
all trembling, almost weak and tired[164]
as it comes nearer the Earth or withdraws.
Growing confident, the current era dares
exceed the ancient times in art and genius
by making the skies (seen as eternal)
turn and turn again all around their
own center, that is, the world's center.   1040
Others, on another path,[165] follow Hipparchus
and Ptolemy, he who almost outrages the
starry spheres by descrying or dreaming
their ways and wheels twisted and strange:
amazing monster! While giving the Sun three
wandering spheres, he without doubt affirms
that the one turning in the middle of them
has not the world's center as its own;
and the last is partly twisted and bent.
He also states that, as the Sun goes   1050
revolving so, it now approaches the core
of the cosmos, now it moves back away.
In the bigger circle he even figures
a smaller circle, which turns all about
its own poles leaving the world's center
far from its own core; and right here he sets
the Sun, now in a high and lofty place,
now below; now approaching the Earth,
now departing; now, by a crooked course,
shifting against the Signs' order,   1060
now following it. He similarly makes

---

[161] Aristotle, again adopting the Dantean definition.

[162] Aristotle conceived a greater number of celestial bodies, but each with just one "intelligence."

[163] A polemic against the neo-Aristotelian astronomers, especially G. Fracastoro (BB).

[164] Precisely this concept, however, will be conveyed in the last lines of the poem.

[165] The anti-Aristotelian school (BB).

the Moon retroverse, and depicts its fine
ring as irregular, not fully round;
both its shape and route he thus twists.
So, of these two discordant schools, the former
does not argue well, leaving us dissatisfied;
the latter does so, but impiously injures
the celestial spheres, unduly depriving them
of their round and perfect shape, and
their simple motion. Nature therefore   1070
disdainfully complains and rebukes.
Here Philosophy fights against appearances,
and, with irrefutable reasons, she throws
both rebelling schools to the ground.[166]
But Sense may still prove to be a friend
of Reason, should others,[167] by traveling
to far lands and countries, reach the sun-burnt
Ethiopians in the torrid zones, where
the greater belt[168] surrounds the world.
There, *if* the Sun irregularly shifted   1080
in that small sphere, the longest day
would not be equal to the longest night;
and if the Moon *did* revolve within
an irregular and not a round circle,
we would sometimes see those spots
staining its surface in different places.
So, let no daring mind ever presume,
most proudly against Truth and Heaven,[169]
to see new shapes and monsters on high.
    What for? Old times still describe to us   1090
their ancient, unbelievable wonders.
Of its thousand and thousand and thousand
and thousand and thousand *lustra*,[170] fabled Egypt
still seems to boast; and in modern books[171]

---

[166] Philosophy is unusually described as a wrestler.

[167] Tasso nods in the direction of empiricism and experimental science—the Renaissance features that would be most successful throughout the following centuries but were then only part of their complex worldview. Tasso assumes that the anti-Aristotelian theories will prove wrong.

[168] The Equator.

[169] The word "cielo" has here been rendered as Heaven, rather than sky, to highlight the hint at Satan. Cf. *Daniel* 7: 8 and *Revelation* 13: 5, both passages including monsters.

[170] One *lustrum* is five years, so the Egyptian civilization apparently dates back to 25,000 years ago. A thrilling hypothesis, but the figure is likely to have simply tripped across Tasso's tongue.

the old memory of famous and infamous
Egyptian lies has not vanished yet.
And some keep thinking and writing[172]
that, in the turning of the flying aeons,
the Primal Sphere moves all around, not
from the bright East to the black West,   1100
but from the Northern point southwards,
so as to show (provided I grasp it right)
how the fast Sun hastens more and more
as it glides down upon its oblique circle.
The same, strengthening their boldness,
say that the Sun rises twice from a shiny
West, and twice again dies in the East,
bringing us the day from where it sets,
ending the day on the opposite side.
The shifting of that point in which the Sun   1110
seems to stop and also extends its course,
then called "solstice" by Ancient Rome,
was perhaps believed to be the external cause
of such a change; and some ascribed it all
to the high genius of Egypt's sharp minds.
They also tell about a change in the solstice,
which once was in the luminous Gemini,
now is in Cancer. Is any point therefore
unstable, that seems so strongly affixed there?
Neither is the order of the sky and art constant,   1120
Nor is the order of bodies: they are of dirty,
rough materials or better-selected and pure ones.[173]
If this were true, then it would also be true
that the upper part of the Northern sky
will be changed, one day, into the South,
and vice versa; the wandering Sun, turning
along the crooked ways of an oblique ring,
would then follow a straighter high path
along this strip where the world is partitioned.[174]
So many changes, and such discordances,   1130
will be seen, in due time, by future ages

---

[171] Renaissance also entailed a (biased) renaissance of Egyptian mystery cults.

[172] According to the ancient Egyptian astronomers, or to Fracastoro at least (BB).

[173] The question mark is not in the text, but it seems to better fit the general sense of the sentence.

[174] The Equator.

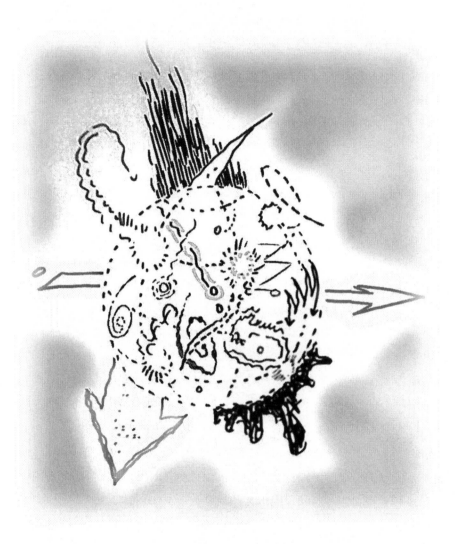

in the upper orders—but such as may be
the sky's vicissitudes, who could ever believe?
Yes, Reason shows off by so figuring,
changing heavenly kingdoms, even kings,
as one was chased away and another[175] came
into power as the high Star Monarch.
While the former, namely Saturn, reigned,
the sky used to move from the now left side.
Then, when Jupiter usurped his seat,   1140
the sky suddenly took the opposite direction,
and by modifying its motion and turning
it forcefully changed all things besides,
those here subject to the sky's influences.
Then, as they tell about a bent, hoary man[176]
already close to death in his old age,
the sky re-wound its years in time
and ran back towards its own heyday,
its perfect age; and later on, step by step,
it became a handsome youth, then a boy,   1150
and then a baby with tender limbs withal;
from infancy it reached the extreme end
of this life, and hid itself in the womb
of the Ancient Mother, *pargoleggiando*.[177]

Oh, the shadowy veil of the old tales,
through which the dim uncertainty of all
bodies transpires, even the loftiest ones!
To which God did give a perpetual
and long-lasting law, but not eternal.[178]
So, in due time, they all will have peace   1160
stopping their continual, certain course.[179]
Clear signs[180] of this will be seen in the sky
before the great Day of the Last Terror,
when this ruinous world's mass will

---

[175] Saturn and Jove, as Tasso explains immediately below.

[176] A cosmic version of the fairy tale featuring Benjamin Button.

[177] Behaving like a child. The verb *pargoleggiare* (from *pàrgolo*, baby) was launched by Dante, *Purgatorio* 16: 87.

[178] Tasso apparently doesn't accept these "pagan" conceptions, but nonetheless agrees with their sense of loss. See again C. S. Lewis on epic cosmology in his *Preface to Paradise Lost*.

[179] Or, "when their . . . course stops," with a Latinizing structure (ablative absolute).

[180] The Biblical prophecies of what follows are well known. Tasso, while reducing them to the laws of Physics (i.e. entropy) echoes them with heartfelt *Michelangelesque* effectiveness.

have to fall, burning and aflame.
Then, lo! The Sun will turn into blood,
and other frightful, fierce signs will
appear on the horrid Moon's face.
In fact, the eternal Forger said,[181] creating,
"Let them be the signs of times, of days,   1170
and years." And such signs actually are
like marks impressed on the Moon
and on the Sun's forehead; and it shows how
to meet the basic needs in the earthly life
of us toiling and stubborn mortals.
Often a perturbed atmosphere forecasts
winds and tempests and stormy rains;
and the dry season is known to a hoary
man whom long custom made expert.
One thing among many did he teach to us,   1180
he who is the true Lord and Master,
when he said, "By reddening, the sky
already saddens, and a storm will rise."[182]
This phenomenon occurs when the Sun
moves behind a dark, shadowy cloud
of dense, impure air: it shines through it
as through a thick red-colored glass.
So the Sun looks bloody, almost hidden,
or else, around it a twin Sun turns,
or even three Suns show off together   1190
in a fierce and frightful manner,[183]
as ancient Rome had already seen
and it still nowadays often occurs
there, below the icy Seven Oxen.
Sometimes we see within dark clouds
outspreading stripes which transform
into the colors of Iris,[184] thus forecasting
a fierce twister, and rain and storm—

---

[181] *Genesis* 1: 14, though here interpreted in a very different sense. In Tasso's Jerusalem poems, stormy or torrid landscapes of this kind are frequent.

[182] *Matthew* 16: 3, but reworked according to typical Tassean moods and scientific interests.

[183] Such phenomena had been described by Pliny the Elder and by the Swede Olaus Magnus (BB). They still "take place" before the eyes of Catholic "seers," often associated with apparitions of the Virgin Mary; reportedly, a vision was beheld by Pope Pius XII in his late years. Tasso opts for a natural explanation in this case.

[184] Sort of a grim counter-rainbow appearing before, not after, a storm. It can be seen in Albrecht Dürer's famous print *Melencolia I* (1514).

a clue, at least, of a changing atmosphere.
To us the inconstant Moon also foretells 1200
by its varying looks the varying of weather:
when subtle and pure on the third day,
it promises and marks stable serenity;
but if it enlarges both horns, growing
nearly vermilion,[185] it then threatens
strong and thick rain, and the violent
assault of the cloudy South wind.
A good helmsman—hoary and shrewd
from experience—can descry the signs
of weather, especially in the North. 1210
And if ever the cloudy corona
surrounding the Sun or the golden stars
happens to fade and fall asunder,
nearly at the same time as it vanishes,
we can expect clear skies and calm seas.
But if the corona breaks on one side,
upon that side from which its fine
texture has frayed, we expect the wind.
If it is torn and rent in many places,
from several directions fierce winds 1220
suddenly rise, struggling and warring
in the sky and at sea—the stormy field
of the noisy and cloudy tempests.[186]
Such signs are made constant or changing
by the sublime will of the All-Mover.[187]

So, may it please Him to show us a calm
peace from on high, clearing away
all that which threatens and lies heavy
on this stormy and uncertain life of ours.

---

[185] The red moon was *the* sign of ill omen in a 1970s "cult" Japanese cartoon, *Grendizer* (known in France as *Goldorak* and in Italy as *Goldrake*).

[186] Recalling the *Odyssey* and the *Aeneid* when Aeolus' winds are let loose.

[187] Cf. the very first and last lines of Dante's *Paradiso*, 1: 1 and 33: 145.

Day Five

The old inhabitant[1] of a foreign land
who plans to go back to his dear country
—after various vicissitudes, sad exile
and many years spent in a hard, toilsome
condition—feels grateful and friendly
towards his helpful shelter and his kind
landlord before he definitively leaves.
Similarly, we who long for our return
to heaven at any time, sooner or later,
from this lesser and opaque[2] cloister   10
of the earth and of the sea surrounding it
—from which, for many years, we have
gotten our food and such a lovely home—
owe the last duties, and words and gifts
of piety and love; we owe the marks
of a memory neither dark nor mortal
to our ancient wet nurse, so pitiful
and dear, who received us babies
in her lap and sustains us now old;
to this sea, which carries and feeds us;   20
to this serene air letting us breathe.
Therefore we will tell how God's hand,
after embellishing each element with
different inhabitants, numerous and happy,
fulfilled all His work on the fifth day,
so that He left no place or climate
solitary and doleful in its vastness,
or wide and lost in unending horror.
     The expert hand of the eternal Master had
painted the sky with fine star-flowers   30
and, as its shining and beautiful eyes,
had created in it the moon and sun,

---

[1] Another autobiographical reference, but Tasso was often less "grateful" than in this simile.
[2] Cf. "this opacous Earth" in Milton, *Paradise Lost* 8: 23. The earth will be described as *quest'atomo opaco del Male* (this opaque atom of Evil) by Giovanni Pascoli in his 1897 poem *X Agosto* (August 10, the day in which his father had been killed in 1867), perhaps mixing *Paradise Lost* 8: 18 and 23.

when He said, "Let now the water issue,
and let the air simultaneously bear
all living beasts who fly and wiggle!"[3]
At His command, with a sudden dart,[4]
all rivers and lakes became fertile,
and the sea produced its wandering shoals
and scaly schools of swimming beings.[5]
The waters full of murky and swampy   40
mire, which, without running or even
moving, stagnate in their own lazy beds,
received both embellishment and honor,
and did not remain slothful and empty
when God created the world afresh;[6]
truly, immediately in being born did
swampy frogs croak in their wet element,
and all those beasts were born together,
so quick and ready the waters proved
to obey the command from On High.   50
All of them—of which we could hardly
list the many different species by words—[7]
just born, in their active, self-moved
existence, competed in expressing
the sublime power of their Creator,
that no human tongue may describe.
Just then the *animal* was first created and
born, endowed with *anima*[8] and sense,
for the plants and the leafy branches of trees
that unfold their foliage towards the sky[9]   60
do have a life through which the green
trunk feeds and grows upon humid roots,
but are not animals: they were not gifted

---

[3] The old Italian verb "repe"—cf. *rettile*, reptile—would literally mean "to snake" though here Tasso refers to fish; it comes directly from the Latin wording used by the *Vulgate* in *Genesis* 1: 20.

[4] "Repente," i.e. suddenly, a clear pun with "repe" in the previous line. The adjective *repentino* (sudden) still exists in Italian. And "to dart" can be said of fish in English.

[5] Cf. Milton, *Paradise Lost* 7: 399-416.

[6] "Di n[u]ovo" means "again" in current Italian. Here it may suggest that, with the creation of animals, the Earth took on a completely different appearance; or, more radically, *di novo* might mean "out of nothing."

[7] Cf. Milton, *Paradise Lost* 7: 492, but in reference to insects.

[8] Soul, here in the Aristotelian sense of the principle of sensory perception; "and sense" is a hendiadys.

[9] Literally, with Tassean intricacy: ". . . and the leafy branches / of the trees that . . ."

by the eternal Father with sense and soul,
whereby we perceive many various objects.
Yet, some[10] do not deny, do not deprive
the wild barks and the rough trunks of some
bowing, of folding themselves, and
of reaching their branches where it fits,
that is almost a motion of leafy arms   70
in a secret longing for hidden love.
In plants, some ancient writer recognized
a "dull sense," or so it seemed to him;
but let this wandering[11] opinion rest
in that silence that plants love so much.
    Be this as it may, on the fifth day God made
animals, whose senses are not lazy, bound,
or hardened by any rough and slow stupor.
Any animal, either snaking or darting,
either on the sea surface or in the depths,   80
was made ready to obey the sound
of the divine and unchangeable Voice.
In those few, brief words none of them was
excluded from the high, eternal command:
not those—dolphins and seals[12]—which litter
by giving birth to new living animals;
nor that little fish[13] by which the fisherman's
hand (the string winding it) is often
shocked and numbed by a secret power;
not those that lay eggs or hide under   90
soft scales or maybe a harder skin;
not those having fins[14] or not having them,
but all of them were meant by those words

---

[10] A recurring view, from Platonism to the Renaissance, even today. Tasso himself was not far from this hypothesis: see below in his descriptions of Eden, as well as the "living trees"—hosting demons or nymphs—in both *Gerusalemme Liberata* and *Conquistata*.

[11] The ancient writer was Pythagoras (BB). Here *errante* should not have its stronger meaning of "wrong." Tasso's caution, seasoned with a pinch of humor, responds to Counter-Reformation attacks against magical and Pagan worldviews. Later (7: 829 ff.), while mentioning the "sentient trees" of Eden, he will ascribe that opinion to Jewish Rabbis.

[12] Mammals, according to modern taxonomy, but then listed among "fish," i.e. water animals in general. With much facetious humor, Melville maintains that whales are fish; at one point quoting an authority (an illiterate sailor) who states all scientific evidence and opinions to the contrary are *humbug* (*Moby-Dick*, ch. 32).

[13] The torpedo, though it is not so little.

[14] "Penne" literally means feathers, but the Italian words *penna* (feather) and *pinna* (fin) are etymologically related. See also verse 181.

and, say, enclosed under a certain law[15]—all
darting, beautiful inhabitants of the coasts;
as well as those that the sea hosts in its depths,
and those that are affixed to the hard rocks,
and those shifting together in great shoals,
and even those dispersed, swimming at will;
and the huge whales and the orcas, 100
as well as the smallest and tiniest fish.
Among them, some[16] support the weight
of their soft, wet[17] bodies on legs; because
of an ambiguous and uncertain nature,
they look for twofold food by land
and water, not wholly satisfied with
one nourishment, one food to eat.
To these do the croaking frogs belong,
the many-legged crabs, then add
the crocodile, the swimming horse[18] 110
who crosses the vast fields of the Nile,
and those[19] undulating along dry banks.
So, the small, big, uncertain and certain ones,
by the decree of one Power, received
different essences and ways of life,
when God said, "Let the waters issue."

Through his prodigious voice, He showed
how much the wandering, wet nature of
the unsteady liquid element fits the fish.
In fact, what the air is to the light birds 120
or to the animals breathing on earth,
such is the water to the sea swimmers
and any beasts writhing in rivers or lakes.
And the reason is clear to our senses,[20]
since the lung[21] has its natural place

---

[15] "Enclosed under the law" is a phrase of Pauline origin, here boldly decontextualized.

[16] The Amphibians, plus a lot of miscellaneous *phyla*, see below.

[17] "Molle" implies both soft and wet. The text literally says "the soft weight of [their] bodies." This introductory description is inconsistent with verses 109 ff.

[18] The hippopotamus, whose name means "river horse" in Greek. Among the marvels of creation that God revealed to Job, there were the *Leviathan* and the *Behemoth*, which modern scholars often identify with the Egyptian crocodile and the hippopotamus. Milton may have had these Tassean verses in mind, see *Paradise Lost* 7: 473-474, but listing three big creatures, not two, see *ibid.*, verses 412, 471, 474.

[19] Snakes, probably.

[20] As explained in verses 137 ff.

on the left among our internal organs,
spongy, thin, and transparent, like a mirror
or anything that receives images
and reflects them; it shrinks and expands
almost like bellows,[22] and the air and the breeze,   130
breathing in and out, it inhales and exhales,
and the ventilating refreshes the heart,
the warm spring[23] of our purple blood
—and by the same "spirit"[24] by which it cools
the internal heat, our audible voice is
formed and shaped into different words.[25]
But to those darting shoals, Nature gave
the curved gills in place of lungs,
and by opening and shutting them,
a fish gets the water in and out,   140
and thanks to them performing such service
which is like breathing water and wave.
    The mute fish, however, sends no sounds,
nor will it ever become a tractable pet,[26]
nor will it love to be moved and caressed
by a human hand that coaxes with touch.
And yet, from some, it has been handed down[27]
that their own nature and features include,
beyond the common rule, an audible "spirit";
some other species have a true voice,   150
and some, quasi-words, in which a badly-
speaking tongue expresses inner feelings.
But sounds need more than the internal air

---

[21] These anatomical images came to Tasso from Plato, possibly via Pico Della Mirandola (BB). With Tasso, scientific data take on poetical dignity; the only great example before being in Dante, *Purgatorio*, Canto 25. Also, compare Tasso's accurate technical descriptions of war devices in the Jerusalem-poems.

[22] As it is often the case, Tasso uses a couple of synonyms: *mantice* and *folle*. Again below: *rezzo* and *aura*, both meaning "air" in old Italian. This linguistic habit here strengthens the impression of the double lung movement during respiration.

[23] To be taken literally, as the heart was conceived as the organ that produced the blood. Cf. Dante, *Purgatorio* 25: 40.

[24] In its original sense: air.

[25] This is a modern concept, i.e. the "evolutionary economy" taking advantage of one organ to develop more than one utility.

[26] Language is rightly associated with any kind of true relationship. Tasso will later stress the intelligence of horses and dogs. C. S. Lewis will develop the idea by showing a new Eve who makes animals evolve through education (*Perelandra*) and by creating Talking Animals (*Narnia*).

[27] Many notions in this section come from Aristotle (BB).

forming them, and the spongy, thin lung,
and the empty and wet cane which is called
fistula;[28] but in fact, the voice is only shaped
and articulated afterward in the throat.
Words also need the tongue and teeth,
so that any being lacking a tongue does not
speak, does not shape its own sounds; 160
while the sound breaks in other organs,
as in the girdle[29] that crosses and tightens
wasps and bees, the internal spirit knocks
and breaks; so, you will hear a hoarse
murmuring that roams about in the air.[30]
Others, by breaking their internal spirits
against the girdle that tightens their bodies,
sing, flapping their wings, and the green
woods resound with the sonorous sounds
of cicadas in the long summer days. 170
But in sea, or river or lake, among fish
—both the soft and the shell-covered types—
none will emit any sound or voice;
some, yes, variously grunt or squeak,
so that the waves often resound with
such squeaking; concerts like these gave
the name to the sea fish called "lyre."[31]
  The "comb"[32] squeaks too, and so does
the sea swallow, as if vying; and both[33]
fly as they squeak, and soar high 180
on long, wide fins, without touching the sea.
In the Achelous River a boar-like fish[34]
not only squeaks but (if one believes) calls,
and the swimming cuckoo[35] has a voice too,
so that it nearly recalls the flying cuckoo.
But this is not a true voice; just voice-like
is the internal spirit, rubbing and breaking

---

[28] Cane, reed, therefore also flute, in Latin; *fistola* in Tasso's Italian. The trachea is called *canna* (cane) by Dante, e.g., in *Inferno* 6: 27 and 28: 68.

[29] Diaphragm.

[30] Another half-parodistic usage of powerful Dantean imagery, *Inferno* 3: 25, 28.

[31] The *Trigla lyra*; from Aristotle (BB).

[32] Or *Pecten*, a name that has the same meaning.

[33] But only the sea swallow does so. The scientific references seem a bit blurred here.

[34] In Greece. BB explains that Aristotle calls it "pig" but suggests no identification.

[35] Maybe a kind of mullet (BB).

against spiky gills, and resounding.
While almost words and a language has
the garrulous frog, in water and mire,   190
the dirty inhabitant of swamps. This
happens because it has lung and tongue
perfectly shaped in all of their parts:
the former is after the manner of fish,
the latter, which emits the hoarse sound,
to the gullet is attached and firmly joined.
Frogs have been heard ululating
underwater; so have other lusty fish;
that howling is a love invitation by which
the excited male entices and calls   200
his female consort to the sweet wedding.[36]
The swift dolphin has both sound and voice
because of not lacking either lung or blood;
but has no tongue to shape and articulate
those sounds we hear murmuring in the sea.
Wet fish can be heard snorting in sleep
and are often seen while they are resting,
even those covered and hidden by hard armor,
although they do not have wet eyelids,
which, lowered in a pleasant slumber,   210
cover the eyes of the tired swimmers.
From this quiet, silent rest of theirs,
in which only their shifting tails move,
an expert fisherman guesses they sleep,
nor does he stab them with his trident,
but he carefully catches them in his hand.
He also often preys upon those sticking
to the rocks, or wrapped in the sand,
or secretly sleeping under a stone, along
a curved shore, or deep underwater.   220
This is how, with a pointed iron tool,
a gilthead bream, or a "wolf"[37] is caught:
it hardly wakes up, still deeply immersed
in its drowsiness, and the end of its rest
is linked with the beginning of death;

---

[36] An interesting insight into ethology. Renaissance writers very often based their natural descriptions not on direct observations but on literary sources, precisely like Medieval authors, but meanwhile they had retrieved better sources.
[37] *Perca lambrax*, a perch (BB).

it indeed passes from the brief sleep into
the never-ending one, almost unaware.[38]
Whereas the swift dolphin and the huge
whale, as they sleep among the waves,
raise their fistulas through the surface,   230
their organs of breath, and empty them;
meanwhile, they just softly agitate
their fins. In the darkness of night, more
than in any other time, sleep pervades
the fish; and also at noon in summer,
when Proteus pastures his fabled
herd in the wide caverns undersea
(as they believed), the *pistrices*[39] and Orcs,[40]
whose lazy beds are made of muddy algae,
snort all day long; next to them,   240
the diviner-shepherd sleeps, after having
counted his scaly flock three times, or four.

    But ancient fairy tales better belong
somewhere else. So, I will leave out[41]
Proteus—and Arion[42] too, who, carried ashore
by a swift dolphin, escaped death in the end.
And I will leave out the disbelieved love
of the devout dolphin and the dead boy,[43]
because of which the sea lover suffered
so much that, broken by his mad suffering,   250
he also died, mourning, on the dry sand.
But if the old fame of such a fact deserves
no confidence, not unworthy of our faith
is that other ancient story, when we read
that Nature instills piety by acting

---

[38] The contemplation of Nature, in Tasso, is not a weekend hobby.

[39] In Latin, *pistris*, *pistrix*, or *pristis* was a sea monster, here in the plural; Tasso uses the uninflected form *pistri.*

[40] In Italian, *orca* means both the mythological Orc and the killer whale (*Orcinus orca*). Here the first is meant; though, of course, there is a linguistic and psychological connection between the two. Proteus' Orc was the protagonist of the most famous episode in Ludovico Ariosto's *Orlando Furioso*, involving eroticism, fantasy and adventure. Here the atmosphere is completely different, midway between myth and demythologization, refined, even elegiac. Tasso loved Arcadian poetry and sea landscapes; now he succeeds in mixing both, again with a bit of humor.

[41] A rhetorical device letting the poet deal with an additional theme by first denying its mention; called *apophasis*; common in Homer.

[42] A citharist, i.e. bard, in Greek mythology.

[43] An ancient Greek myth that Tasso could have read in Renaissance sources (BB).

as the teacher and[44] mother of fish.
She in fact gave dolphins full mammae
to feed their beloved offspring; they can
even gather the calves into their round
wombs,[45] so that the newborn infant   260
can re-enter where he had come out from,
when the roaring sea turns too stormy.
Growing up among tempests and clouds,
he learns how to swim across the sea
without fearing foamy waves and twisters,
taught by his father. And together they prove
trustworthy guides to our bold sailors,[46]
so that the good, wise helmsman can foresee
the frightful war of the opposing winds,
and lead the tossed ship into port.   270

    But who—what white-haired, tired fisherman
growing old by the Thyrrhenian Sea, or
the Adriatic, the resonant Aegean,
or along the Caspian or the Black Sea,
or by the Red Sea, or where the Great
Father Ocean washes Germany and France,
Scotland, Britain,[47] Ethiopia and India—
who, I say, after spending his whole life
on the infertile[48] and solitary sands
and around the hard and cavernous crags,   280
casting in the sea now the hook, now the net,
could ever tell about the many species
of the wet swimmers, by which their
natures and old progeny are distinguished?
And about a thousand different modes
and ways of life, habits, and all-varied
works, and their different anatomies?
For some fish are known by the Egyptian Sea
and the Eritrean,[49] whose waves are blood-red,

---

[44] The "a" (to) in BB must be edited into "e" (and).

[45] This legend comes from Aristotle, then repeated by St. Basil and St. Ambrose (BB).

[46] In ancient times a widespread legend about dolphins.

[47] "Britain that would afterward be called England." Ludovico Ariosto, *Orlando Furioso* 2: 26, verse 4.

[48] That is, non-cultivable; also reflecting the beliefs of the ancient Greeks. Tasso who, following *Genesis*, has described the sea as the very origin of life, transfers the adjective *infeconde* to the sea coasts.

[49] The Red Sea, on the basis of the etymological meaning of *erythraios* (red, in Greek).

some by the Caspian, Assyrian, Persian Seas,   290
some there,[50] where Atlas washes his feet,
and where Indus and Hydaspes foam white:
species either wholly foreign to our sea[51]
or, for the great part, rare and unknown.
How many more are begotten and fed
by the Ocean below the Bears, or below
the sky devoid of the Plow and Bears![52]
They'd look like wondrous monsters[53] to us;
but in the beginning all equally
were brought to life by the divine Voice   300
differentiating them in so many ways.
Thus, some species in generating lay
eggs, but do not warm and brood over them
as birds do, nor do they build a nest
or nurture their offspring with much toil,
but the waters receive the falling mass
and make a living, swimming, wriggling beast;
some[54] bear already fully-shaped animals.
Unlike the mule on earth, unlike many
lusty birds of the air which mix   310
their offspring, the unmixed phyla of fish
will last long, and ever-fecund,[55] thanks
to legitimate weddings, since Nature has
certain laws and inbreeds similar types
(yes, Nature mixes the Moray with the fierce
male Snake,[56] but he lays down his poison
so that she does not flee; otherwise she would).

   No species of fish presents a mouth
partially equipped with sharp teeth
and the other side harmless, bare,   320
as with the sheep and oxen among us.
And no fish, so far as it is reported,
ruminates when it is satiated with food,
except the scarus; in fact,[57] all of them

---

[50] In the Atlantic Ocean, off the coast of NW Africa.
[51] The Mediterranean.
[52] The Southern hemisphere.
[53] Coupling the original meaning of the Latin word *monstrum*, i.e. something amazing, with its current sense.
[54] Let's remember that Tasso's concept of "fish" included sea mammals.
[55] While hybrids are generally not so.
[56] A legend coming from the Latin philosopher and essayist Aelianus (BB).

have white teeth like those of a saw,
set tight in two rows, and their food varies
accordingly.[58] Some get nourishment from mud,
some others from fungi and weeds,
others from plants of the sea and swamps, or
from those which make the riverbeds green.   330
Some hurriedly run towards the crumbs[59] that
human hands have thrown into the water,
showing therefore they like human food;
some swallow a smaller fish and the hook.
But a major part of the greedy fish
devour and destroy one another, the
smaller ones as the meal for the bigger.[60]
And it often happens, likewise, that
no sooner has a fish greedily eaten
a smaller one, then it will in vain flee away   340
from a bigger one now in pursuit;
it will finally be caught by the predator
and two fishes[61] will then fill one stomach.

    This occurs even more often with Man,
when a potentate chancing[62] to exert
hard, unjust power over the humble plebs,
greedily feeds on the "smaller's" blood,[63]
of whoever is his subject and servant.
Is there any difference[64] between a fierce
heart, which the greed for wealth and gold   350
always spurs and makes insatiable,
and a huge sea monster chasing thousands
of weaker fish so as to fill with them

---

[57] "A prova" usually refers to vying, but on some occasions it rather means "as a demonstration."

[58] Once again a modern concept.

[59] Here *esca* must be interpreted in its original meaning of something to eat (from the Latin verb *edo*, cf. also *esurio*, "I am hungry"), not technically as the bait, as in line 334.

[60] A very old saying. Tasso found it in St. Basil (BB). The anthropological parallel becomes obvious in the following lines.

[61] The smaller one, and the still smaller one it had eaten in its turn.

[62] "A cui fu dato in sorte," where *sorte* has several nuances: to have the fortune to..., one's lot being..., to be given the power... The translation hints at the basic Renaissance concept of chance, in all senses of the word.

[63] Echoing Dante, *Paradiso* 27: 59, in that case in reference to the decadence of the Papacy. The metaphor likens the powers attributed to vampires (cf. *Dante Was a Fantasy Writer, op. cit.*, pp. 17-18).

[64] Faintly echoing Dante, *Inferno* 19: 113, also against greed.

its deep, all-devouring stomach?[65]
Such a man, growing unjust, ungodly,
seizes the property of a poor neighbor—[66]
and *you*[67] enjoy the goods of him, who has been
forcefully taken away, and those old thefts
you gnaw and destroy with tyrannical teeth,
adding to your wealth, as a due fruit,   360
what he had been usurping for many years,
so that you prove greedier than a greedy
man, and more unjust than the unjust.
Mind that the same end does not await you
which the unwise fish incurs, getting
itself caught, while pursuing others,
by a sharpened hook, or creel, or net.
O proud man, you won't escape, you
won't, after so many committed crimes,
the final penalty, long-looming   370
like a hanging and threatening rock.

    Now pay attention to the snares and the
cunning frauds of a tiny, low animal,
and shun such base examples of fraud.
The crab craves for the sweet, exquisite
flesh of the noble oyster of the sea,
a difficult, precious, and dear prey;
but Nature made a hard wall of defense
surrounding that soft food all around,
two valves[68] which slide together and clench   380
so strongly and firmly that the lumpy[69]
appendages cannot break through.
What will the crab do?[70] In a calm sea,
in the clear light of a serene sky,
the oyster enjoys the sweet sunbeams
and beautiful landscape—she opens up;

---

[65] The Latinizing word *vorago* employed here (*voragine* in current Italian) conceptually means a chasm, a gulf, but has the same root as "to devour." Cf. Dante, *Inferno* 6: 27.

[66] Cf. King Ahab and Naboth's vineyard in *I Kings*, ch. 21.

[67] Tasso now addresses the second-level evil-doers, who rob the robbers. Classics are ever-modern.

[68] The word *testa* appears here, literally "head," but *testo* could—and still can, somewhere—mean "pot."

[69] Translation of the adjective *orride* according to its original Latin meaning. Translated intuitively, "rough" seems a usable alternative.

[70] The story makes one think of a sexual assault, as *granchio* is a masculine word, *conca* (= *conchiglia*) feminine.

he, laying hidden, stealthily throws
a stone inside her valves, preventing her
from closing them and covering herself.
In this manner a cunning mind   390
can fill the gap of debilitated strength.
Ha! The evil[71] teachings and mute frauds
of wickedness, of unjust and shrewd men,
but also of a rough, non-eloquent[72] tongue.
If you aim to learn industry and art
for profit, do not harm your neighbors,
do not commit outrages on your brethren!
Shun the low examples of the reprobates
and, happy and satisfied with meager things,
humbly put self-sufficient poverty before   400
annoying pleasures and servile honors,[73]
put it before glory and magnificence;
triumph and reign in and over yourself,
a greater kingdom than Scythia and India.

   Nor will I leave out the octopus' thefts
and cunning frauds: if it ever clings
to a sea rock of whatever kind, it
suddenly paints and dresses itself with
the colors of the rock, and looks like it.
So, if a swimming fish passing by,   410
misled by appearances, comes close,
it thinks it a hard underwater rock,
and becomes an easy prey and food.
Such habits are well known by the flatterers
in the palaces of august emperors
and noble kings; in this manner they
all too readily bow to honor the glory
of Fortune, and often change themselves
through a thousand different colors and shapes
according to customs, or times,   420
or the Lord's will and his pleasure, by
varying attitudes, faces and gestures,
words and manners. With modest people

---

[71] "Oh di malizia . . ." sounds like "odi malizia . . . !" in Dante, *Inferno* 22: 107, describing a case of fraud.

[72] "Infeconda," infertile, but here possibly in the sense of *non-faconda*, that is, the tongue of an animal. Alternatively, *infeconda* means non-creative.

[73] Lofty words, but, especially in his last years (when he was working on this poem) Tasso often petitioned his friends and protectors for money and other purposes.

they are modest, overtly sighing[74] with
the suffering, joyful with the joyful,
arrogant next to arrogant. They follow
the others' ideas and tastes as a law,
so that it is no way easy to skip any
treacherous and dangerous meeting
with them, so as to avoid the harms   430
that impiety often causes by hiding
under the opposite mask of piety.[75]
Greedy wolves with such habits often
put on the white fleece of the meek
lambs, appearing therefore to others
as simpletons.[76] Shun, O my friend, shun
such a two-faced and perverse habit!
Follow Truth. Love and prefer
the sincere candor[77] of an innocent
soul, and faith unbroken and pure.   440
    Variable[78] is the serpent-snake,[79] therefore
an ancient, just sentence condemned it
to lay and drag its body on the ground.
Sincere are the just, not lying or feigning,
like Jacob; therefore they are welcomed
by the Most High to His eternal seat.
This ever-varying, equivocal place
in which we spend our lives, this vast sea
is big and wide,[80] and snakes and dragons
and fierce monsters roam it endlessly;   450
small animals are mixed and mingled
with the big ones—but, all together,
the swimming population is curbed by

---

[74] "Sospirosi in atto," with Dantean reminiscences, cf. *Purgatorio* 10: 78 and 33: 4.

[75] Tasso (see Pittorru, *op. cit., passim*) had a hard time trying to adapt to court rules.

[76] "Semplicetti," a Dantean word from *Purgatorio* 16: 88.

[77] Etymologically meaning whiteness, here in reference to the lamb. In Italian, the word *candore* conveys innocence, even naiveté, rather than frankness.

[78] "Vario," a very simple adjective with many shades: varying, varied, [skin-]changing, deceitful (that's how BB interprets it), and, more distantly, maze-like, snaking (cf. the puzzling *vago vago* in Dante, *Purgatorio* 32: 135).

[79] To make the Biblical citation more solemn and/or to stress the theme of duplicity, Tasso doubles the subject by pairing two synonyms (often, a modern term and a Latinizing one): "'l serpente e l'angue." Milton, and the Church Fathers, see a special link between the Serpent and sin because of the former's shape and behavior, though *Genesis* does not mention this; see PL 4: 347-350, 7: 495, 9: 161 ff., 10: 164-170, 867-871.

[80] The frightful side of Dante's "great sea of Being" (*Paradiso* 1: 113).

a wise Ruler, a just Law; so here you
may find some rare examples to follow.
Just do not blame Him if you see in them
the faults and flaws of an imperfect nature.[81]
You should recall and admire, first,
how places are parceled out among
the fish as their own dwellings   460
and kingdoms,[82] so that they do not pass,
but seldom, from one place to another,
usurping the others' fields, beds, food;
and all, closed within their boundaries,
only move across their proper lots.
No geometer[83] divided those vast spaces
among them, nor, with any kind of walls,
surrounded their wet, cold territories,
nor limited them; so, on every side,
what they need is fully available,   470
like a destined portion to each.
This basin hosts and feeds these fish,
that feeds the others. No river, no mount
with serrated rocks and long ridges
divides them or blocks their roads;
but a certain law of Nature shares
with all, in an equal and just measure,
the places and dwellings as most fitting
to each, where they may gather and feed,
and have enough food for the day.[84]   480
  Not such are we, the infected offspring
of our father Adam; proud against God:
we do shift the limits that were fixed
by our ancestors, and keep amassing
wealth by occupying others' lands,
adding house to house, field to field,
city to city, kingdom to kingdom,
stealing them by force from our neighbors.
  Whales and killer whales knew at first
the place that Nature had prescribed for them,   490

---

[81] Cf. Dante, *Paradiso* 13: 76-78; compare also the sea metaphor in verses 121-123. King
Solomon in person speaks.
[82] Once again, Tasso's modern interest not only in "Nature" but ecology, ecosystems.
[83] In the etymological sense of "Earth-measurer." Of course in English this person is called
a *surveyor*.
[84] Cf. the Lord's Prayer.

and the prepared meals; and the deep sea
without islands, beyond inhabited
countries they dwelt, where no firm land
is left in all directions, where no coast
or mountain can be seen anywhere,
where no vast fields can be plowed
on the un-navigable sea, where no bold
sailor ever came seeking new peoples,
new kingdoms, and new glory;[85]
where no old story or ancient fame,   500
no boldness, no noble human thought
leads the ship of crazy imagination.[86]
But that same unknown, immense sea was
occupied by whales as huge as mountains
(as the experienced helmsmen tell),
and no island or city is ever damaged
by them; they never demonstrate their own
hostile, harmful, obnoxious strength.
Each animal of such behavior and kind,
as in a friendly town or land,   510
a homeland indeed, obeying old laws,
lives in that sea district in which
God's will and its own nature placed it.

   But there are fish going on pilgrimage,
and voluntarily in exile from home, they
are bound to unknown, foreign zones.
They leave together, united in a swarm
—in the manner of warriors who leave
their tents and their former encampment
at a given sign, following the trumpet's   520
blare—when the destined time approaches,
awakened by the old, powerful law
of Nature, swiftly and hastily
they turn their course northward.
One may see them, like a torrent,
together, run from *Propontis*[87] to the
Black Sea. Who guides and rules them?
Which king's command? What edict,
promulgated with the herald's trumpet,

---

[85] Another allusion to the *Conquistadores*.
[86] See Dante's Ulysses in *Inferno* 26, especially lines 97-98, 118-120, 125.
[87] The Sea of Marmara. *Propontis* means "before Pontus," the Black Sea.

shows them it is already the right season?   530
Who leads the pilgrims? Can you not see
the Eternal Order,[88] penetrating
the tiniest parts, fulfilling the Whole?

The divine law is not opposed by the
obedient fish, but he who opposes it
is Man, reluctant, and rebelling in vain.
Mute as it may be, do not despise
the reasonless beast, for a greater fool
are you, resisting the high command
of the heavenly King. So listen to   540
the words and speech of the silent fish!
Yes, movements and acts almost speak,
inviting and waking us up to wander[89]
and leave these turbid, bitter waters,
looking for sweeter[90] waters elsewhere,
in the Northern zones[91] where the sun heats
less with its rays, and more weakly attracts
the water's lightest parts upwards.[92]
No greedy desire for goods and gold
leads them to cross seas and rivers,   550
as men do,[93] but only the love and zeal
for their unmixed,[94] legitimate offspring.

But let us wonder why the haughty Giants[95]
are no longer produced by Nature, or born
from the pregnant Earth[96] in a horrible birth,

---

[88] *Sanatana-dharma* in Sanskrit. The Renaissance was at the crossroads of ancient cosmic order and modern crisis. See the very beginning of Dante's *Paradiso* (1: 1-3), with the same verb, *penetra*. Cf. also *Wisdom* 7: 21 ff. (one of the so-called "apocryphal" books of the Old Testament, traditionally included in Catholic Bibles).

[89] "Peregrinar," to wander abroad and, more specifically, to go on pilgrimage.

[90] In Italian, fresh water is called *acqua dolce*, "sweet water." In fact, the most famous migratory species of fish—eel, salmon—travel from seas to rivers, so ethological details fit in well with the moral metaphor.

[91] Literally "kingdoms."

[92] A circumlocution for evaporation. Metaphorically, it should mean that the soul reaches a less "hot," less "exhausting" place; but this would imply that the sun plays a negative role, contrary to many passages in the poem.

[93] But on other occasions, as we have seen, Tasso exalts the explorers.

[94] Without infertile hybridizations; but especially as a moral teaching—quite odd from someone like Tasso who never married; not even, as was often the case in Renaissance Courts, for the sake of appearances.

[95] He will answer no sooner than in 6: 1384 ff.

[96] "Pregna" in the English sense of the word (*incinta*, in current Italian), cf. Dante, *Paradiso* 13: 84.

while she does not regret having elephants
and whales.[97] If these also are creatures
and works of the eternal divine hand,
they are good, as made good by Him,
who made them as big as mountains   560
and islands;[98] He thus aimed at humbling
our pride, and frightening us to death
by their monstrous, fierce appearance
and their hideous, measureless mass.[99]
When God, in fact, first created so many
animals, and so different and varied
in works, in motions, and in appearance,
He made some useful to us on earth
for our necessities, and obedient to
our calm or, at times, harsh command.   570
For His own greatness and glory also
He made other beasts, in them showing
His wonder-accomplishing divine art
and divine power, which, near and far,
more or less clearly shines upon us.[100]
The foolish minds of the ingenious Greeks
turned the marvels of the eternal
Lord into games, trying to imitate them
with their many embellished lies,
when describing, beyond the marks of the   580
invincible Heracles, the fabled kingdoms
of a happy people, the once famous
Islands of the Blessed,[101] and the long course
of one bold ship;[102] moreover describing
the measureless, wide-bellied fish
which holds within itself whole peoples,
so that its deep and gloomy stomach
works as a perilous battlefield for
the cruel weapons of adverse forces.

---

[97] A paraphrase of Dante, *Inferno* 31: 49-53.
[98] Cf. Milton, *PL* 1: 201-208.
[99] Against naive creationism, Tasso does not think that "all creatures have been made for Man." His cosmos, indeed his Earth, is theocentric, with some hints at biocentrism. Cf. *Job* 41: 1-4, 25-26 and 42: 1-3.
[100] Again echoing Dante, *Paradiso* 1: 2.
[101] Also "Fortunate Islands" depending on the source.
[102] Odysseus', according to non-Homeric traditions (BB), also followed by Dante.

But ships being wrecked by fish,   590
indeed the fierce attack waged by one
fish against a thousand superb warships
was no fairy tale, no joke or game.[103]
No fairy tale is Jonah, thrown into the sea
and swallowed by a voracious monster.
But the High Lord's supreme power
can be discovered in the small things,
not only the greater ones. Lo! with sails
unfurled, a well-equipped ship crosses
the resounding sea, pushed by the wind.   600
Suddenly, a most tiny fish
slows down and stops its fast run,
as if it had put down roots in the sea
depths, and so from "delay" the fish
was given its name.[104] Very fearful are
not only whales and killer whales,
or the sea saw with pointed teeth,[105]
or the dogfish, or the sword-like one;
there also is a sea fish[106] that, once
killed, remains frightful: it stings   610
so as to cause quick, inevitable death.
The small sea hare[107] suddenly kills, too;
but if you compare the cons with
the pros, usefulness abounds more,
and the examples of fish do help us.
    But if you well evaluate yourself,
Man, you are fish,[108] and life is the sea,
and like a net[109] being cast into the depths,
there collecting many kinds of fish,

---

[103] It happened to Alexander the Great's fleet, according to Pliny the Elder (BB). Cf. *Moby-Dick*. The very dangerous art of whaling was known in the Renaissance; see the Paladin Roland killing the "orc" in Ariosto, *Orlando Furioso*, Canto 11, and the "monsters" pictured in sixteenth-century sea maps. The philosopher Tommaso Campanella (1568-1639) in *The Island of the Sun* would list whaling among the proofs of man's incredible skills.

[104] From the Latin root of the name "remora." This is a deeply-rooted legend.

[105] The saw-fish. With a rare example of Greek Accusative: ". . . la sega marina acuta i denti."

[106] Stingrays.

[107] BB mentions the gastropod *Aplysia leporina*, but the reference is perhaps less precise.

[108] The metaphor turns into a sort of brief treatise on theological anthropology. Curiously enough, the statement that "Man is fish" would also make sense from the viewpoint of the theory of evolution.

[109] From *Matthew* 13: 47-50.

so is the great heavenly Kingdom,   620
which gathers and grips us in its strings,
then receives the chosen ones in vases
and selects and throws the others away.
And behold, when the world is burned up,[110]
the angels will come out, the holy ministers
of divine judgment, and the sinners will be
divided from the just; those damned to fire,
these destined to their glory in heaven.[111]
There are, therefore, good and bad fish.
The good are not entangled in the net   630
but lifted, and no hook kills them; they
are washed with the innocent, pure Blood
from a precious wound.[112] Man: you are fish,
you are that fish whose open mouth
showed the "stater" hidden within,[113]
and free will, that you own in yourself,
is your—leaning or even—scales.
Man: you are fish, Peter the fisherman,
or he who has Peter's role and place;[114]
this sea, the Gospel, the very foundation   640
of the Church, God's sacred dwelling.
O good fish, do not fear nets and hooks, for
She[115] does not kill anyone, but consecrates!
You are a fish, but now rise high[116] over
the turbid waves, so that no stormy billows
submerge you; if the open sea is stormy,
swim boldly, or take shelter at bottom;
if it is calm, play among the waves;
and if there is a noisy tempest or twister,
mind that the thick, violent clouds do not   650
knock you against the rocks ashore.

---

[110] The Gospel parable is "contaminated" with *II Peter* 3: 10.

[111] Here *Matthew* 25—especially verses 34, 41, 46—takes over.

[112] A typical Baroque devotion. *Sanguine tuo pretiosissimo*, ". . . by Your most precious blood," in a hymn. In this same vein, immediately after composing *Il Mondo Creato*, Tasso would write a poem on Jesus' tears (*Le lacrime di Gesù Cristo*).

[113] A coin, from *Matthew* 17: 27. Tasso found this allegory in St. Ambrose (BB), the Greek word *stater* meaning "balance, scales."

[114] See *Matthew* 16: 18.

[115] The Church; *Chiesa* is feminine.

[116] Like a sea swallow, see above.

But now rise, rise out of the depths
—may our speech emerge from the waves!
Let us look upwards, up towards the sky,
we will see the shore wonderfully adorned:[117]
the salt, drawn by the waves, nearly hardens
into white marble,[118] and like deep-red stone
the beautiful coral glows in the air,
which formerly was soft grass underwater;
and among the shells, the hard pearl   660
shines white; and on the sandy wastes
flames the gold, and like most precious gems
some stones are painted in many colors.
Underwater the "golden fleece"[119] grows too;
and waves have their flowers, strewn and carried
to the shore; here the glossy purple shell
also shines. Yes, what adorns unconquered
chiefs with a joyful triumphal glory,
what is revered in the powerful kings
or, now, honored in our purple Fathers,[120]   670
is a beauty, a treasure, a dear commodity
from the sea—its courteous gift, indeed.
It adds a thousand beauties and feasts,
and a refined,[121] superb, maritime splendor.
A gentle wind blows; a placid breeze, sweetly
murmuring, whispers and wanders about,
and ripples the waves, which look like
foamy silver among the rocks or by the
curved coasts; often with the color of shiny
sapphires the sea is tinged, and like   680
pyrope[122] under the sun's gentle rays.
Scattered sails fan out far away,
shining white in hundreds, in thousands,
faster than running horses and chariots;
painted ships unfold their old, famous

---

[117] Echoing and reversing Dante, *Inferno* 21: 6.

[118] From St. Ambrose, possibly describing the cliffs of Dover (BB).

[119] A mollusk, again after St. Ambrose (BB). But perhaps Tasso wanted to make these lines even more "precious" with a hint at the myth of the Argonauts.

[120] The Cardinals. Tasso is—officially, at least—far from Dante, *Paradiso* 21: 133-134. The Baroque Era was often scandalized by Dante's attacks against the Church authorities, as prophesied in *Paradiso* 17: 127 ff.

[121] "Vaghe," once again this basically untranslatable adjective.

[122] A fire-red stone, from Greek *pyr*, fire.

ensigns, and with pointed rostra furrow
their flat ways; all around, the wet fish
thrash, and often the swift dolphins
show off their hunched backs in the air.
Happily they echo with the sound of trumpets: 690
the shores, waters, arsenals, harbors
full of ships and other boats made of wood
variously shaped. An old, beautiful ship
paves a wide way for illustrious knights,
curbing the wrath of Neptune and his pride;[123]
and again, the rewards, the winners'
honored palms I see; and I bow before
the glorious Crown[124] standing out on masts.
     As a man who dives into the wavy bosom
of the Adriatic Sea during a feast[125]   700
with honor celebrating an old glory,[126]
and searches the dark, most secret depths
among hard rocks lying underwater
and the most hidden sea mysteries
in order to take back the thrown gem
to the old *Doge* and the red-clad leaders;
I now reascend from the sea depths,
and from those black, gloomy gulfs
the beautiful Truth, who is brighter than
any gem boasted by Arabia or India,   710
the beautiful Truth, who seemed to lie
there underwater, I bring to light;
and I show her to the mortals' eyes
to be admired, with no cloak to darken her
beloved body, no veil to cover her hair.[127]
     Now I will dare… I will try to take off from
the wavy fields to the windy plains of air.

---

[123] In *Gerusalemme Conquistata* a huge sea devil appears, based on Neptune/Poseidon.
[124] Of the King of Spain, then ruling Naples (BB). Neapolitan aristocrats honored and helped Tasso much in his last years; see again Pittorru, *op. cit.*
[125] The "Wedding of the Sea" in Venice, when a ring was thrown by the *Doge*—the City Leader, from Latin *dux* (verse 706)—into the Lagoon, and retrieved (BB).
[126] A victory against pirates, about the year 1000 (BB).
[127] The clearest "manifesto" on the sense of the whole *MC* project. Tasso's source of inspiration, Truth, has no cloak and no veil, unlike Dante's Beatrice (*Purgatorio* 30: 31-32). Possibly with a hint at the water nymphs/fairies of the Arthurian saga and poems of chivalry in general.

Who will give me wings like a dove[128]
so as to let me soar above the clouds
and winds, sweeping among the birds[129]   720
just below the sky? May He who led us
beyond the sky[130] support and carry me
through this stormy, doubtful kingdom
of Fortune—varying and changing in so
many ways, and hosting and feeding
twisters, winds, rain, snow, and flames
which perturb the birds' flights.
   The sky was adorned, the sea filled,
woods, meadows, mountains were green,
when God commanded the sweet[131] birds   730
to wander flying above the earth
in the air, in which wet vapors gather
and condense, then evaporate upwards[132]
from the cold womb of the opaque Earth.
Hence immediately did the feathered beasts
start their flight and song across the air.
Will those[133] who stayed awake among
mute fish now dare yield to sleep among
the voices of so many songbirds, thus
slothfully handing over the praise of   740
the supreme King to the beautiful birds,
or the thanks to Him who feeds us?
Twice as in competition—both before dawn
and when in the evening the sun withdraws
its rays, and the East dims and darkens—
they make a fine concert of gentle notes;
will we choose to have a silent dawn,
leaving the two ends of day unsung,
which opens and closes with ringings,[134]
and precisely this merry din prepares   750
us mortal men for our tiring work?
God forbid! But let us go on recounting

---

[128] From *Psalm* 55: 6 (not 14: 7 and *Song of Songs* 2: 8 as noted in BB).
[129] "Volanti," flying beings, following closely the Latin term *volucres*.
[130] The Risen Christ, cf. *Colossians* 3: 1, or the saving God in general.
[131] "Vaghi."
[132] A common phenomenon, but the Italian wording specifically echoes Dante, *Purgatorio* 5: 109-111.
[133] Readers.
[134] At the sound of bells; cf. Dante, *Paradiso* 10: 139-144.

the good and noble works of Day Five.
  The beautiful birds are like fish,[135] between
the "swimmers" and the "winged fliers"
there is a sort of kinship: to those
Nature destined swimming; to these, flying.
The one and the other cross liquid paths,
either with feathers or by swiftly
moving or almost coiling their tails,   760
which in place of a rudder steers their course.
But they are different as the fish's food
is provided by the ever-shifting waves,
and the birds' by the firm, steady soil.
Therefore, swimmers need no legs
as fliers do, and this is the reason why
the former lack, but the latter have them.
To the crocodiles, too, which often
come to prey on the sandy shores
of the Nile, Nature gave short legs   770
(*piedi*, feet or legs, comes indeed from "soil,"
that was called *pedon* by the Greeks).
While one bird[136] flies, sweeping through
the sky, carrying and supporting nonstop
on wings the weight of its weak body,
to which Nature denied feet; as if
She were teaching it, in the sublime flight,
to aim above, to despise the earth,
thus giving an example to noble souls
who long for heaven and sneer at the soil.[137]   780
This bird looks like our little[138] swallows;
among rocks suspended in green grottoes
it makes its nest with sticking mud,
in which it can hardly make its way:
kypselos[139] it was called by Ancient Greece.
Other birds have been given feet that

---

[135] Both this insight and that in lines 762 ff. come from Aristotle (BB), but they have maintained their freshness from a scientific viewpoint, too.

[136] Its Greek name, from Aristotle (BB), will be mentioned in verse 785.

[137] Richard Bach's *Jonathan Livingston Seagull* has a long tradition. See also Dante, *Paradiso* 22: 133-138.

[138] The tender diminutive form *rondinella* is here employed instead of the scientific name *rondine*.

[139] The swift; its Greek name appears wrongly spelled in BB's footnote. Tasso renders it as "cipselo."

are unfit[140] for preying on others and
hunting for their food, so they look for it[141]
in the air. Among these, one can count
the ever-wandering[142] swallow, whose   790
low flight acts in the place of feet,
grazing the ground close on wings;
and the bird which lives by the grassy
shores,[143] therefore called *riparia*.[144]
Different are the birds in many other
fashions, in their sizes and their shapes,
varied in their colors and ways of life,
varied in their work and in their habits.
Now, omitting the many ways in which
their feathers are split or joined together,   800
or enveloped as in a skin or sheath,
or incomparably soft and weak, I will
tell about their being "clean" or "unclean."[145]
The former, meek and harmless, search
for their food on earth: seeds and grass;
the latter long for fiercer meals,[146]
greedy for raw meat and dark blood,[147]
since they received sharp talons and
a hook-bill as their weapons, and wings
faster than the others', so their prey   810
are swiftly seized and torn to pieces.
Such fierce species have no flocks;
they habitually wander alone and
plunder,[148] only uniting and mating for

---

[140] The pun "feet/fit" only works in English.

[141] Insects, that is.

[142] "Peregrina," an adjective that—has we have already seen—also suggests other things: a religious spirit (as on a pilgrimage), a sad condition (exile, cf. Dante and Tasso himself), beauty (rarity). Here the term *rondinella* is again used.

[143] "Rive," shores. Pronounced somewhat like "reeve-hey." From Latin *ripae*.

[144] The sand martin, *Riparia riparia*, in English "riparian."

[145] Birds were divided into clean and unclean in the Old Testament with reference to their edibility, see *Leviticus* 11: 13-19, but, interestingly enough, here a different criterion is followed, a clearly scientific and ethological one (see verses 808 ff.), according to what *they* eat. N.B.: In the Middle Ages, occupations having to do with blood, e.g. the butcher's, were considered unclean in both senses.

[146] "Fero pasto," from Dante, *Inferno* 33: 1 (where it was spelled "fiero," but Tasso re-Latinizes it).

[147] "Atro sangue," as in *Gerusalemme Liberata* 4: 7, verse 8, describing Satan's mouth.

[148] "Rapina," plunder, robbery. *Rapaci*, birds of prey, are also called *uccelli di rapina*.

the ardent love[149] of their dear eyries.
The others gather in various flocks,
longing and glad for friendly company,
though not safe,[150] as rapacious predators
upset, scatter, and often kill them.
Such are the doves, white as snow,   820
to which Nature gave a fine, precious
ornament, full of colors and gold-hued;[151]
so are the peregrine cranes, the slim starlings.
Among these, some are not subject to
any hard commander: a free and quiet
life they lead, obeying old laws of their own;
others, having a leader, in squadrons
follow their guide flying in the air.
Some have been living in their native
lands for a long time; others fly   830
far away to foreign places, looking for
a warmer sun before winter comes;
others return, when still in frigid days,
migrating in advance in view of summer.
So do thrushes in late autumn on the wing,
on the lukewarm threshold of chilly winter,
where a thousand ambushes are laid
in an inhospitable land. Man cheats them[152]
with his deceitful, treacherous cages,
or catches them with sticky[153] mistletoe,   840
or entangles and binds them in a net.
And when storks finally return,[154] Spring
raises her green standards again.
Some birds know the hand's caresses that
sweetly flatters and cajoles them,
and are accustomed to a Lord's table.
Others are timorous; others make

---

[149] "Amoroso desìo," sexual instinct, but literally "amorous desire," cf. Dante, *Inferno* 5: 82-84, 119-120.

[150] Once again, note the anthropological, existential implication.

[151] Tasso loved this iridescent effect, see *Gerusalemme Liberata* 15: 5.

[152] Here Tasso writes *le*, i.e. the feminine pronoun in the plural, logically referring to *specie*, "species" (but the word has been left implied in the original text), not exclusively to thrushes (*tordi*, masculine). Grammatical concord in this whole section is quite fluttering.

[153] "Tenace," from *tenère*, to hold; quoting Dante, *Inferno* 21: 8. Mistletoe was the natural version of birdlime, and in Italian the two are still called by the same name, *vischio*. Tasso's poetical and moral insight into fowling is deeper than Dante's, *Purgatorio* 23: 1-3.

[154] "E la cicogna ritornando," imitating the Latin ablative absolute.

their beloved nests in human houses;
still others, like savages and highlanders,
prefer the most solitary places.   850
A great variety and difference is
created among birds by voices and sounds.
Some are taciturn, some loquacious;
some without any music and song,
some singing. Some even learn from
teacher Nature to imitate the many
kinds, uses and arts of sound, sweetly
lowering and raising their flexible
voices. Others, either shy or unlearned,
perpetually maintaining one tone,   860
will forever emit the same voice.
Boastful is the peacock, proud the rooster,
while peaceful and lustful the dove;[155]
wicked and jealous is the partridge,
which helps the hunters go plundering.
Some species love to be joined together,
thus uniting both strengths and homes
as if in a city, common to all
under their king. Others refuse the rule
and the pomp of a proud nobleman,   870
so that each must take care of itself.

    Let us[156] start from those whose example
we may usefully follow in human life.
The bees[157] have common towns, and roofs
of soft wax and sweet-smelling cells;
common flight and labor, and the works of
a superb skill, and the daily pastures;
they even have common children
—not born with a painful delivery
after lustful love that unites and joins   880
unclean limbs sweating together,
but sucked and chosen by their mouths

---

[155] Symbolizing many things, the dove represents such contraries as lust and chastity.
[156] Here, as in many other places, Tasso translates from St. Basil (BB).
[157] The creation of "birds" includes all flying animals, unlike in Milton, *PL* 7: 475 ff.

out of sweet-smelling, dewy flowers.[158]
Then, all together in a beautiful parade
under a sole order, they follow the
sole command of their beloved king.
No bee would leave for the meadows,
which are dressed with grass, painted with flowers,
if at first the king had not started the flight.
And this king is not chosen by chance   890
or by Fortune, which often raises the
unworthy and vile to a supreme power;
nor is he voted by the erring plebs;
nor by inheriting an ancient kingdom
does he sit on his ancestors' superb
throne, puffed up with paternal glory,
softened by flattery and courtliness,
though rough and ignorant of liberal arts.
But of Nature he acquires his noble reign
and from Nature he wears royal insignia   900
of shiny gold to adorn and honor him,
and he exceeds all others in greatness,
figure, and the meekness of temper.
Though the king is armed with a sting,
he does not use it to take revenge,[159]
for—according to laws not engraved
or written on paper, or on dry leaves,
or frail bark, or the hardest stone,
but imprinted by Nature in the mind—[160]
where there is more power and valor,   910
more clemency and piety must abound.
But a bee that does not follow the king,
or proves reluctant to obey his will,
will soon regret its foolhardiness
or arrogance, and receive a stroke of
its own sting, and die self-stabbed:
a fierce and sour self-punishment

---

[158] Bees are shown partly in a realistic way, partly on the basis of legends. The idea that society is ruled by a "king" (verses 886 ff.) comes from Virgil's *Georgics* 4: 68 (BB) and *Aeneid* 1: 584-594.

[159] "Far vendetta," maybe from—and against—Dante, *Paradiso* 6: 90, 92, who justified the ways of God "taking vengeance" by means of the Roman Emperors.

[160] Possibly the boldest theological reinterpretation in the whole poem, starting from a basic doctrine of St. Paul (see especially *Romans* 2: 14-15 and *II Corinthians* 3: 3) and turning it into a biological phenomenon.

once used by the ancient Persians,
who voluntarily killed themselves.
No barbarian king of Persia or India   920
or Sarmatia,[161] recent or old, ever saw
his devoted people kneeling with as
much reverence before his royal scepter
as the tiny people do in the presence
of the happy king of the busy bees,
who never uses his natural weapons
against his subjects and against the humble.
  Here may Christ's servants heed! They
who should never render evil for evil,
but overcome evil through advancing good.[162]   930
Listen to the holy example of chaste bees,
and let no one scorn to imitate it:
they, in fact, while getting their food,
do not damage or spoil the others';
but of wax, collected and mixed from various
flowers, they shape their sweet homes.[163]
To the ingenious bees, flowers and grass,
exhaling scents all around, also provide
the first foundations for their roomy
though small palace, sprinkled over   940
with dewy drops of celestial humor,
liquid at first, later thick and sticky.
With thin wax walls, they divide and partition
their tiny cells, above which, in the upper
part, suspended and concave, they
build barrel vaults; and the cells adjoin
one another, both united and divided,
so that the sticky mass may link
and bind them more strongly with
a support that will not collapse: 950
it will easily bear all that sweet weight;
no honey store is in danger of crashing.
The ingenious bee really proves to be
an architect of such wonderful labor

---

[161] Current Poland, more or less.

[162] *Matthew* 5: 39-40; *Romans* 12: 21.

[163] The example we should follow includes a motley list of things. See also the bee metaphor in Francis Bacon's *The Advancement of Learning* 2: 91, and Jonathan Swift's "The Battle of the Books."

and work; wise, and fully aware of what
geometers have discovered and teach.[164]
It makes the cells in a fitting shape,
all with six equal angles and sides,
not one perpendicularly against the other
but adapting the lower spaces   960
to the upper concave parts, so that
no floor and no roof suffer damage.

But how shall I tell and enumerate
the different lives of our dear birds?
The far-off living cranes[165] carry a stone
in a clawed foot so as to balance their
troubled flight in the unsettled weather,
when in the brief, cloudy days, they
leave Thermodon and Hiberus[166] behind
and cross the wide seas to winter   970
on the sunny banks of the ample Nile;
as a ballast, among winds and waves,
in search of new shores and new lands,
helps a tarred ship to hold its course.
In the night, cranes have guards and
sentries go on patrol[167] while the others
safely sleep in a tranquil stillness:
quick, ready, on each side they check
the nocturnal dangers and the winds.
When their guard and time of vigilance   980
are over, with the sound as of trumpets
they awaken their sleeping comrades,
then take a brief nap, and the others
take their place in that tiring duty.
One walks at the head, as if preceding
the raised banners, then, in due time,
it turns back and passes to another
the role and the place of the chief.[168]

---

[164] Bees were usually sung in poetry because of the sweetness of their honey, made with a great variety of flowers, as a symbol of good choices. Here a more modern technological approach emerges, cf. Leonardo Da Vinci.
[165] This legend comes from Pliny the Elder (BB).
[166] Two rivers in the Mediterranean area, respectively in current Cappadocia and Spain.
[167] This section comes from St. Basil and St. Ambrose (BB).
[168] The precise description of military life is among the thematic differences between Tasso (plus Ariosto) and Dante; armies in the modern sense of the term are a late Renaissance/Baroque institution.

Much reason, many skills are shown
by the storks, too, who all together,   990
as with flags waving, come to our lands
from a faraway and unknown clime;
and our crows as friendly guards[169] fly all
around them, united into a great flock.
They are the storks' trustworthy convoy
against the enemies in their long flight,
as English and Scottish soldiers do,
or Germans and Spaniards in a league;
during that time, no crow can be seen
anywhere; then they come back   1000
with feathers red with honorable wounds,
showing the signs of the help they lent.[170]
　　Oh, who prescribed them such certain laws
and such a merciful duty? Who threatens
heavy charges or just penalties against
those who, in the battlefield, desert
their orders and places out of cowardice?[171]
Follow this example, O weak mortals!
Let man learn from the flying birds
the holy laws of hospitality;   1010
let no greedy, proud host shut the doors
in the face of the wandering pilgrims
at midnight, or deny them their food,[172]
if, for the sake of foreign birds, our birds
do not refuse to risk their lives in war
by taking part in others' dangers.
What other cause of fierce death, in fact,
in Sodom, poured down a frightening rain
of burning flames from an upset sky,
than the law of hospitality being   1020
broken, and that scandalous outrage?
But merciful, dear Providence, who
teaches storks to love old relatives,

---

[169] According to St. Ambrose (BB). A scene like this will occur a little lower in Tasso's lines on the Phoenix.

[170] In *MC*, human protagonists almost disappear, but Tasso creates a smaller, and nonetheless serious and even moving Animal Epic.

[171] "Per viltade," from Dante, *Inferno* 3: 60.

[172] Possibly with reference to Jesus' birth or, more probably, the poet's own (alleged) misadventures.

can arouse the sweet love of human
children towards their old, tired sires.
Storks, around a languishing father,
whose long age makes his wings
and lesser feathers fall to the ground,
stand pitying; the suffering limbs
—bare of any downy, light covering—   1030
of the now weary flyer they warm up,
very gently, with their own feathers;
and they bring him some food to eat,
and on both sides they finally lift
the old, slow parent on their wings,
thus reawakening the old functions
of his limbs, helping him to fly again.
    But who of us does not look annoyed, tired
for having to lift his invalid father?[173]
Who carries his weight on one's shoulders   1040
(it hardly sounds believable in old stories[174])
rather than disdainfully entrusting
his weakened limbs to others' arms, offloading
one's own duty onto the servants?
Let us now look at a praiseworthy example
of maternal love; let no one moan
about poverty or utter destitution, nor
give up hope of one's life and cry,
if they recall the teachings and works
of the industrious, compassionate swallow.   1050
Yes, the swallow, small in build, but
great for her luminous, sublime love;
being poor and needy, she assembles
and shapes her nest by herself,
more precious than gems and gold,[175]
as the value of any treasure is low
in comparison with a place in which
wisdom nests. Truly wise and shrewd
is she, preserving her precious freedom
of flying while she feeds and raises   1060
her still little and frail children safe

---

[173] A rhetorical question, as Tasso deeply loved and honored his father.
[174] Aeneas carrying Anchises during their escape from Troy.
[175] Cf. *I Peter* 1: 6-7 and, for the following lines, *Proverbs* 3: 13-15. The simile comes from St. Basil (BB).

from the snares and the attacks of other
birds beneath the same tall roofs
which protect man, and she accustoms
them to the presence of human beings.
Marvelous also is the engineering
by which she builds her home without
the help of any architect or smith.
She first chooses and prepares the straws,
then spreads sticky mud on them   1070
to glue them; and whenever she cannot
carry liquid slurry upwards in her feet,
she sprinkles her wings with water, then
combines dry, light dust, producing anew
the mud she needs for her humble home.
With this adhesive she compacts together
the chosen straws to shape a nest
for her chicks—and if one is pricked in the eye
and made blind, she will restore to it
the lost sight with her medicinal skill.[176]   1080
Let those who complain about their misery
look at the swallow and hope for the grace
of that Lord who gave her such a rich
dowry, such a rich gift of mind and skill,
so that she may offset any disgrace
of destitution and fortune, any need,
in her happy and praiseworthy poverty.
    The halcyon, a small bird of the sea,
shapes her sweet nest as a ball with
dried flowers that grow undersea;   1090
right in mid-winter, her little chicks
are freed from their soft, frail shell
onto the sandy shore, where the mother
had laid the dear weight[177] of her eggs.
This happens when fierce winds beat
and hurl the sea against the coasts,
and, shining with white foam, the waves
flood the soft sands and the hard rocks.
But at the halcyon's longed-for delivery,
the frightful wind's fury is calmed,   1100

---

[176] By using celandine, according to St. Basil and other ancient writers (BB).
[177] The Italian wording partially echoes Dante, *Purgatorio* 20: 24, describing another wonderful winter birth.

the stormy waves subside, all around
the clouds clear, and the sky, brightening up,
with a face now quiet and happy, smiles
to the faithful[178] birds' offspring.
In the first seven of those happy days
will the feathered mother sit on the eggs,
and in the other seven feed the young.
To such a fortnight, experienced sailors
gave the name of "halcyonian days,"[179]
distinguishing and marking them from all   1110
for the brilliance of their clear serenity.
May this reassure and comfort us
when we ask God for graces and gifts:
He, if for the sake of a tiny bird,[180]
calms down the big, vast, and frightening
sea in the midst of a hard, stormy winter,
curbing it, making it quiet and flat,[181]
what will He do, if He comes to our rescue
—He who gives man His anointed[182] Son,
His Godhead's image and likeness?[183]   1120

The turtledove,[184] separated from her love,
does not want any new love or consort,
but chooses a sad and solitary existence
on a dead branch, and with muddy water
quenches her thirst, renewing by this
the bitter memory of her dead husband.
To him she preserves her chastity
and to him the dear name of "wife,"
for cruel death cannot break the holy
laws of modesty and the contract   1130
to which she first voluntarily subscribed.
Let this be an example to the widow
not to rush boldly to a second wedding,

---

[178] "Fidi," literally trustworthy, etc., often referring to dear friends.

[179] *Alkyonides hemerai* in Greek, seven days before to seven days after the winter solstice. "Midwinter" (line 1091) will therefore mean the solstice, as in Shakespeare's "Midsummer," rather than "in the middle of."

[180] Cf. *Matthew* 6: 26 and 10: 29-31; *Luke* 12: 24.

[181] Cf. *Matthew* 9: 26 and parallel Gospel texts.

[182] Literally, "chosen" as the Christ ("anointed"). Cf. St. Paul, *Romans* 8: 32.

[183] Cf. *Colossians* 1: 15; *Hebrews* 1: 3. All these cross-references may show Tasso's familiarity with the Bible, as surely was the case; more directly, they come from St. Basil (BB).

[184] In the diminutive form *tortorella* instead of the plain *tortora*. Cf. above, *rondinella*.

plunging into profound oblivion
her first love and her first promise.[185]
   The eagle, in raising her[186] noble offspring,
proves incomparably disdainful, unjust:
out of three eaglets, she drives away two,
hitting them hard with her strong wings,
and so raises the third with enough   1140
food, which the flying predator provides.
But maybe a better and more just reason
is what drives her: not shortage of food,
but a severe test by which she shows
that unworthy children would not fit in,
for she will lead them towards the sun,
suspended in midair in her curved talons.
The one not turning its half-blinded,
weak eyes away from the burning rays,
but fixing them boldly on the sun,   1150
is chosen; the others, abhorred and disdained
(as unworthy of royal honors)
by her generous and great refusal.[187]
The outcasts are welcomed in the nest
of the bone-breaking eagle, and hence is
given this name,[188] perhaps a crossbreed, born
of a misshapen parent or another bird;[189]
she will not let them cruelly starve, but will
feed and keep them among her own sons.
Such[190] are those hard, harsh[191] fathers   1160
who "expose"[192] their children, or unjustly share

---

[185] Quick second marriages were quite usual, especially because women were not economically independent.

[186] Lines 1160 ff., suggest that the male eagle is meant; however, following Tasso, in lines 1136-1160, "she" is used. The matter invites further analysis.

[187] "Gran rifiuto," again from Dante, *Inferno* 3: 60, where, however, it was meant as a brand of infamy.

[188] "Ossifrage" [to be here identified with *Gypäetus barbatus* (BB)] comes from *ossa* and *frangere* in Latin.

[189] Solidarity among outcasts; again from St. Basil (BB), one of the best animal stories here collected. It also conveys the typical Tassean tension, especially obvious in *Gerusalemme Conquistata*, between the Renaissance neo-pagan ideal of the "Superman" (see Nietzsche) and Christian values.

[190] To be linked back to verse 1137. After defending old fathers, now Tasso protects little children.

[191] "Acerbi," literally unripe; Dante used it in reference to sinners (*Inferno* 25: 18) and Satan (*Paradiso* 19: 48).

[192] That is, abandon their newborns by a monastery or the like. *Esposti* were the foundlings.

goods and food among family members.
All other birds having hooked talons,
when their children first try, timidly,
to fly, hardly spreading their wings
with uncertain and shaky remiges,
quickly push them out of the paternal nest;
and if one proves too slow in leaving,
by hitting it with his wings, the fierce
father drives it out, down the cliff.   1170
But worthy of high praise are the love
and zeal of the crow for her offspring:
she, acting as a good, trustworthy mother,
leads her weak children in their first,
bold flight, and keeps feeding them for
a long period to let them grow strong.
    Yet there are many and diverse birds which
do not need the males for procreation,
for breezes and winds fertilize them[193]
—but then their children will be sterile: 1180
no perpetual windy race will come from
the progeny of Eurus, Notos, Auster.[194]
Even so, without mixing, without coupling
in conjugal love do vultures conceive
and litter, and enjoy a very late death
(a rare, wonderful marvel on earth)
by leading one-century-long lives.
Now, if some[195] dare mock the sublime
mysteries of our divine, undying faith,
or disbelieve that the Son came   1190
out of the intact Queen's virginal cloisters,
preserving the flower of her virginity,
let them see this well-known, sure example
that noble Nature provides of things divine![196]
Let them believe that, what a flying bird
can do, the Omnipotent God can, too.

---

[193] In Ariosto's *Orlando Furioso*, not a bird but a very fast horse, Rabicano, had been conceived so.

[194] The SE, North, and South winds.

[195] The Jews. Jesus' Virgin Birth is also accepted by Muslims. According to a traditional Catholic tenet, not only did Mary virginally conceive Jesus, but he did not "damage" her "flower" when he was born.

[196] This *outré* sample of Apologetics comes from no less than Origen and St. Ambrose (BB).

These same vultures have a nearly
divine sense that lets them forecast
the warriors' death; they at times, indeed,
accompany the armed squadrons since   1200
they already foresee the bloody carnage,
the painful end of the horrible battle.[197]
Or who may effectively tell about
the frightening armies of locusts?[198]
As at a horrible war signal, they
rise high in the air in huge formations,
then encamp and occupy a country
as far as it stretches, but touching
no sweet fruit before the headquarters
allows them to plunder the fields?   1210
Do I have to describe how in summer
afternoons the reeling cicadas, as with
a lyre inside their chests,[199] make the green
woods echo with their trills in repetition?
Or how some screen or shield against the sun
in gloomy places, in a nocturnal life,
is sought by the bird[200] sacred in ancient
Athens to their goddess, and by them fed?
It alone, among the many flying birds,
uses teeth and stands on all fours   1220
(while two feet has the African bird,[201]
however big and heavy it may be),
though supporting its light body on two
when it spreads its leathery wings.
Joined with one another, they hang
like a long chain with many links,
and in this fashion, Nature, you show
the firm knots of reciprocal love.
And the eyes of this nocturnal bird are
like those of a man wholly devoted   1230

---

[197] Cf. Milton, *PL* 10: 273 ff.

[198] Cf. *Exodus* 10: 5, 14-15 and *Joel* 1: 4 ff.

[199] Tasso's physiology here is incorrect.

[200] In this section, Tasso—quite unbelievably, however much his sources may have misled him—mixes up the owl and the bat. It is noteworthy that he does not show the bat as a trite devilish symbol but quite the opposite, on the basis of an accurate ethological description.

[201] The ostrich. During the Renaissance, more accurate pictures of it were available than before.

to the vain study of human[202] wisdom,
since the former's sight is powerful
in the deep gloom of night, but weak
when the sun disperses the shadows,
and the latter's intellect seems sharp
in his vain thoughts, but in the True Light
the weak mind will be overshadowed.
Do I need to recall the trilling voice of
the little songbird[203] prompting us to work?
It echoes widely and[204] calls the sun   1240
and awakens wayfarers and good farmers,
the former to their hard, tiring journey,
the latter to reap the ripe wheat sheaves.
Our sweet sleep may also be broken,
inviting us to keep attentive watch
against the snares of the ancient adversary,
by the slow bird[205] that already saved
the Great City, the queen of the world,
by unveiling the nocturnal fraud:
cruel barbarians, hidden by night,   1250
were climbing up along dark ways
toward that high, triumphal top[206] where,
in august majesty, there stood the high
rock of[207] power and Jupiter's temple.
What about the white swan and its
divine omen and sweet song before
its foreseen and serene death—so that
the immortal soul may trust and hope
in eternity by grace, beyond the sky?
Or the Indian worm,[208] wonderfully   1260
adorned with horns and wings by Nature,
exhibiting so many changing shapes?

---

[202] In the sense of "merely" human, without the light of God's grace. Cf. Dante, *Paradiso* 11: 1 ff.

[203] In general; while his source, St. Basil (BB), referred to the rooster.

[204] The *a* (to) in BB must be edited into *e* (and).

[205] The goose. About 390 BC, according to a now proverbial legend, these birds raised the alarm when the Gauls tried to attack Rome by stealth.

[206] The Capitol. The current square, dating back to the Renaissance, was designed by Michelangelo.

[207] Here, *e* to be edited into *a*. Literally, "the high rock [consecrated] *to* power [as the temple was to Jove]." *Imperio*, or *Impero* in contemporary Italian, might also mean Empire, but surely not in this case, in the fourth century BC.

[208] The silkworm, though it more properly came from China.

So, you noble ladies[209] who sit down
weaving and re-weaving precious
works with trees, flowers and even more
wonderful figures, with dear threads
sent you from afar, from far-away India,
to adorn your dear bodies with soft,
beautiful dresses—in doing so, ladies,
please recall to your high minds[210] what   1270
you already heard on other occasions:
that we will rise again, putting back on
the cloak of humanity, and be eternal.
All wrapped in light and gold, you will
shine before the soul-enlightening Sun,[211]
sitting on a high, glorious seat, adorned
with something better than pearls and purple.

***

---

[209] "Donne" currently means women, but the term here keeps the Latin sense of *dominae*. It
is worth remembering that Tasso decided to write *MC* after his theological conversations
with a noblewoman. The passage sets forth themes and images that can be construed as
foreshadowing the story of the phoenix which is the subject of the remainder of Day 5.

[210] Being spinners did not necessarily imply being "subdued" as Dante seems to want them
in *Inferno* 20: 121-122. To be sure, Dante lists learned women among his readers in
Convivio, Part I, ch. 9, but not so in the *Divine Comedy*.

[211] Cf. *Matthew* 13: 43, reworked in a very refined way.

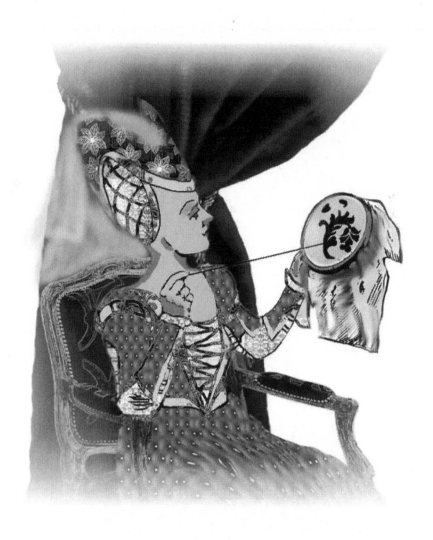

The Poem of the Phoenix [1]

I will now address you, and you will receive
the utmost honor in sublime verses,
O immortal, resurgent, unique bird.   1280
Poetry will provide a worshiped pyre[2]
of high praise, so that ancient Fame may be
renewed worldwide and spread her wings,[3]
and through this clear, serene sky she
may happily and gloriously sweep,
now disdaining the Arabian mountains.[4]
Among the other beautifully painted birds,
who on that first day spread their wings
in the pure air at the sound of His voice,
God also forged the phoenix, as it   1290
is believed, if old fame prove trustworthy.[5]
By such a shape-shifter (a mortal, unique,
ever-born-again bird) the eternal Father
wanted to show, as by a rare example,
His only, immortal, born-again Son,

---

[1] For the first and last time, an editorial division is made here that does not follow the original text. The reason is that there begins, at this point, a true "poem within a poem," not strictly a long poem but nevertheless as long as three Cantos of the *Divine Comedy*. The protagonist is the Phoenix as a symbol of Christ. Dante had chosen another mythological creature, the griffin, as his own Christ-symbol, insofar as it hinted at His two natures, human (the lion) and divine (the eagle); see *Purgatorio* 30-32. For Tasso, however, the central theological tenet is Jesus' death and resurrection: not by chance did he write two long poems dealing with the "reconquest" of the Holy Sepulcher in Jerusalem. His "Poem of the Phoenix" mixes several ancient sources, both classical and Christian, Dante included, in a complex balance among theological teachings and refined descriptions for poetic effect. See the introduction for remarks on the issue of the bird's gender.

[2] As those of the dead heroes in Greek and Latin epic poetry.

[3] Fame, in the Renaissance, was portrayed as a winged woman, plus other details: many eyes, a trumpet, etc.

[4] The verb *sdegnare* might simply mean "to leave" a place, but here a dig against Islam is possibly implied: the "true phoenix" is "our own."

[5] Another taste of Tasso's skepticism—quite possibly—here marked by dry parody and a *soupçon* of facetiousness? Already many times Tasso has scoffed at false learning and philosophical credulity. Such facetiousness is central to Milton's anthropology and satire, but was it inspired by Tasso? See Milton's "Manso" lines 42-43, "*Gens Druides antiqua sacris operata decorum / Heroum laudes imitandaque gesta canebant*" (Unless ancient times handed down groundless stories); Cf. *PL*, book 1, The Argument: "...was the opinion of many ancient fathers." *Passim*.

destined to rebirth since the Father let
His eternal Offspring be born for us.[6]
    There is a place[7] in the remotest zone
of the scented and luminous East,
where the Sun opens his golden doors   1300
in coming out, crowned with the day.
This place is not near the spot in which
the sun rises in summer, or else, where,
encircled by clouds, it appears in winter,
but at the point where it appears in rising
when it equalizes the nights and days.
There, with open fields, a vast plateau
spreads in all directions; no valley, no hill
slopes down or rises in that spaciousness,
but the place is believed to raise   1310
its green, shadowy head twelve times
higher than our most famous rugged mountains.
Here, ever-unlit, a thick[8] forest is sacred
to the Sun,[9] and the wood is green with the
unending honor of non-deciduous leaves,[10]
circled by the swelling ocean all around.[11]
Even when the burning signs of fire were
left in the sky by the charioteer[12] Phaëton,
the place was safe from those flames;
when the world sank in the great   1320
Flood, it overcame those frightening waters.[13]
Pale Diseases will never arrive there,
nor unhealthy Old Age and ungodly Death,
or Greed, the infamous hunger[14] for gold,

---

[6] Jesus Christ's birth and work of salvation (death/resurrection), cf. e.g. *Matthew* 1: 21; *Acts of the Apostles* 2: 22 ff.; *Galatians* 4: 4-5. It is remarkable that Tasso envisions Jesus' resurrection especially as a second birth.

[7] "Loco è," echoing Dante, *Inferno* 18: 1, but in a very different context.

[8] "Opaca selva," similar to Dante's *selva oscura* in *Inferno* 1: 2, but here in a positive sense.

[9] Often a symbol of God and/or Christ; here, more strictly, of God the Father, as the phoenix is the Son.

[10] A Baroque periphrasis to say "evergreen." Leaves are termed "honor" probably in parallel with man's beard, that was traditionally called *l'onor del mento*, "the chin's honor."

[11] Like Dante's Edenic mountain of purgatory and Lewis's neo-Edenic island in *Perelandra*.

[12] Lit.: "charioteering." The verb *carreggiare*, referring to Phaëton, comes from Dante, *Purgatorio* 4: 72.

[13] Not so according to Milton, *Paradise Lost* 11: 829 ff.

or further, wicked Sin, or fierce Mars,
or the insane love of a cruel death.[15]
Far are Wrath, Suffering and Mourning,
and Poverty wrapped in her horrid clothes,[16]
and the troubling thoughts, and pungent,
thorny cares, and scanty shortages.   1330
Here no storm or the horrible force
of a turbid wind ever shows its fury,[17]
nor do shadowy clouds spread their black,
gloomy veil across the countryside,
nor does any violent rain ever fall.
But in the middle, murmuring, is a lively
spring, shiny, transparent and pure,
rich with sweet and crystalline waters,
which each month overflows and floods,
so that it waters the wood twelve times.[18]   1340
Here, a leafy tree[19] raises its branches
from a lofty trunk; sweet, non-caducous
fruits[20] hang down among the verdant leaves.

Among such trees and in that very forest,
by that spring, the one phoenix dwells,
who from death is born again and lives:
a bird equal to the celestial substances,
her life matching the stars, she consumes and
overcomes time by virtue of re-made limbs.
As a servant[21] dearest to the Sun,   1350
she has this duty and gift from Nature:
that when in the sky a new dawn begins

---

[14] With a pun in Italian: *infame fame*. Moreover, here Tasso "edits" Dante, who in *Purgatorio* 22: 40-41—precisely in the cornice of Greed—had clumsily translated from Virgil, *Aeneid* 3: 56.

[15] Suicide, probably. These verses list Tasso's worst nightmares.

[16] Tasso was not St. Francis of Assisi; cf. Dante, *Paradiso* 11: 58-60, 73-78.

[17] As in Dante's (purgatory) and Milton's terrestrial paradise.

[18] Cf. Milton, *Paradise Lost* 4: 223-230.

[19] The palm tree. According to ancient Egyptian and Phoenician traditions, Rabbinic translations of Job 29: 18-20, as well as ancient writers like Pliny, the phoenix was associated with the palm tree. The etymological relationship between the "palm tree" (*phoenix dactylifera*) and the "phoenix" is based on Biblical and Egyptian legends (see note 32). See also Dante, *Purgatorio* 22: 131-132 and 24: 103-104, 116-117; Milton, *PL* 4: 195. Milton's *Epitaphium Damonis* ll. 195-189 clearly reflects Tasso. See Rudolf Gottfried, *SP* 30 (1933): 497-503.

[20] "Pomi," a term whose prevailing meaning is "apples."

[21] "Ancella," feminine (from Latin *ancilla*), recalls Virgin Mary; see *Luke* 1: 38 in the *Vulgate*.

211

to flare, stained with the color of roses,
and chases the tiny stars from the sky,
she three and four times plunges her body
into the water, and seven times drinks
the sweet liquid from the whirling stream.
The phoenix then takes off and sits atop
the leafy tree, whence she overlooks
and watches the forest all around;[22]   1360
and turning towards the rising sun, waits
for the newly-born sun's rays and light.
As soon as the breeze blows, and shines with
that very gold that makes the sun blaze,
the bird starts to impart her sacred song
in sweet tunes, thus calling and hastening
the new light with her wonderful voice[23]
—which no voice from Cirrha,[24] no sweet
harmony from Parnassus will ever match,
nor will the resonant lyre of Hermes   1370
resemble it, nor the voice of the dying swan.
But after Phoebus[25] has crossed the bright,
open fields of the heavenly Olympus
and has turned around that wide circle,
the phoenix beats her chest thrice with her
golden, painted wings, praising the sun
with steady sounds every day and night
(she herself also distinguishes the fast-
running hours). After worshiping thrice
the blazing face, she is finally silent,   1380
like the solitary priestess of that holy,
dark wood[26] and those deep, gloomy
shadows—to her the secrets of the sky
as well as those of Nature are well known;
therefore she deserves respect and honor.
When a thousand years[27] have passed,

---

[22] These lines were probably a direct source for Milton, *Paradise Lost* 4: 196-201. The Fall (looming in the episode in *PL*) mirrors the Bliss (here in *Creation of the World*).
[23] Cf. Hinduism, according to which "without the daily sacrifice, the sun would not rise."
[24] The harbor of Delphi, consecrated to Apollo, the god of music.
[25] Apollo, often identified with the Sun, though the original god of the sun was Helios.
[26] "Sacro...bosco," perhaps with a pun on the astronomer Giovanni Sacrobosco, i.e. John Holywood.
[27] "Two hundred *lustri*." Other sources—e.g. Dante, *Inferno* 24: 108—indicate five hundred years.

she, made slow by her now old age,
she, who succeeded in flying beyond
the clouds and the dark, sonorous storms
to renew her tired life, and her time   1390
now encompassed within narrow limits,
shuns her sweet home in the familiar wood.
Longing for rebirth, she leaves the sacred
places behind and flies towards our world,
where hateful Death has his kingdom.[28]
Grown very old, the bird slowly flies
towards that famous part of Syria
called *Phoenicia* precisely after her;[29]
among deserted forests, she looks for some
secret room along untrodden ways,   1400
and hides herself in the wood's depths.
High in midair, she chooses a strong,
lofty date-palm (to which also she
gave the happy name of *Phoenix*), [30]
forever unbreakable by the teeth
of any scaly snake[31] or bird of prey,
or any horrid and dangerous beast.
And so enclosed in grottoes, the winds are
quiet among rugged cavernous cloisters,
so as not to upset with turbid spirits   1410
the sweet face of a beautiful purple air;
no condensed cyclone covers the empty
fields of the sky, preventing the happy
bird from seeing the gentle sunbeams.
Here she makes her nest—either nest or grave
where she dies to be born again and live,
as he who is father and son of himself,
who by himself is made and created.[32]

---

[28] "...we cannot share God's dying unless God dies; and He cannot die except by being a man."—C. S. Lewis, *Mere Christianity*, Part II, ch. 4, a perfect synthesis of the theology of the Church Fathers.

[29] This fantastic etymology comes from the Pseudo-Lattantius. It may be worth remembering that, according to some legends, Syria, namely Damascus, was the place in which Adam had been created before being taken by God to Eden.

[30] The scientific name of the date-palm, but the etymology is a bogus one (from Epiphanius).

[31] Satan and men acted as mere instruments; Jesus died because he had divinely planned it, *John* 10: 17-18.

Here the bird chooses from the rich forest
the sweet juices and the gentlest spices[33]   1420
being picked in Tyre or Felix Arabia, or
by the fabled Pygmies, by sunburnt Indians,
or what the sunny land of the fortunate
Sabeans[34] produces in its well-watered bosom;
and gathers the spicy-smelling cardamom
and balsam with its reed-like stems,
not without cassia, fragrant acanthus,
and the tear-like drops of incense,
the newly-born sprouts of soft nard,
adding the dear essence of myrrh.   1430
He then quickly lays down his changing body,
sets and positions his already still limbs
in the lively bed of his happy nest,
and in a false sepulcher, before dying,
prepares a burning cradle to his birth.
With her mouth, he sprinkles sweet juices
all around, as well as on his own body.
Here the dying bird celebrates his last rites;
and already weak, with a song of praise
he hails, worships, appeases[35] the Sun.   1440
He mixes humble prayers and humble song,
asking God for the flames that will let him
rise again with a newly-acquired strength.
Among the many spices, he commits his
expiring soul[36] to the sepulcher, undoubting,
harboring bold trust in such a dear pledge.
Meanwhile,[37] his dead body burns with
Vital Death: its heat gives rise to flames,
also triggered by the faraway lamp,
so that he keeps burning beyond measure,   1450
glad to die so, insofar as he expects
to be born again in a very short time.

---

[32] The divine *Logos*, equal to the Father, by whom the Father expresses both Himself and the whole creation. Spiritually as well as grammatically, the phoenix transforms into the symbol of rebirth. Cf. lines 1561 ff.

[33] The word *odori*, literally "smells," still means spices or herbs in some regions of Italy.

[34] The inhabitants of southern Arabia. The Queen of Sheba, who met King Solomon, came from there.

[35] Cf. *Luke* 23: 34, possibly.

[36] Cf. *Luke* 23: 46.

[37] "Parte" in its Dantean sense.

The pyre shines as with blazing stars,
consuming the aged and tired phoenix.
The moon slows down and restrains its course,
and in that wonderful birth, Nature,
the worn-out Mother, seems to be afraid
that the immortal bird may be lost, but
distinguishes and divides the uncertain
border between the twin lives in that fire.[38]   1460
After having turned into still warm ashes,
he now gathers his own ashes together,[39]
into one mass condensed—a hidden
power here acting as the inner seed.
Thence the animal is firstly re-born
in the encircling shape of an egg; then
re-shapes himself into his primal image,
and out of his new, torn-open shell,
the immortal phoenix finally springs up.
The rough chick little by little starts   1470
to clothe himself with beautiful feathers,
as some butterflies, sticking to stones
by a thin filament, change their outsides.[40]
But our world offers no fitting food
and nobody cares about nourishing him,
so he meanwhile drinks celestial dews
fallen from the golden stars and silver
moon like sweet and crystalline rain.[41]
These he gathers, and amidst a thousand
scents, until he reveals his mature shape   1480
with grown limbs, he will feed on them.
And when he flourishes as a young bird,
he goes back flying to his first home.
What remains of his former, dead body
and of his burnt and incinerated skin,
he anoints with a precious, scented juice
in which he mixes balm, incense, and myrrh:[42]

---

[38] These two lines are not very clear; "Nature" has been considered the grammatical subject
because other alternatives seemed even less likely.

[39] From Dante, *Inferno* 24: 101-111. But it is not *how* Jesus rose again, cf. *Acts of the
Apostles* 2: 31.

[40] Literally, "[ex]change feathers," a phrase invented by Dante, *Paradiso* 27: 15.

[41] In the Catholic tradition, the Eucharist is called "the bread of the angels." Cf. *John* 6: 31
ff.

piously with his beak, he shapes them
into the round form of a ball or sphere,
and carrying it with his feet, he heads   1490
for the shiny Orient, and hurriedly so.
An innumerable flock of flying birds
accompanies him; a long, thick squadron,
a great army indeed, almost making
a cloud all around, encircling him.
None of all these warriors would dare
counter that Chief in his pilgrimage,
but adore the path of the Burning King.
No fierce falcon boldly wages war
on him, nor does the bird that brings   1500
(as of old tales) the lightning to Zeus.
As horrid barbarian troops were inspected
along the Tigris by a Parthian King
—proud with his precious gems and golden
pomp, his hair adorned with a crown,
purple his mantle which was embellished
by Syrian needles with pearls and gold,
he who with golden reins used to guide
the dusty gallop of his frothing horse
across Assyrian cities, sublime and superb,   1510
where he had his vast, happy empire—[43]
just so the born-again bird goes, wonderful
to be seen,[44] when with royal dignity
and royal bearing he spreads his wings.
His color is deep red, making him look
like a supple poppy when, opening
its petals skyward, it shines red in the sun;
this, covering him like a veil, displays
his body, his neck, his head, and his back.
He unfolds a tail resembling sparkling   1520
gold, stained and painted with purple.
His feathers are also adorned and painted
—as one can see in a dewy, curved cloud—

---

[42] Cf. the newborn Jesus (*Matthew* 2: 11) and the sacred oil of the Covenant (*Exodus* 30: 22-31).

[43] This passage, in its powerful imagery and complex syntax, is as gorgeous as a description by Milton. Tasso translates from the Latin poet Claudianus in this case, but he is well familiar with this epic style.

[44] "Maraviglioso in vista," with Dantesque wording, as well as *vanni*, wings, in the following line.

by the rainbow: there variously mix the
verdant color emerald with white marks,
and other beautiful cerulean flowers.[45]
His eyes are big and like hyacinths,[46]
shining outwardly with lively flames;
like a gem is his hooked beak, too.
An even crown encircles his head,   1530
like the blazing rays which enclose the sun.
His legs are scaly and adorned with gold,
his talons rosy; his noble shape resembles
partly the peacock, partly the bird that
nests on the banks of the Phasis River,[47]
so large that hardly any bird or beast
across all Arabia may match his size;
yet not slow at all, but swift and ready, he
with royal dignity in his speedy flight
openly displays his royal majesty.   1540
An ancient city in green Egypt was
sacred to the Sun in primordial times;[48]
here a worldwide famous temple stood,
great and superb with a hundred pillars
quarried from Thebes'[49] rugged mountain.
Here—according to Fame—he laid down
his precious bundle on the smoking altars;
that dear load, destined to the fire,
he gave to the flames, worshiping three
and four times the Sun's burning image.   1550
The lighted seed flames, and the sacred smoke
waves and blows with scented clouds until
it reaches the stagnant fields of
Pelusium,[50] and diffusing its fragrances,
it fills Ethiopia and India with itself.[51]

---

[45] Using the flowers as patterns of color may come from Dante, *Purgatorio* 7: 73-76.

[46] Not the flower, but a precious stone (BB) whose color was basically orange.

[47] East of the Black Sea; the bird is the pheasant, whose name comes precisely from Phasis.
Tasso describes the phoenix not at the beginning, but, with a climax, in his glory *after* the
resurrection—and rightly so, both from a literary and from a theological point of view.

[48] Called Heliopolis in Greek, meaning "Sun City." The Christ-phoenix worships the Sun as
a symbol of God the Father, but it is curious to remember that Tasso had formerly attacked
the Sun cults.

[49] In the area now corresponding to Karnak and Luxor.

[50] A city at the mouth of the Nile, near the modern Port Said.

Wondering about that wonderful sight,
the whole of Egypt rushes, merrily greets
the pilgrim bird, immediately celebrating
and honoring him;[52] his shape and name, with
that date, are sculpted in sacred marble.   1560
  O fortunate, happy bird, the father and son
of yourself and the heir of yourself,
being both fed and feeder, undistinguished
by sex;[53] whom old age will never
lead to an end like everybody else,
neither will Venus corrupt—nor will she
weaken and dissolve one's beloved one.[54]
Instead of venery there is a happy death,
whence you are born as "the same" and "another,"[55]
and through death you gain immortal life.   1570
Although the Ages have modified the seas
and mountains, and changed the world,[56]
you remain perpetual and nearly[57] eternal,
forever equal in the likeness of yourself.
You are the only witness of the turnings
of the world's eras and its[58] many centuries,
of so many things, so many glorious
accomplishments, O fortunate bird!
All the more fortunate because you show us,
as in a painted and golden picture,   1580
the only Son of God the Father, God as
the Father, equal in the likeness of Him.
Through your unique example, Nature
to our spirited minds—if they chanced

---

[51] Ethiopia and India were thought to be the same place, but faraway in SE Africa, so these lines must be interpreted as "the scent reaches Pelusium in the one direction, and Ethiopia in the other." Cf. St. Paul, *II Corinthians* 2: 14.

[52] A scene like this takes place in *Gerusalemme Liberata* when the seductive witch Armida joins the Muslim army.

[53] Not because the phoenix is androgynous but because there exists only one specimen.

[54] Tasso's theological and existential longing for an ultimate Principle transcending both biological generation and entropy. See the verbal roots *gen-* and *genn-* in Greek: both "to become" and "to be born" entail transience, as it was stressed by philosophers and Church Fathers. Cf. *Letter to the Hebrews* 7: 3, 22-28.

[55] Like the Risen Christ; see *Luke* 24: 39; *I Corinthians* 15: 42-45; *II Corinthians* 5: 16-17, etc.

[56] Tasso exhibits a very modern sensibility in geology.

[57] The phoenix is consistently just a symbol, not the true thing.

[58] The world. This is probably an original Tassean take on the myth of the phoenix.

to doubt—teaches how He did rise, now
eternal, from his death and sepulcher;[59]
and although our pure, invincible faith
receives light from a brighter source,
it does not dismiss you, and perpetually
honors your name before your Maker,   1590
the supreme Sun giving light to the sun.

    The eternal Father had by now made all
the liquid fields,[60] those swept by winds
or waves, with their own inhabitants
—if truly inhabitants of the wandering air
are the birds: they rather belong to the earth
that provides them with food and flight.[61]
When He saw his own works, and that
all were good, even the wild beasts then
being good[62] since His goodness was   1600
imprinted on them as the Master's mark,
He therefore blessed them by saying,
"Increase! May your prolific offspring
fill all waters, and on earth, as well,
may each breed of the flying birds
grow and spread beyond number."
The holy command of His voice remains
these days a certain, unbreakable law,
for—after so many years, decades, and
centuries that have already flown past   1610
after the world's origin, up to this late
and last era,[63] whose end is close at hand—
no seed of theirs,[64] no animal stock,
either because of any flood or fire,
or of any long, deadly, horrible plague,
or of their own ferocity, or of man's
cunning snares and terrible weapons,

---

[59] Cf. *Letter to the Romans* 6: 9.

[60] Both the seas and the atmosphere.

[61] A foray into the theory of (or, in Tasso's case, a "feel" for) evolution. One of the main hypotheses on the origin of bird flight is that feathered dinosaurs used their rudimentary wings to jump; or, to glide down from trees, according to another hypothesis.

[62] A typical Edenic *topos*, from *Genesis* 1: 30 but especially *Isaiah* 11: 6-7. Cf. Milton, *Paradise Lost* 4: 340-344.

[63] The end of the world has been expected "for certain" from the first civilizations onwards. Cf. among others, Dante, *Convivio*, Part III, ch. 14.

[64] The animals. But, elsewhere, he remarks that some species have disappeared. The Renaissance was the epoch in which people started to wonder about the meaning of fossils.

were ever extinguished or in danger,
but they all are kept almost eternally.
So great is the power of that divine, 1620
holy Voice which guards and preserves them,
so that this vast world may be fully
adorned everywhere, as embracing
and welcoming all in its wide bosom.
And so it was. Linking evening to morning,
God then put an end to the fifth day.

Day Six

T here, where the celebrated Olympus
—the blazing seat of the Gods, they said—
above all clouds and above the winds
raises its serene forehead in the calm air;
there, where Alpheus used to carry
on its shiny waves the glorious dust
of winners, whose limbs it cleansed,
various prizes for famous games were
given in old[1] Pisa. The fastest and strongest
athletes were frequently seen toiling in dubious   10
wrestling or racing, and charioteers turning,
with fervent wheels, around the high
metae, and in many other competitions
people seeking honor and clear fame;
also seen were the most sublime poets
vying with each other—whose sweet
songs and gentle, eloquent tongues
were listened to in awe. They all knew
there was no comparable prize or palm.
Sometimes, the first days of those   20
ancient contests passed in uncertainty,
nobody being crowned; only in the end,
when greater were the toils and risks
of competing, or shameful the scorn
in being defeated, inflexible juries
would give dear prizes to the happy winners,
and their glorious names now resounded
all around at the blaring sound of trumpets.
   But in this—as it were—arena and field
of wisdom, where we revere, sitting   30
on a lofty seat in the likeness of God,
him[2] whom God let judge us on earth,
though not a severe judge, but Clement,
an even more pressing, more serious
concern for uncertain honor weighs on us,

---

[1] To distinguish it from the current city of Pisa in Italy; see above, 3: 219.
[2] Again Pope Clement VIII, with reference to *Matthew* 17: 19.

in this last[3] day and last race, in which, after
such a wearing, bitter competition,[4]
a crown or prize is now set before us;[5]
otherwise, a very hard penalty looms.
The game and fruit are not the same   40
as for those who fight the enemy or sing
at the sweet sound of resonant strings,
in this my—so to speak—unworthy attempt;
for, there, the peril is only scorn and sneers
from the audiences; here, harm and death.[6]
   So, friends,[7] please show pity and help me,
I beg, by supplying strength and spirit!
Together with me, enter this adorned
wonderful, great, and spacious theater
of the created things,[8] where, admiring   50
the art of the great and eternal Father,
by degrees we may raise our pure minds
to His invisible and happy Kingdom,
where He keeps his ultimate rewards.
Nor am I asking for a green garland
of luxuriant laurel,[9] so swiftly stripped
of its leaves, losing its beauty and value;
or of pale and forever famous olive,
like the one brought by Amphitryon's son[10]
from the great sources of the cold Danube;   60
but let my prizes be health and peace
on earth, and more in the starry cloisters.

---

[3] Suggesting many possibilities: Tasso's fortunes, the end of creation, judgment day; the poem, of course, will include another day, the seventh.

[4] In his last years, his poetry was often attacked by "competitors" or "enemies."

[5] Tasso was to be crowned, in Rome, as "Poet Laureate," but he died before this could happen.

[6] The "death of poetry," according to BB; but Tasso also had material reasons to be afraid. When he lived in Rome, he ran the risk of being kidnapped by the thugs of the Este family (see above the notes at 1: 475 and 3: 1106) and dragged to some prison or "political" asylum; the Pope in person—Sixtus V, a predecessor of Clement VIII—after being informed, stopped the plan. See Pittorru, *op. cit.*, ch. 12.

[7] Calling upon friends for aid could already be found, though in a less tragic key, in Ludovico Ariosto, *Orlando Furioso* 46, stanzas 1 ff. It is interesting to highlight the difference with the solitary Dante, who addresses his readers as "readers," not as "friends."

[8] Again a declaration of his own poetics.

[9] This statement is not completely sincere. As mentioned, Tasso was about to be crowned Poet Laureate in Rome.

[10] Heracles, who actually was the son of Jove and Alcmena, Amphitryon's wife. This "agricultural myth" of his had been sung by Pindar (BB).

Meanwhile, this glorious crown is set
before you,[11] and I now wish to crown you
for your worthy works, in the wake of your
sound judgment.[12] So, my faithful friends,
with benevolent attention listen and learn
of the complex[13] natures of the wild beasts,
of the humble flocks and earthly herds,
and of Man, whom the eternal Father   70
last[14] created out of clay, from a humble[15] soil,
making him fit for scepter and kingdom
and for immortal life—if his own sin
was not to him the harsh cause of exile,
full of hard work and of hateful death.

    After the great God had rolled out the sky
supreme and spread the lower earth,
and fixed a barrier[16] amidst the waters,
dividing the upper and the lower ones;
and had commanded that unstable,   80
wandering element to gather into one,
and given names to the sea and earth,
and adorned the dryness with plants and herbs,
He turned to embellishing the world.[17]
So, to the day and the icy night He gave
the two major and most shining lamps,
and He adorned the first[18] bodies with
stars and with gold, with different figures
and beautiful turnings; and with perpetual
harmony made wonderful sights and courses.   90
Then, producing the various fish in
the wavy womb of fresh or salty waters
and the light, flying birds in the air,
the Creator said—and those words were
a certain command, an unbreakable law:

---

[11] Plural: his readers.

[12] These lines probably adapt Dante, *Purgatorio* 27: 140-142.

[13] "Aspra," cf. Dante, *Inferno* 1: 5. The adjective usually means sour, bitter, rough, harsh, etc.

[14] "Da sezzo," a rare expression coming from Dante, *Inferno* 7: 130.

[15] Recalling that *umile* (*humilis* in Latin) makes etymological reference to the soil.

[16] The firmament (*Genesis* 1: 6).

[17] In the story of creation, the Church Fathers—echoing the Rabbinical sages—distinguished between the "work of distinction" in days one to three and the "work of embellishment" in days four to six.

[18] Celestial.

"Let the Earth produce all kind of souls
of living beings[19] (let some of them support
their heavy bodily weight on four legs;
let some drag it on the ground and snake;
let her produce the offspring and children   100
of any other creeping beast), and with
predators, let her yield flocks and herds."
So, God made the wild earthly beasts
and the horned and the woolly herds of
the meek species, and those that slither
in oblique turns, adhering to the ground.[20]
But is this Ancient Mother truly living?
Has Earth a soul, so that she was longing
and ready for giving birth, like a woman?
Were the Manichees therefore right, proud   110
with vain *gnosis*, and right the old lies
of those who, philosophizing,[21] gave a mind
and spirit to this vast earthly mass?
A spirit that blows and penetrates her,
according to them, and feeds the sky
and the earth, and the beautiful, blazing
sphere of the sun, and the moon globe,
the golden stars, the large fields of air and sea;
in various fashions mixed with her vastness,
it stirs and moves her manifold limbs.   120

Those who dared dress the Earth with
a breathing soul,[22] or gave the world a mind
and made it a god—not simply a breathing,
living being, embracing all in itself—
ill understood those holy words of God
and twisted His sentence for the worse.[23]
The dry Earth had in fact no soul at all,
but He who commanded her also gave
her the power to produce new life.

---

[19] The etymological meaning of "animals," from Latin *anima*, soul.

[20] Cf. the list of animals in Milton, *Paradise Lost* 4: 340-352.

[21] The -ing form (gerund, *filosofando*, in Italian) already had a pejorative sense in Dante, *Paradiso* 29: 85-87. Such worldviews, duly updated, have become fashionable once again in the manifestation of diverse "New Age" formulations.

[22] In many languages—see Sanskrit, Hebrew, Greek, Latin—the word "soul and/or spirit" is linked to breath.

[23] Tasso uses the words *sentenza* and *torcere* that Dante used to describe theological controversies, see *Paradiso* 4: 55 and 29: 90.

When He said, "Let the grass germinate,   130
and also the green trunks be fruitful,"
she did not produce them as if already
keeping them hidden in her bosom.
Nor palm, oak, holm-oak, or nice cypress
did she yield unto the untilled soil,
as if drawing them out of her fertile womb;
but of all things that are or were made,
the Divine Word is the nature and life.
So, when the Lord said "germinate," He
meant in his sublime, divine speech: 140
"Let her not give that which she is pregnant with,
but let her acquire that which she has not,"
and the eternal Father gave her the force.
Similarly, He now commands her and says,
"Produce the soul," not meaning an innate
soul, but a power which He himself bestows
with his divine and wonderful voice.
He did not command the water like that;
He ordered it to produce the creeping
beasts *with* their souls, while He ordered   150
the Earth to give birth *to* living souls.[24]
God said so—if I understand it right—
for, upon those wet swimmers underwater,
He wanted to confer a less perfect life,
a less worthy nature; that is why in that
thick, impure and mixed[25] element they
enjoy far less sharp and pure senses.
Weak is their hearing, rough their sight,
absent their memory, unimpressed in their
inner sense are the images of fantasy;   160
they nurture no knowledge, no notion out
of experience; in such a coarse existence,
their flesh and belly are their only Lords.[26]

---

[24] This may look like a futile argument to us, but it has a long philosophical and theological history, from Democritus to St. Basil, as it is summarized in BB's footnotes. Through this distinction another premonitory sign of the theory of evolution (see line 154) will surface.

[25] Unlike the "pure" and "unmixed" air. From Aristotle, who supplies Tasso with his doctrine of sensual perception in this section (BB). We have here, besides, another clear example of the de-structured nature of the poem, only mildly following the sequence of days in *Genesis*.

227

While the Empress of the land animals
is the soul, to the extent that she is believed
to have a vast dominion and large dowry
of reason and of immortal minds.[27]
Their senses are perfect, sharply perceiving
present objects; the past leaves deeply
impressed traces, memories are not blurred,   170
nor uncertain. Their powers are lively,
with unambiguous voices they can express
the signs of their inner sentiments.
With merry, or sad, sorrowful sounds
they demonstrate happiness or show pain,
or they reveal their longing for food,
or voice the love that burns inside them
and cannot lie hidden in a bestial heart
under soft wool or any other veil of
hard bristle; of all which—the sheep's   180
bleats, the neighs, the snarls—are like marks
(like the barks and howls in the mountains
and woods, or by clear and running rivers,
and moos and roars) of inner sentiments.
A thousand more feelings and voices
can Nature show through such variations.
Whereas the wandering inhabitants of
the wavy kingdoms are not only dumb
but untamable; they avoid any familiarity
with us, never getting used to caresses   190
or kindness, nothing learning or taking
from humanity; they will forever shun
being partners of the Ruling Animal.
That way did God in the waters create
soul-equipped bodies, while on the earth
He rather made *souls ruling their bodies*.
Therefore the ox could know its owner,
the donkey recognized the humble manger
of its Lord,[28] but the fish does not recognize
its feeder—so deep, underwater, proves   200

---

[26] Implying a moral teaching on man, see *Philippians* 3: 19 and Christian tradition, e.g. Boethius and Dante's *Convivio*. In *The Last Battle*, C. S. Lewis will show Talking Animals reverting to plain animals.

[27] Tasso recognizes true intelligence in the superior mammals, such as horses and dogs.

[28] *Isaiah* 1: 3, traditionally read as a prophecy of Jesus' birth. Here with a pleasant witticism.

the stupor of slow and laborious senses.
A donkey can recognize a familiar voice,
and recognize the path it walks on too;
it even chanced to guide an errant man[29]
who got lost along an uncertain path.
And of a better and subtler hearing
—if here fame is true—no land animal
with such rough limbs will ever boast.
While in the camel, the exotic carrier
of heavy weights and ugly riders,[30] deep,   210
tenacious is the memory of injuries,
and strong its wrath, ready to take revenge.
Sometimes, having been beaten, it keeps
its anger hidden within for a long time,
as if it had subsided, then it draws it out,
thus rendering evil and the injuries back.
    Listen, all you, who—as if it were virtue—[31]
secretly feed the memory of offenses
with disdain and grudge and resentment!
Listen to this comparison[32] that you   220
apply to yourself by keeping your wrath
hidden like the still burning sparkles
buried under deceitful cold cinders:
catching fire again with dry wood
or tinder, they can suddenly flame
and renew the half-extinguished fire.
In such fashion a very proud soul was
produced in the brutes, and you follow
the example of the haughtiest beasts.
    But of the immortal soul created   230
in the beginning, we will speak later;
now I tell you about the animal soul.
The soul of the animal is life and blood;[33]
the blood condenses and turns into flesh,

---

[29] The prophet Balaam (*Numbers* 22: 22 ff.), but also possibly hinting at commonplace episodes in which a donkey may have helped its owner find his way again.

[30] Literally, "misshapen Africans." We will not try to gild the pill: this is plain racism.

[31] To take revenge of one's "injured merit" was a "duty" not only for Milton's Satan. The protagonists of Ariosto's and Tasso's poems of chivalry provide a good example. Not even Dante was immune, see *Inferno* 29: 19-36.

[32] That of the camel (lines 227-229), although Tasso interposes the simile of cinders.

[33] According to ancient physiology—the Bible, Aristotle, Galen—life was conveyed and operated through the blood.

and the flesh, finally decaying, dissolves
into earth. Therefore, mortal is the soul
of the wild beasts, or rather, I would say,
it is something "dead." Hear therefore
why God made the Earth produce
the soul of the living beings, and how   240
then the soul changes and turns into blood,[34]
the blood into flesh, the flesh into earth;
and in the same way, the earth will turn
back into flesh, then the flesh into blood
and the blood into soul[35]—thus you find out
that the animal soul is blood and earth.
Do not think that the animal soul may be
older than its body and so may survive
after the mortal body lies dead,
but understand the ever-changing shapes   250
and the varying cycles,[36] and meanwhile shun
the deafening chatter of quibblers
that[37] would better lie hidden in silence.
    Such people are not ashamed to say
that the soul, by which man reasons,
is the same which makes the dog bark
as it runs, and the ungodly[38] serpent hiss.
They imagine that they have passed through
many shapes: not only servants and kings,
with very different faces and limbs,   260
they have supposedly been, but charming
women, or sea fish, or plants, or bushes.[39]
So saying, they showed themselves to be more
mind-less and soul-less than a fish or tree.
    But among so many proud, sundry minds

---

[34] More precisely: the principle of life, contained in the male's sperm, supposedly modified the female's blood.

[35] Through nutrition and metabolism.

[36] Of matter.

[37] Syntactically referring to the chatter.

[38] Again a sort of "natural proneness" to sin.

[39] The belief in metempsychosis can be found in various religions and ancient philosophies, although it is sometimes improperly ascribed to Hinduism and Buddhism. BB highlights that "plants and bushes" did not belong to the list of possible incarnations, but that this novelty was based on Dante, *Inferno* 13. It should be added, in terms of literary sources, that this inclusion of *flora* goes back to Virgil, who (apparently) believed in metempsychosis *and* described the murder and metamorphosis of Polydorus into a plant in the *Aeneid*, which inspired Dante, Ariosto, and Tasso.

in those ancient times, no one appeared
who deemed the soul to be earth or mud.
By following the vestiges and signs
of motion or senses (untrustworthy guides)
some saw it as "spirit" or light air, 270
others as a thin fire and a quick flame,
others deemed it as an inborn humor,
or a smoking and mixed vapor from these;
as earth, no one. So the Ancient Mother—
the Earth, I say—who produces and bears
the animal souls as untilled seeds,
was therefore defrauded of her honor
by such proud, dispute-loving thinkers,
such discordant minds going in reverse.[40]

We, however, to the old, great Mother 280
pay due honor for her noble abundance
by calling the wild beast's breathing soul
her "daughter."[41] Now, it does not matter
if we dare affirm nothing, either
old or new, about the shape of the vast
Earth with irrefutable evidence,[42] as if
we may be fair judges on such a great issue.
According to some, its shape and figure is
that of a sphere; others,[43] seeing it differently,
imagine it like a cylinder, or like a disk. 290
Others[44] see it as a basket or barnyard,
empty and hollow in the middle, equally
polishing and embellishing it on each side.
And he[45] who, imagining, was abducted
to heaven, as he wrote in his Tuscan
verses, saw—or believed he saw—from up there

---

[40] "Ritrosi" as in Dante, *Purgatorio* 10: 123, where it is spelled *retrosi*.

[41] The Italian word *anima*, soul, is feminine.

[42] We still hear people parroting the legend according to which Columbus had to defend "his" idea that the Earth was a sphere; but the shape of our planet had been well known at least since the ancient Greeks. In Dante's *Convivio*, for example, the precise length of its diameter was supplied. But Tasso never takes anything for granted. On the other hand, William Blake will also argue that the Earth's shape depends on the way we look at it (*Jerusalem*, plate 83).

[43] Anaximander and Anaximenes (BB).

[44] Leucippus and Democritus (BB).

[45] Dante. Probably for the first time in literature, the author of the *Divine Comedy* appears in somebody else's poem as a character—and because of his *Paradiso*, not *Inferno*. See *Paradiso* 22: 135, 151.

this Earth that makes us so fierce: it was like
a base, contemptible-looking flowerbed,[46]
but he describes it as having round[47] form.
Still another,[48] both in its polar strips   300
and in the large, wide zone in the middle,
made it uninhabited and solitary,[49]
which he depicted as a dismal place,
horrid to see, while picturing the extreme
poles as buried under high snow and ice.
Because of the major belt[50] aflame,
he left only two zones[51] subject to the sun,
which never directly heats and warms them,
in the two hemispheres; and in each phase,
it shines more mildly with oblique beams.   310
One of them is where we live, limited
on both sides—within a very narrow space—
by perpetual cold or excessive heat;
the other zone, under another sky, hosts
barbarians bereaved of Bear and Plow.[52]

But the New Era discovers and shows
that each part of the Earth, icy or torrid,
hosts and feeds Man—this tough, enduring[53]
animal since his first earthly birth.
Now the inhabited Earth no longer   320
seems a drum[54], as had been taught by

---

[46] Dante wrote *aiuola*, i.e. a "small *aia*," a small farmyard or "threshing floor" as in the Longfellow version, but Tasso seems to interpret it in the current sense of the term, possibly having the geometrically arranged Renaissance gardens in mind (against which, see Milton, *Paradise Lost* 4: 241-242.)

[47] The term may mean a circle or a sphere. Dante anyway conceived the planet as a sphere; see line 325.

[48] Macrobius (BB), "he" in line 307.

[49] Before the discoveries of Renaissance explorers, only a small part of the Earth was thought to be able to host human life: the strip between the Arctic Circle and the Equator, plus a small section of Sub-Sahara Africa. The Southern hemisphere was conceived as being mostly occupied by the sea (see e.g. G. Sacrobosco, *La sfera*, 1230).

[50] The Equator.

[51] The two temperate zones.

[52] Cf. Dante, *Inferno* 26: 127-129 and *Purgatorio* 1: 23-24, "through imagination," and the actual reports of the explorers, whose facsimiles are collected in Luigi Firpo (ed.), *Colombo, Vespucci, Verazzano: Prime Relazioni di Navigatori Italiani sulla Scoperta dell'America* (The First Reports of Italian Navigators on the Discovery of America), Turin: UTET, 1966.

[53] "Costante" as in Dante, *Paradiso* 11: 70. An interesting definition of our species.

[54] *Timpano*, literally "eardrum," but according to Tasso' likely source here, Aristotle's *On the Heavens*, II, 13, 293b: "Some think that it [the earth] is spherical, others that it is flat

the great master of those who know,
nor does it look like a shield[55] to our eyes;
it rather turns around itself in a circle,
like a fruit, one of those we cut and open.
Not an island, as it does not lie inside
the great father Ocean, but encircles it,
as the New Era dares to affirm—which
sees too much, and therefore aims too low.[56]
Be this as it may, according to what reason   330
and senses can show in the nearest objects;
let us leave out its shapes, and not measure
its wide spaces all around like geometers;[57]
let us not proudly try to level ourselves
to the heavenly King's science and power.
He, in fact, held the Earth in His hand,
and with His hand measured the seas,
and all waters and the sky with His palm.[58]
Who placed awesome mountains on the scales,
yoked woods, and weighed rough cliffs?   340
Who holds the wide ring of the vast Earth,
and there placed—as small as locusts—[59]
its scattered inhabitants, and built the
high sky as a vault over His own chamber?
Who, if not the King who supports the globe?
Let us not state, vain with our pride,
how far the opaque and gloomy Earth
may cast and spread its freezing dark shadow;[60]
nor how it deprives the wandering moon
of splendor when it intercepts the sun,   350
or whether the Earth dims the beautiful
face of Venus,[61] darkening its brilliance.
But let us rather listen, in wonder,
to God's voice, which runs to and reaches

---

and drum-shaped." Later, in II, 14, 297a, Aristotle writes, "Its shape must necessarily be spherical" (JT). According to the *American Heritage Dictionary*, *Tympanum* in Medieval Latin means "eardrum," in Latin, "drum," from Greek *tumpanon*.

[55] And/or a turtle shell; the term *lorica* means both, cf. Loricates.

[56] Another interesting remark on his own times.

[57] "Qual geometra," cf. Dante, *Paradiso* 33: 133.

[58] From *Isaiah* 40: 12.

[59] Cf. *Numbers* 13: 33.

[60] The "cone of shade." In the following lines, eclipses are mentioned.

[61] Here called *Ciprigna*, i.e. the goddess of Cyprus; cf. Dante, *Paradiso* 8: 2.

all created things, and completes the world
in both its middle and extreme parts.[62]
    As a voluminous sphere or marble ball,
being struck and pushed by a strong hand,[63]
reaches a slope, and thence downward
goes, dragged by the very downhill   360
ground and by its own rotating shape,
thus rolling with faster and faster turns
until its run happens to be stopped by
a flat land, where it will now roll still;
so, moved by the sound of that holy Voice,
Nature proceeds, in depth permeating
everything that is born and decays,
preserving every progeny and spawn
equal to themselves until they reach their goal.[64]
Nature gives the horse a running   370
successor in its father's likeness;
of a bull, a hard-horned bull is born;
of a superb lion, with a hairy back
and having sharp claws, a lion is born.
Together with the lion, his rush and rage
are born,[65] and that magnanimous disdain
by which he passes a humble enemy
lying on the ground, without harming it.
Thence also comes its love for loneliness,
so that it shuns, nearly abhors, comrades,   380
wandering across deserted sands or high
forests in Mauritania or Numidia,
on its own, among hunts and perils;
or between Nestus and swift Achelous,[66]
where Europe used to give birth to lions.
And like a powerful and tough tyrant,
proud and indomitable by nature, it
wants no peers nor accepts food from others
to sate its cruel and profound hunger;
so much its disdainful taste[67] loathes   390

---

[62] Echoing several lines in *Wisdom*, ch. 7—an O. T. Greek book included in Catholic Bibles.

[63] The example comes from St. Basil (BB), but also will be used by Galileo to describe the act of creation.

[64] A somehow Linnaean insight into extinctions, cf. line 385.

[65] One of Tasso's main natural concerns: behaviorism.

[66] Two rivers in Greece.

the remains of a rotten, unconquered prey.
Nature also gave it such a wide throat,[68]
and so resonant is its frightening voice,
that its powerful roars fill the nimblest
and fastest-running animals with fear,
so as to stop and catch them, stunned.
But after a meal,[69] it is happy and playful;
celebrating, it frolics with its friends,
not fearing or suspecting anything.
Then, growing heavy in its old age   400
and slow in hunting, the old fierce beast
dares dangerously attack man's towns
and stalks men among their very walls.
But this beast, so horrid and fierce, even
when it is most proud and, becoming
more savagely cruel, inflames its rage,
fears and shuns the flame of a torch;
dismayed, it also flees from the rooster,
frightened by it the more if the beautiful
whiteness of the bird's spread wings shines bright.[70]   410
    While the panther, an impetuous beast
that can suddenly stir, has a body matching
the various motions of its quick soul, being
equipped with slim and flexible limbs.[71]
And painted with spots, the beautiful
leopard displays its variegated[72] coat,
and hiding its fierce nature, with its painted
appearance it thus succeeds in alluring
the simplest and most imprudent beasts
and catches them: treacherous fraud   420
is more useful to it than running fast
or jumping quickly after its wild prey.
Meanwhile, the she-bear is lazy and slow,

---

[67] "Disdegnoso gusto," from Dante, *Inferno* 13: 70; noticeably bringing back the word *gusto* from its metaphoric sense to its literal sense, because in Dante it referred to suicide.

[68] "Canne," plural, as if this lion were as frightening as Dante's Cerberus (*Inferno* 6: 27).

[69] Quoting—and in contrast with—Dante, *Inferno* 1: 99.

[70] From Lucretius (BB). Tasso combines modern science and old "legends," in the etymological sense of *legenda*, i.e. nice stories "to be read."

[71] Corresponding to the description of the *lonza* in Dante, *Inferno* 1: 32-35. The Medieval term may also indicate a leopard.

[72] "Variata," Dante termed it *gaietta* or *gaetta* (depending on codices) in *Inferno* 1: 42. The symbolic meaning of Dante's *lonza* has been thoroughly debated by scholarship. Tasso's lines entail fraud rather than lust.

with secluded habits, hiding in high places.
With such a shape she cloaks and dresses
her fierce soul:[73] a body rough and heavy,
almost an indistinct, ill-arranged mass;
and inside a cold, horrid-looking cavern
she dwells, here hibernating and sleeping.
But later inflamed in fury, feverish,   430
she seeks harsh vengeance for every injury:
against the weapons she hurls and defends
herself in the mounts, adding wound upon wound,[74]
as if running towards voluntary death.
With her tongue, however, she skillfully
shapes her misshapen cubs,[75] like a forger.
    What about you, rougher than a wild bear?
Your children's uncultivated, coarse habits,
so long as they are of tender age—
won't you shape, polish, adorn them?   440
Are your words sweet in promoting virtue,
or pungent and harsh while being pitiless?[76]
    To her own wounds, besides, the she-bear,
as resourceful Nature teaches her,
knows where to find a cure to recover:
when most seriously wounded, she uses
mullein as a bandage, and that dry herb
wipes up and cleanses the bleeding limb.
A snake whose eyesight is feeble and dim
feeds on fennel,[77] and thus expels   450
that bad humor that mists its eyes.
The eagle too, by using rustic lettuce,
strengthens its weak and failing sight.
The turtle, when the snake's cruel poison
is killing it, while the absorbed venom
snakes inside,[78] looks for health and life

---

[73] An animal's body is the "embodiment" of its soul and "character": a Platonic approach that will surface again in Schopenhauer's philosophy, see *On the Will in Nature*, ch. 2.

[74] Bear hunting is exalted as a proof of courage in *Gerusalemme Conquistata*.

[75] Here called *orsacchi*; *orsatti* in Dante (*Inferno* 19: 71); their "sum," i.e. *orsacchiotti*, in current Italian. The habit of shaping cubs with their tongues was also ascribed to lions, with a Christological allegory.

[76] After—duly—defending the rights of parents, Tasso—more unusually—defends the rights of children.

[77] Cf. Milton, *Paradise Lost* 9: 580-581.

[78] These verses are also interesting from a linguistic viewpoint. Tasso, as he already did on previous occasions, plays on the two meanings of one word (*serpe*: a snake, it snakes); and,

from the wild marjoram, not in vain.
A sick fox, to drive away death that
looms over it, against illness uses
two droplets[79] from a resinous pine.   460
While the mountain goat, when it is stabbed
right in its flank by the hard iron point
of a feathered arrow, knows to heal itself
by virtue of the art that Nature teaches;
and by eating dittany,[80] the cruel dart
comes out of the deep, dangerous wound.
A weak, sick lion will greedily try
to get a monkey for its fierce meal;[81]
a leopard will drink goat's blood instead,
and a deer will feed on olive twigs.   470
    And you, of the languid, dying soul,
will you not find a cure? Do you not know
the true medicine? Will you not savor
the vital juice of the sacred books?
    The signs of weather are also taught[82]
by Mistress Nature: the sky turning
from hot to cold, and from clear to cloudy,
or threatening a storm or twister,
so that to forecast the rains and the winds
and the turbid, whistling tempests   480
man's mind often proves to be less able.[83]
At the approach of winter, the sheep
see to it that they eat abundant food,
as if foreseeing the shortage to come
brought on by the cold and darkest season.
The oxen, enclosed in the coldest weather
in their warm—albeit filthy—cowsheds,
as soon as spring comes back to us,
stirred by an inborn and certain sense,
they stretch their hairy and tamed necks   490

---

vice versa, he uses two different terms, a strictly Medieval one (*tosco*) and a still currently used synonym (*veleno*), to indicate the same thing (venom).

[79] "Lacrimette," literally: little tears; from Dante, *Purgatorio* 5: 107.

[80] One of the most famous—and legendary—medicinal herbs, very often employed in poetry, from Virgil (to cure Aeneas) to Tasso himself in his Jerusalem-poems (to cure Godfrey of Bouillon).

[81] "Fiero pasto," a bit ironically from Dante, *Inferno* 33: 1.

[82] Cf. *Matthew* 16: 2-3.

[83] Less able than Nature and animals taught by her.

beyond the mangers, and gaze longingly
for the air outside, tepid and clear.[84]
And again, the hedgehog in its den
engineers two entrances to breathe:
one looking on to the cloudy Auster,[85]
the other on to the cold North wind,
so, when it fears Boreas'[86] fierce spirit,
it plugs the opening facing North; but
if an African wind brings a disturbance,
it closes the hole in that direction   500
and hides itself on the opposite side.

Here to our senses it clearly appears that
God's sublime Providence everywhere
sweeps, filling and adorning the Whole;
and the more perfect and more sublime things
will not make Him ignore the lowest ones;
even in the vilest beasts He will stir
a feeling for the future, letting them
provide[87] for their needs. And will only man
mind and pay attention to the present,   510
without thinking of his future existence?
Let him see the rare, praiseworthy example
of the ingenious and hardworking ant,[88]
that in summer puts away the food to eat
in the cold winter. However faraway the
icy days of the harsh season are, the black
throng does not lazily stop nor does it
slow down, it indeed gets accustomed
to toil; in the sunburnt fields the work
is not less fervent than the hour and day,   520
until the wheat is all stocked in their nests.
With their nails,[89] they cut and saw the precious

---

[84] A charming description; arguably superior to Dante' celebrated pastoral scene in
Purgatorio 3: 79 ff.
[85] The South wind.
[86] The North wind.
[87] Keeping the link between *Provvidenza* and *provvedere* (Providence / to provide, attend,
take care). The dimension of *future* intrinsically implied in the so-called "animal instincts"
has been studied by Schopenhauer, *op. cit.*
[88] *The* exemplary animal in western literature—together with the bee, that Tasso has already
praised. Here, he reworks and expands his sources, St. Basil and Plutarch (BB). But the
society of ants may also be seen as a nightmare, see H. G. Wells' *The First Men in the
Moon.*
[89] Actually, ants use their mandibles as working tools.

fruits,[90] still wet, so as to have them dry
in the sun. Waiting for the sky to clear up,
they forecast the best days in this way.
When they expose the grains to the sunlight,
no rain will be dropping from dark clouds
—they provide a sure sign of fine weather.
They put away that dried harvest in their
tiny cells, then save and divide it   530
as most diligent keepers and dispensers.
This occurs as the sun burns the fields,
but the round moon also can admire
their nocturnal labors from above:
those serene and hot nights are thus
taken away from sweet rest, from still sleep,
and added to long, unending toil.[91]
Into a tiny body, such industry of
an ingenious, untiring spirit was
put by Nature, the wondrous Mother;   540
or, rather, Nature's supreme Father[92] did
give them such virtue as a rare gift.

How great are your created works, how
sublime, how wonderful, eternal Master!
All your works that You have made
with your infinite wisdom and art![93]
We also, the grandchildren of old Adam,
as gifts and dowries from Nature
have many personal powers, born
together with the naked infant from   550
the same seed, out of the mother's cloisters.
No law, no art, and no ancient tradition
or present example shows and teaches
it all[94] to the still simple, confused[95] soul,

---

[90] Grains.

[91] Modern field research has scaled this down. And yet, in this long description of the ants' habits, an intriguing detail is missing, namely the exchanges of communication, as reported by Dante in *Purgatorio* 26: 34-36.

[92] Tasso is likely afraid of (being accused of) pantheism. Nevertheless, he does not strike out the proceeding line.

[93] Paraphrasing *Psalm* 104: 24.

[94] Those "powers," "dowries," tendencies, inclinations, etc.

[95] The umbrella word *vaga* is employed. Here its translation as "confused" comes from Tasso's source in this section, i.e. Dante's anthropology as developed in *Purgatorio* 16-17 (see esp. 16: 87-88 and 17: 127). On the other hand, *vaghezza* will appear again in line 556,

which plays like a little child in soft limbs:
its own tendency and desire incline
and move it with a friendly feeling.
Who teaches us to hate[96] fever and the
illnesses that follow, making humankind
weak and sick? And to abhor death,[97]   560
even without any teacher or counselor?
Not art, not reason, not custom or law,
but it is our nature, cajoling and sweet,
which makes us the closest friends of ourselves,
and teaches and dictates all this to us.
Here is the reason why the noble soul
shuns vice, and voluntarily flees it
without any more drive, teaching or habit.
Seeing how beautiful Virtue is, it[98] falls
in love with her, then seeks and follows her,   570
so that shunning vice is the first move
by which it turns its steps towards heaven.
Each vice is an inward evil, a sickness of
the weak soul, burning with vain desires.
And virtue, forever opposed to vice,
is the soul's health, therefore constant
and firm in all its works and duties.
Therefore justice is dear to everyone,
so is prudence, and grateful and praised is
modesty;[99] and fortitude, even more   580
wonderful, the virtue of unconquered souls
—in spite of ungodly and proud fortune—
is honored and worshiped: statues, arches,
sacred altars and temples are erected to it.
Such are the faithful and dearest friends
of the well-trained[100] Soul, who adorns her limbs
with them more than she does with health.

---

in that case in parallel with "desire." Tasso makes the most of the polysemy of the term: desire is simply the other side of spiritual uncertainty.

[96] In the Hebrew and Scholastic sense of shunning, as opposed to "loving" i.e. tending towards something.

[97] Cf. Milton, *Paradise Lost* 11: 466 ff. for Raphael's explanation of Death.

[98] Both *anima* and *virtù* are feminine, so the erotic metaphor is a bit forced. Dante (*Purgatorio* 16: 88-90 and 17: 91 ff.) describes the love story of the soul and *God*. In fact, in line 585, Tasso will turn to "friendship."

[99] That is temperance. The four classical "cardinal virtues" are listed.

[100] "Domesticata," literally: tamed, with reference to its "wild" side.

Love your fathers, O you devoted[101] children,
and you, devoted fathers, love your children
without arousing the youths' resentment,   590
as Nature both teaches and forces you.
If the lioness, a frightening beast, loves
her own cubs, and if the fierce wolf
defends its cubs by fighting for them
till death,[102] how can a cruel human father,
crueler than beasts, despise his offspring?
Can there be such great hardness, hate,
and oblivion of nature in man's heart?
    Oh, the sweet, sublime strength of maternal
love! It even bends the fierce tigress,[103]   600
and from her prey—that she, already tired,
pursued, panting—suddenly turns her
back to defend her beloved offspring.
And when she finds out that her dear
cubs have been kidnapped from her den,
she immediately runs after the tracks
imprinted by the hunter, who carries them
along as precious prey. He flees at full speed
headlong, riding his fast-running steed;
and to evade the swift feline, since   610
no other escape or trick will help,
with fraud based on a shrewd device, he
baffles the angry one and saves himself.
He, in fact, throws a sphere of clear,
transparent glass right before her eyes,
so that, deluded by a deceiving image,
she mistakes it for a cub, slows down,
and cools down her fury, longing to seize
her sweet child in that lonely land
and carry it back to her cold den.   620
After having been stopped by the deceit
of those false features, she sets out again
much faster, quickened by her own ire,
after the still fleeing predator—now

---

[101] "Pietosi" in the sense of Latin *pietas*, the devotion to one's duties, especially towards one's family and God. These verses summarize *Colossians* 3: 20-21.
[102] Perhaps with a hint at Dante, *Inferno* 33: 29-36.
[103] A widespread legend, but Tasso specifically follows St. Ambrose's *Exameron* (BB), turning it into a "cinematic" pursuit.

she is at his heels in a towering rage.
But he, again, with a deceiving object,
a mendacious mirror, slows down
the tiger's run, and finally vanishes.
But no oblivion will make the mother
forget her solicitous care and ready   630
love: the unhappy beast wanders around
that vain and deceiving image, almost
trying to nurse her cubs with her milk.
This is how the great wild cat, cheated,
loses in one fell swoop her dear offspring
and vengeance, that is so wanted, so sweet.[104]

If so strongly can a tigress love her cubs,
and so can the mate of the proud lion,
as well as the ravenous bear, what wonder
would it be if you could see love   640
in the meek and innocent mother sheep
and in the wild and ever-fleeting hind
for their tender, newborn children.
In a great flock, among the many sheep
the simple-minded lamb, jumping lightheartedly,
comes out of the closed fold, and from afar,
he soon recognizes his mother's voice
and, looking for the sweet springs of
his milk, he quickens his wobbly pace
to where the udders are that he longs for: 650
finding them empty, he is satisfied.
He does not flee from others, more heavy and full,
but ignores them, looking and yearning
for the food he needs only from his mother;
and the mother recognizes her little,
sweet baby son's bleat among thousands.
In this fashion, the lack of true reason
is made up for by a powerful sense that,
by nature, is well developed in sheep,[105]

---

[104] BB reports a verse by Juvenal as the source of this not-very-Christian sentence, but Juvenal's concept is quite different: "Vengeance is a more joyful good than life itself." Dante provides a better grounding, see *Purgatorio* 20: 94-96, in the circle of greed, also denouncing the use of deception (line 64) and the decline of family values (lines 82-84, 104). The "Tale of the Tiger," far from being mere folklore, includes all the basic elements of Tasso's worldview: action, strength, heroism, tragedy, illusion, failure, and elegy.

and perhaps keener than our intellect. 660
    The solitary doe, at the time of delivery,
shows more skill and shrewdness than any other
animal that has any seed or share
of foresight and of resourceful reason.
Therefore, rather to the parental care[106]
of humans she will give her newborn fawns,
fearing predators. The craggy cliffs,
the wild dens, the untilled fields are left
behind by the timid beast; but where
there are tracks imprinted by human feet 670
on the paths they tread or run through,
she trustfully exposes her newborn,[107]
and there also feeds on *siselian*[108] herb.
Sometimes she shelters in a cowshed
away from a predator's fangs and claws;
or seeks a hard cradle among broken rocks
where only one small opening exists,
so she can watch and defend her fawns;
she gives them milk from four udders
—or two, in those females with which 680
Nature proved sparing on nourishment.
Since this animal has no bitter gall,[109] she
enjoys a very long life, and sometimes
her skin appears white, and in this old-age
color she is venerated by friendly people,
as that doe who once used to wander,
untied and free, in a secluded corral,
after being freed by her happy king.[110]
Fame also depicts and portrays
a renowned doe with antlers of gold,[111] 690
and puts a necklace around her neck.

---

[105] Indicated by the standard poetic periphrasis *umil gregge*, humble flock. The idea of super-developed animal senses which can practically attain the same results of reason in man is typical of Tasso.

[106] Again *pietade*, or *pietà* as in current Italian, in the sense of Latin *pietas*.

[107] "Il suo portato," from Dante, *Purgatorio* 20: 24, significantly referring to the Infant Jesus.

[108] A herb Pliny the Elder more precisely called *seselis* (BB).

[109] One of the four basic "humors" in ancient medicine.

[110] The Etruscan king Capi, the founder of the city of Capua in Southern Italy (BB).

[111] Antlered, but a female specimen; to catch her was one of the toils of Heracles. Misled by other zoological enterprises of the Greek hero, BB wrongly claims Hercules killed her. The animal was sacred to Artemis.

Without the honor of branching antlers,
without this innate, superb ornament[112]
does were left by Nature, a mean mother,
more liberal and generous with stags,
which often renew their own: leaving
the old ones on the ground (their own weight
makes them fall, dense and full), they
develop new ones on their proud foreheads.
Every year, they will add a new, long   700
outgrowth to their branching antlers;
and sometimes, the shape-following ivy
sprouts out of them, leafing upwards.[113]
Oh, the marvels of Nature,[114] increasing
the beauty and glory of a timid beast;
yes, timid, fearful, and cowardly,
in spite of its fierce and proud appearance,
armed with its long and useless weapons!
Its big heart, such as Nature shaped it,
does not harbor any pride nor proud   710
boldness, but faint-heartedness and fear.
As in the case of the most timid hare,
the deer's diluted blood is poor in fibers,
so that it does not clot and condense,
sticky and strong; it rather looks like milk
coagulating, rennet-less, and flows away.
But sometimes,[115] burnt and spurred by love,
in the season in which the warmed-up Earth
opens up her womb, and the lazy ice
soon vanishes, and the snow melts   720
letting the torrents run turbid and swift,
the stag's heart awakes his warrior spirit,
and he battles, and he dares to attack,
if he chances to meet another in a wood.
Then, not only the tigers and wolves,
the misshapen bears, the painted lynx,[116]

---

[112] The antlers.

[113] Apparently, many kinds of things can sprout out of a deer's forehead: a cherry tree (see the eighteenth-century *Adventures of Baron Munchausen*), a cross (see the Medieval legend of St. Eustace)…

[114] The paradoxical nature of Nature is a keynote of the Renaissance worldview. Here maybe with an echo from *I Corinthians* 12: 23?

[115] The following set of sections is quite thorny because Tasso keeps mixing sources and situations. Especially puzzling is the constant shift from male to female deer.

and the boar—that, rubbing its hairy flanks
against a trunk, applies a coarse armor
of sticky mud to its hard shoulders—
but the fierce mother too, longing for love,   730
roams, forgetting her helpless children,
which are still lacking claws[117] and a coat;
even the most timid ones are now driven
by sharp spurs, burning with inner fury.
An unbounded fury drives and leads
—beyond the roaring Ascanius,[118] the ridges
of high Ida, the Euphrates, the Taurus—
the randy mothers of the bellicose herd.
They cross mountains, they swim across rivers,
they spring among precipices, and rocks,   740
and deep valleys. Not, O Sun, towards
your birthplace, nor towards Eurus,
but Boreas and Caurus,[119] and the direction
whence Auster darkens the sky with rain.
Here they finally distil a fluid poison,
called *hippomanes*[120] in the old parlance
of ancient shepherds; often gathered
by cruel, ungodly stepmothers,[121] together
with malignant herbs, then used and mixed
while uttering non-innocent words.   750
So powerful was love and the sweet zeal
in their fierce hearts for further children,
so ardent the longing for wanton mating!
By nature, lust stirs and becomes inflamed,
and leads, in the horrid forests, not only
the wildest beasts but even the leaders[122]
of the most docile herds to hard battles.
Waiting[123] in suspense on uncertain duels,

---

[116] Dante, *Inferno* 16: 108.

[117] Maybe—as, above, he mixed up bats and owls—Tasso here confuses passages referring to deer (which remain the main subject, see line 738, etc.) together with the descriptions of a different species, maybe lions.

[118] A river in Bithynia, in the Northern part of current Turkey. The places mentioned in line 737 are more famous.

[119] The NW wind.

[120] Literally, "mare's mania/folly," i.e. estrus.

[121] Witches, as in 3: 1038. Cf. *Inferno* 20: 123, where, however, Dante omits the basic element of formulas.

[122] Suddenly, the text focuses on stags again.

248

that fill and shed the males' hairy chests and
proud foreheads with wounds and blood,   760
are the silent wives and antlered throngs,
waiting for which command, which victorious
and haughty guide they have next to follow.
To separate such fierce fighters, their very
masters[124] do not dare, and gaze astonished.

    If the love for children, or the love that joins
a lustful couple for procreation, can
be so strong in a feral heart and tough soul,
how much can it be in those whom our human
reason and arrogance make proud
and selfish? What wonder, therefore, if once   770
and twice, indeed three and four times,
for one and the same reason, there burned
an inextinguishable fire of ancient hate?
Asia and, against it, proud Europe,[125]
armed with steel and furor for war, mixing
slaughter and ruin and devastating
fires, filled land and sea with all this.

    In the trusty dog,[126] if you mark it well,
where reason is missing, sense abounds: 780
what the loftiest minds, by philosophizing
in the ancient schools, could hardly grasp
about the subtle art of the syllogisms
—weaving various figures in various
fashions with them, in entangled knots—
precisely this, I say, a dog immediately
and easily learns by his own nature.
In fact, detecting the traces of footprints
of a timid hare, or perhaps a deer,
the dog finally comes where the path   790
divides itself into more paths; and he

---

[123] To get a text making sense, it is necessary to add a period at the end of line 757, and to edit *sospesi* (literally, "hanging," masculine) into *sospese* (feminine: both *spose*, wives, and *torme*, throngs, in line 761).

[124] The stags who taught the younger deer to fight; cf. the "unstoppable" duels between the strongest knights.

[125] From the Trojan War to the Crusades. In *Gerusalemme Conquistata*, Tasso presents nearly all the world's peoples—Vikings to (Asian) Indians—taking part in the First Crusade, on both fronts, turning it into a "clash of civilizations."

[126] BB discovered that among the sources of this section there was a "forbidden" book, i.e. an esoteric one: Valerian's *Comments on the Egyptian Hieroglyphs*, published in 1556. Another intelligent dog will be described in lines 845 ff.

keeps roaming about their entrances,
scenting the ways or the scattered prints.
Meanwhile, he does seem to syllogize
to himself: "The wandering wild beast
went in that or the other direction,
or took that other one, and there runs.
But it did not follow this or that path,
therefore it hurries up along the third."
Thus infers the dog by deducing;   800
his quick sense replaces a prolonged art,
by which he rejects errors and finds the truth.
No greater truths did the various schools
discover by writing, with a stylus or a reed
on the sands of the coast or in the dry dust,
the different forms of argumentation.
Out of three things that were submitted,
they, "sentencing to death" two as false,
approved the third, therein was imprinted
the truth, which, however, would be deleted   810
by the blowing wind, by the swelling waves.
The arrogant minds of men, of the proud
and wretched mortals, do not realize
that dust and the thinnest sands are
the basis of truth that man's mind finds
without God's soul-enlightening light;
so that, in the darkening of a brief day,
"truth" will be dispersed by the wind and sea.[127]
Even though the Ancient Age[128] boasted
of its sacred signs and lofty pillars   820
in which the noble arts were displayed
in that adorned temple sacred to Hermes,[129]
and other pillars are famous and celebrated,
in which the Ancients tried to preserve
a thousand old memories safe from floods
and fires, and yet they collapsed long ago...
in each case, after the turnings of time,
no trace or dust heap is left of them;

---

[127] Cf. Dante's final revelation in *Paradiso* 33: 64-66, with the snow and the Sybil instead of the sand.

[128] Again from an esoteric source, Iamblichus' *Mysteries of the Egyptians* (BB). As already mentioned, during the Renaissance the first attempts to decode the hieroglyphs were made.

[129] Hermes *Trismegistos*, i.e. the "Thrice Great," was considered the author of esoteric texts.

a long night hides those names and works.
But[130] against the swift hounds' senses   830
the timid animals have senses and skills,
and they are often wont to mar their
own footprints so that their hidden
getaway may leave no clear sign behind;
they even know the winds and breezes
that to the sniffing hounds could carry
their well-known smell, thus betraying them.
So God's Providence flows and stretches
everywhere: it sometimes takes care
of the hasty fleeing of the timorous   840
beasts, and often[131] gives them as a due quarry
to the brave ones, thus honoring the feral
virtue with the spoils[132] of the vanquished,
and feeds their strength with that plunder.
   But what memory is as strong and firm
as that of the trusty dog, sometimes?
Or, who may deserve a higher praise
for having a grateful and steady heart
than the trusty dog, who fiercely dares
drive the evil thief out of one's home,   850
thus preventing the night robber's crimes?
He is ready to fight and die together
with his dear owner, or *for* his dear
owner, at least, and to save his life by
offering himself to a glorious death.
Often, before the high, superb seats
of the severe judges, the faithful dog
even accused the culprits by barking,
and often that speechless witness was
deemed trustworthy; and justly the feared,   860
horrible sentence falls on the criminal.
   Once upon a time in Antioch, they say,[133]
in a lonely place, a man was murdered

---

[130] A surprising resumption. Day 6 shows the poem's "messy" style in an even clearer way than the preceding Days.

[131] "Sometimes . . . often": quite significantly, the odds are not even.

[132] In two senses, as *spoglie* also means skins.

[133] The anecdote comes from St. Ambrose (BB), but Tasso could find here something very congenial to his worldview: the intelligence of animals and his own passion for detective stories. In *Gerusalemme Liberata*, he builds a whole "case" on the armor of Rinaldo, who is reported murdered, with evidence, witnesses and all.

—he had his most trusty dog with him—
at that uncertain hour,[134] between darkness
and light, that noisily[135] divides the still night
from the day and calls the weary mortals
to their work, or else calls them back
from their labors to a friendly rest.
The murderer, a certain mercenary,   870
was a cruel man of blood and hate,[136]
and meant to hide that hideous crime
under the dark and tenebrous cloak
of the cold and caliginous night;
then, covered with the same cloak, he went
to a more distant and safer place.
The murdered body lay in its dark blood;
the face looked pale, dirty, death-stricken.
People gathered around to have a look.
The dog, wailing in a tearful way,   880
mourned the horrible death of his owner.
Meanwhile, he who had hence left after
infecting himself with that cruel deed,
in order not to rouse suspicion and get
the faith of innocence, came back there
to talk—really, a brazen-faced[137] fellow!—
about the atrocious case to others:
so great can fraud be in human minds!
Joining that thick and wide circle of
various people, he, looking distressed,[138]   890
came near the prone murdered man.
Then the trusty dog, suddenly stopping
his miserable, sorrowful wails, took
the frightening weapons of vengeance,[139]
seized and held him with his sharp fangs;
and once again murmuring miserably,
he made all bystanders shed painful tears.
To make his wonderful act trustworthy,
the dog seized only that man, not letting go

---

[134] The twilight, either at dawn or at sunset.
[135] Because of roosters crowing and/or bells ringing, etc.
[136] From Dante, *Inferno* 24: 129, also referring to an unmasked robber.
[137] "Con sicura fronte," literally "with a sure forehead" in Dantesque parlance.
[138] "Pietoso in vista," again a Dantean expression. Tasso gives this anecdote an epic tone (the quotes from Dante are obviously missing in St. Ambrose's text).
[139] Cf. above, line 636.

of him nor loosening his strong bite.   900
At last the killer, disturbed by such
clear sign, could no longer unload on others
the heavy sin of his own hate and fury,
of that serious and injurious crime,
nor uproot the suspicion of his evil
deed, now fixed in everybody's minds;
he might perhaps hit back, but not defend
himself from a dumb, barking[140] accuser.
He is caught, tied, and sentenced to death.
    Who may ever tell the dogs' ancient   910
marvels and the rare, famous examples?[141]
And show them buried in one grave with
their owners? Or honor those who, next
to their owners, burned on one pyre? Or exalt
their inborn, unfailing trustworthiness
in war, among thick formations and arms?
Who will, one day, dedicate the blood-stained
spoils of the killed tyrants and enemies
to the dogs' glory, and in the living rock
carve them, and inscribe the deeds and names   920
of those heroes who, triumphing over
long wars and long exiles together with
their trusty friends,[142] finally traveled back
to their noble homeland amid the sea?
All this was well known in Ancient Greece,
enclosing many islands in its watery bosom.
Not to speak of the dogs' victories, old
and new, among tall peaks and mountain woods;
of their heads being cut off and impaled;[143]
and of the hides of fierce, horrid beasts[144]   930
hanging on the walls as hunting trophies.
    But now, how could I leave you behind,
or tell—condensed and in brief—about you:
O fast steeds and illustrious carriers
of the knights in the glorious wars;
you, in dusty paddocks and vast fields,

---

[140] Lines 907-908: two Baroque oxymora in a row.
[141] Again drawing on Valerian (BB).
[142] "Fidi amici," a common phrase to indicate dogs. *Fido* is the "classic" name of dogs in Italian stories.
[143] Dogs' heads placed on top of military labara; from Valerian (BB).
[144] Chased and killed with the help of hounds.

255

their comrades in both honors and risks!
You are true warriors: springing forward
at the clear sound of a blaring trumpet,
you partake in the blood-stained pursuit,   940
in the golden spoils, in the honored palms.
This was not only seen in the older[145] Pisa
during the Games, and on famed Olympus,
but in Thebes and Troy too, in those areas
and times which were named after Olympus;[146]
and in Marathon and Leuctra, on both sides
of the plains and mounts of noble Pharsalia
—everywhere carrying your young riders
to the battlefields on your strong backs,
like a new wonder[147] never seen before,   950
you looked like the tall, biform centaurs.
Who could list, as you well deserve, your
spoils and qualities, your toils and merits?
Not only did you shed abundant blood
in noble deeds alongside your wounded Lords,
but, if one may believe so, you also shed
abundant tears, with human sentiments,
mourning their dire, untimely deaths.[148]
You shared both the triumphs and the graves
with the kings and the heroes of old;   960
you gave the name to that famous, buried
city,[149] whose fame still resounds nowadays.
You were not the proud offspring born
of the earth, struck off by a trident,[150]
you were not shaped by an earthly hand;
but the sublime call of the eternal Lord,
more blaring than a trumpet, caused your
birth even before His powerful hand
shaped Adam on earth, out of earth.

---

[145] Again, to distinguish it from the Italian city.

[146] But see BB: "Tasso misunderstands. The Olympic Games—that were held every four years—were named after the city of Olympia, not after Mount Olympus."

[147] "Mostro" in the Latin sense of *monstrum*; though, in this case, both senses apply. This is the standard explanation on the origin of the myth of centaurs. In *Purgatorio* 32: 96, Dante uses the Latinizing adjective *biforme*, two-shaped, to describe the Griffin, a symbol of Christ as God and Man.

[148] Compare Achilles' horses in the *Iliad*.

[149] Bucephala, in India—now Gialalpur—named after Alexander the Great's horse Bucephalus (BB).

[150] Poseidon's, according to Greek mythology.

That Voice, which sounds clearer and   970
clearer through Nature, His obedient servant,
perpetuates your progeny and name.
But let that proud, warlike spirit in you,
nearly equalizing your honor with man's,
be humbled by the heavenly King's choice;
He who, among a thousand olive and palm
branches, deigned to ride a donkey,[151]
leaving you to the glorious emperors,
the noble kings, the undefeated chiefs.[152]
Thus, let grandeur and magnificence   980
and any other earthly, sparkling pomp
yield the highest honor to humbleness
and to that humble, tranquil patience
which prepares the meek's shoulders,[153]
and whose most sublime seat is a manger,
therefore beside the heavenly Sovereign,
who has no horse (or its deceiving image)[154]
in the sky among fabled and vain honors.

    But... what study or desire leads me astray,
making me late along the planned route?[155]   990
Let us go back to admiring the providence
and art of the last works created by God.
Providence it was, in fact, not luck or chance,[156]
that made the proud and untamed progeny
of the cruelest and less docile beasts nearly
infertile, limiting them to few specimens.
The other way round, it made the fleeting
offspring of the timid species very fertile,
among which a varied, abundant game can
easily be hunted. This is why the shy   1000
hare usually begets a very large
number of whelps. Each time in birth

---

[151] *Matthew* 21: 1-8, but with an eye on Catholic liturgy: olive (much more seldom palm, in the Western countries) branches are still currently used in the Mass of Palm Sunday, one week before Easter.

[152] An experienced courtier, Tasso lists the rulers in hierarchical order, with God at the top.

[153] To carry the cross as Christ did.

[154] BB interprets it as the coats of arms. The words "sky" and "fabled" may also suggest the figures and mythological origins of some stars and constellations, e.g. Pegasus.

[155] Dante, probably with a hidden purpose, said something similar in *Purgatorio* 29: 97-105 and 33: 136-141, but Tasso can hardly be believed to have a problem with length in this "wild" poem.

[156] Nor the blind law of natural selection, he would perhaps add today.

the mountain goat delivers pairs,
while the wild sheep is often pregnant
with twins simultaneously conceived,
so that their stocks shall be preserved
against predators. On the other hand,
the fierce lioness, barely fertile, conceives
but one cub, born by ripping her belly
with its claws; in such a fashion,   1010
killing its mother while being delivered,
its birth makes a blood-splattering passage.[157]
The viper also will pay a cruel reward
to its mother, coming out by gnawing
the very bosom of the pregnant snake.
Moreover, if you examine the various parts
of the various beasts,[158] you will discover
the master art of the eternal Maker,
who made nothing needless or lacking in them.
It was He who adapted sharp teeth,   1020
on both sides of the mouth, to the fierce
predators feeding on sanguineous[159] meals,
while only one side of the mouth is filled with
teeth in those that eat from different pastures
upon the green fields: He gave rumination
to the easy-living and harmless species.
Throats and skins and bellies and bosoms
and the networks[160] with other uncertain parts
in which the food is gathered and flows,
and that which is pure and light matter feeds   1030
the various limbs, and the impure-and-heavy
finds an open way so as to be expelled:[161]
these are not vain, useless devices at all,
but indispensable; the use and pros of each
are apparent—preserving the lives,
either long or brief, of the earthly beasts.

---

[157] A nonsensical datum coming from St. Basil (BB); at its very least, it contradicts line 592. But Tasso probably likes the "splatter" side of it, on which he insists. It also echoes Dante, *Inferno* 13: 102.

[158] Again, with a modern scientific approach: comparative anatomy. Mark the now technical term "to adapt" in line 1020.

[159] According the Aristotelian biology, animal and human tissues were "synthesized" by the blood itself. Cf. Dante, *Purgatorio* 25: 42.

[160] Systems, apparatuses.

[161] Cf. *Matthew* 15: 17.

Long is the neck of the African camel,
matching the legs' length, and the animal
can thus browse on the grass and live.
A short neck hooks the shoulders   1040
of the bear, the lion, the voracious
tiger, and the other beasts whose natural
food does not consist of grass and fruit,
nor must they bend towards the ground,
but simply live by blood and plunder.
    What is the usefulness and the purpose of
the hideous nose of the huge elephant,
which Italy also calls *proboscide*?[162]
To such a big, indeed massive, animal
overcoming any superb earthly beast   1050
in size, the trunk was given cleverly
to cause fear and fright. It practically
performs the duties of a neck, because
the elephant has a short one, unable
to reach its feet; and if it were longer,
it could not support the head's weight.
So, it uses its nose instead and seizes
its food by means of it—a strange nose
indeed, empty inside, inhaling and storing
(as it were) lakes of amassed waters   1060
in its hollow so as to quench its thirst.
It then sprays them like a river, like
a polished fountain in white marble,
sculpted by an experienced master's hand.[163]
As an urn designed like this very beast
—with its grotesque, actually horrid look—
out of its nose, or maybe its open mouth,
or somewhere else, pours and pours large rivers
of waters, sprinkling the ground all around;
so the immense Indian[164] beast gathers   1070
the liquid and then splatters abundantly,

---

[162] A very long section is devoted to elephants, which during the Renaissance became very popular animals in Italy because of living specimens that could be seen (see lines 1155-1156). They were portrayed in painting and sculpture, see especially the monument in *Santa Maria Sopra Minerva* Square, in Rome, which still in the 20th century would inspire Salvador Dalí.

[163] A two-way simile between an elephant and a fountain.

[164] Indian elephants appear in *Gerusalemme Conquistata* in a war context (see here below, lines 1125 ff.).

a wondrous scene: so that its nose seems
a fountain, and it imitates Nature and Art.
But that same nose will often function
as a pliable hand, so many are the ways
in which the elephant folds and stretches it.
Keeping it still, relaxed, and harmless,
the pachyderm[165] often walks among
the docile and simple-minded flocks,
without bothering the humble sheep,   1080
which make room on both sides for it;
but it can seize the fiercest beasts and
throw them in midair, then frightfully
knock them down to earth by force,
as a big rock does, at first lifted high
by a machine,[166] then crashing down
because driven by it or by its own weight.
Its cervix then is as short as the throat,[167]
or else, the head would prove too heavy
for its huge body, that rests and stands   1090
over quite badly-built and rough feet
showing no joint to articulate them,[168]
and its four legs function as the beams
or columns beneath that imposing mass.
It bends them after a man-like manner
only when it sits down, but forced—alas—
to turn on its right or left side, since,
hindered by its own extreme weight,
it cannot keep its balance on both;
that is why it is seen leaning on one   1100
side when it is sitting and resting.
Or rather, it only bends its hind knees,
and in so doing, it does resemble man;
the other two remain firm and stiff,
so that it leans against the wild trunk
of some strange tree. There he now rests
and sleeps a hard, deep, and lazy sleep;
but the tree bends under such weight and snaps.

---

[165] The subject has been added in English, to avoid a too frequent use of "it" as either the elephant or its trunk.

[166] Technological devices play a key role in Tasso's Jerusalem-poems.

[167] According to ancient medical terminology, *collo* (neck) meant the anterior part of it; *cervice*, the back part.

[168] Another sudden jump into Medieval bestiaries.

Sometimes, however, it has been cut down
by hunters, who from the long teeth seek   1110
ivory—[169] a very precious merchandise
suitable to turn into wonderful works
and masterpieces in barbarian hands.
The support breaks, and now at once
there falls the fierce animal down,
as a building, because of the quaking
of the earth,[170] staggers and collapses
to the ground, encumbered with ruins.
While not being able to pick itself up,
it is betrayed by its wailing and killed   1120
by the weapons that transfix its soft belly;[171]
nor could man pierce with lances and arrows
the bristly back and the other external parts[172]
of the elephant, which thus dies with a moan.
But on its huge and horrid shoulders,
during a perilous war, it often carries
a tower filled with armed people; and
carrying such a weight, it smashes down
anything it meets. A self-moving mountain
or living fortress the fierce monster seems,[173]   1130
which ancient Africans[174] and Indians used
to array to rout the enemy armies
and trample on the scattered, bloodstained
weapons and on the fallen soldiers.
This big animal, provided it does not die
during a tearful war or a fierce hunt,
lives three hundred years; it has a sense
and spirit of piety, therefore worships
the cold and night-illuminating moon.[175]

---

[169] Starting from a Medieval legend on hunting, Tasso rapidly shifts to a very modern perspective, in which a concern for the elephants' fate, or doom, is at least implied.

[170] The Italian word *terremoto*, from Latin *terrae motus*, has been here divided into its original elements: "di scossa terra / il moto," the motion of the shaken earth. An earthquake hit the city of Ferrara during Tasso's lifetime, in 1570.

[171] A scene also described in *Gerusalemme Conquistata*, and possibly based, in its turn, on *I Maccabees* 6: 46 (a book accepted in the LXX and Catholic Bibles, but rejected by Luther).

[172] As with the Leviathan, cf. *Job* 40: 31 and 41: 4-5.

[173] During the Renaissance the first tanks appeared, at least on drawing boards: see L. Da Vinci and others.

[174] That is Hannibal.

Another animal[176] exists in the North,   1140
where the celestial Bear freezes the rivers,
whose piety and size are truly peerless.
This beast, foreseeing the shortage to come,
keeps the food it has meanwhile fed upon
in a large vessel it is provided with,
and keeps it there for the times of need;
retrieving it later, the beast feeds itself.
So, the latter being supplied with food,
the former[177] with water, they suffer no
shortage; as a city, forecasting siege   1150
and war, takes in provisions and fills
many houses and depots and store-rooms
with any food that the people may need.
But even this beast, so big and fierce
—which Rome, happy and triumphant,
saw when Lion[178] sat on the High Seat—
is tamed and subdued by man.[179] In this way,
God, who made all, wanted to show us
that the wild beasts are subject to Man:
to Man, His living and beloved image;[180]   1160
Man, whom He chooses as the immortal
heir of the divine realities[181] and calls to
the high glory of the heavenly Kingdom.
Not only in the biggest and fiercest beasts
is it possible to see and admire
this divine Providence and divine art,
for it shines in small creatures as well.
Not less wonderful than a very tall
mountain that towers towards the clouds
in the sky, a deep valley seems to be—   1170
where, shunning the fierce pride and wrath

---

[175] Elephant behaviors suggesting a kind of "social religion," like honoring the dead, have been reported in recent times too. Cf. C. S. Lewis, *That Hideous Strength*, ch. 17, section 6; as well as Tarzan films and the myth of the "Elephant's Graveyard."

[176] As shown in BB's notes, its identity is controversial (camel, yak,...?). Its "piety" is not clear either.

[177] The elephant.

[178] Pope Lion X, in 1514; a gift from the King of Portugal (BB).

[179] Cf. the basic "ideology" in Kipling's *Jungle Book*.

[180] Paraphrasing *Genesis* 1: 26.

[181] *I Peter* 1: 4, etc.

of the Winds,[182] who often search and haunt
the loftiest peaks, one may seek refuge
in some quiet place, under a clear sky
that keeps itself tepid and serene.
The elephant, though so fierce and huge,
is frightened as soon as it chances to see
(who would believe it?) the low, little mouse.
The scorpion also, armed with sharp arms[183]
and poison, is frightful to the biggest beasts.   1180

But, because of this,[184] let no reckless tongue
spit his poison against God, and reproach
Him for making the snakes and dragons,
and the worms,[185] and that little serpent[186]
that, by throwing bitter venom from afar,
kills man with a most painful death.
That would mean to blame the Master
who, in these bold and arrogant times
rebelliously resisting the divine law,[187]
urges us to fear Him with the lash   1190
and with dire blows and dire wounds;[188]
it is like blaming the very Physician
who tries to find a medicine for our ills.
But if you trust God, trample safely
on the poisonous basilisk and the asp;
crush both the lion and the dragon,[189]
that will forcefully subdue their tamed
necks to your righteous and safe foot.
Trust the celebrated example of Paul,[190]

---

[182] Personified—and dangerous—as in the classical epic poems. They survived as "the Powers of the air," i.e. devils, in the New Testament and Christian tradition, Tasso's poems included.

[183] Another of those puns only existing in English, but surely Tasso would like them as Baroque *agudezas* (subtleties).

[184] Again against Gnosticism. Later on, however, a dualist view of creation will surface.

[185] For the identity/difference between snakes and dragons (and worms), see *Dante Was a Fantasy Writer*, op. cit.

[186] A snake called *iaculus* by Lucan; maybe the black mamba (BB). The name *iaculus* comes from the Latin verb *iacto* meaning precisely "to throw"; *iaculum* was the arrow.

[187] The word *ragion(e)* meant not only reason, with its many nuances, but also Law as a code, see e.g. Dante's *Convivio, passim*. See also *Inferno* 1: 125. Here, as elsewhere, Tasso echoes the style of Counter-Reformation (and Reformation) preaching.

[188] Plagues were not only a symbol; some spread through various areas of Italy during Tasso's lifetime.

[189] From *Psalm* 91: 13 as it sounded in the *Vulgate*, where it was *Psalm* 90 because of a different textual division.

to whose holy, immune-made hand, 1200
while he, after having landed on Malta's
sunny coasts, gathered wood for a fire,
the viper caused neither pain nor death;
that lethal poison, which so easily clings[191]
and creeps, did not bite his hand at all
—powerful is Grace in the innocent soul![192]
Should I here recount a trying, fierce
history of cruel vipers and horned vipers?
Of Hydras, who exhibit a thick, hissing
barrier of snakes around their swollen, 1210
cerulean necks and horrible heads?
Or, of asps, deaf to the enchanter's song?
Or perhaps, *phareae, cenchri* and *chelydri*?[193]
Or *alphasibaenas*?[194] Or that fiery serpent[195]
that looks like a dart and, like a dart, upon
mortals violently hurls its killing poison?
What about *you*,[196] deserving the top palm
of victory among the African plagues
as a killer? You steal not only the spirit
and soul, but the very corpse from Death 1220
—you "kidnap" it, and by force burn it up.
    As a painter,[197] who portrays the pallor
and bleakness of a dead body, adorning
a bloodless face with the hues of death,
also adds there horrid beasts and frightening
monsters, and verisimilar ones at that:
though, as true-to-life, he may frighten you,
the mere illusion of those painted features

---

[190] *Acts of the Apostles* 28: 3-6.

[191] "S'appiglia" like one of Dante's hellish serpents, see *Inferno* 25: 51. The verb *apprendersi* (line 1205, here rendered as "bite") also comes from Dante, *Inferno* 5: 100.

[192] The line may also be translated as: "*This* can the grace of an innocent soul do!", but it seems less likely.

[193] From Dante, *Inferno* 24: 86-87.

[194] *Sic.* Clumsily misspelling *amphisbaenas*.

[195] The already mentioned *iaculus*, here "recalled" by the quotation from *Inferno* 24: 86-87, but mixing its description with *Inferno* 25: 83.

[196] A reptile called *seps* in Lucan's *Bellum civile* (BB). Dante had reworked this in *Inferno* 24: 97-103.

[197] The second out of three very brief essays on painting. Tasso had already described the technique of Eastern icons (2: 276 ff.), and below (lines 1722 ff.), will deal with early Renaissance art. Here "strict" Baroque art is concerned. These verses match strikingly a painting made by Goya two centuries later (1795) but set in the sixteenth century: *Saint Francis Borgia at the Death Bed of an Impenitent*.

and his craftsmanship can delight you;
so, by means of these colors and lights   1230
of poetical style, together with these
shadows of poetry, I create dreadful
shapes, and I thus try my best to please
the most sublime minds, and from deep horror
draw such delight that satisfies the more wise.[198]
But,[199] lest I incur annoyance and scorn,
I will not expand any longer on these
dry, sunburnt, frightful sands, and these
wild beasts and snakes; at more joyful things, like
a new Cato,[200] I will look on in passing.   1240

　　But my hurried paces are now delayed by
a large number of strange, horrid monsters[201]
and by various animals flying in swarms,
produced by the rotting limbs of dead
bodies; or else, seedless and fatherless,[202]
conceived and begotten by the Ancient
Mother out of her warm and wet womb.
Such species, wandering numberless, cause
annoyance rather than terror or pain.
How many, how many do I see, flying   1250
around me in a cloud, darkening the sky!
Who will chase them away as they pass by?
May your light do so, O eternal Father!
I ask You, here where the Holy One seems
against the Holy One and partly opposing:

---

[198] Among the "manifestos" we have already come across, this one is the most radically Tassean. Cf. *Gerusalemme Liberata* 1, stanza 3, but capsizing it: there, beautiful descriptions aimed at attracting readers and making them "drink" (that's the verb Tasso uses) the more serious contents; here, a frightening surface calls the readers to a paradoxical discovery of Light and Beauty at a deeper level—in poetry as well as in life. Melville assumes a like posture in *Moby-Dick*, ch, 1: "Not ignoring what is good, I am quick to perceive a horror, and could still be social with it—would they let me—since it is but well to be on friendly terms with all the inmates of the place one lodges in."

[199] This proviso makes the "Great Statements" (as the *Veda* would say) somewhat lighter, with a bit of humor. See lines 1241 ff.

[200] Of Utica, as told by Lucan (BB); he crossed the dangerous desert areas of Northern Africa, where he had moved after Julius Caesar won the civil war against Pompey, whom Cato supported.

[201] As it happened to some knights in the islands of the witches Alcina (Ariosto) and Armida (Tasso).

[202] The belief in the "spontaneous generation" of some animals was still alive until the nineteenth century; see Schopenhauer. Cf. Dante, *Purgatorio* 28: 103-117, with reference to plants.

Were you, O God, the Creator of flies?[203]
Insofar as human reason, enlightened
and "in-formed" by God's light can say,[204]
I dare affirm that You created, then,
mature animals in their perfect age.   1260
    The *phyla* and the different species
of plants and animals came out perfect
in that beautiful land[205] of clear light
at the sublime sound of His holy
command, with nothing left behind
of both the wild, infertile plants and
the fertile ones. From the beginning,
in being born, each one was adorned
and laden with its leaves and fruits,
unlike what happens today: now, as each   1270
season alternates in its turn, no longer
in unison are[206] the plants generated.[207]
Today, the fertile seed[208] is first sown,
its root is driven deep into the soil,
then we can see trees and herbs sprout
and keep growing; on the one side,
they send their roots deep underground
like foundations, while, on the other side,
they lift their trunks and branches skyward,
then the leaves and flowers germinate.   1280
Last comes the fruit hanging in midair,
but, not yet ripe nor in its perfection,
it slowly metamorphoses and changes
into different appearances and shapes.
First, it is so small that it baffles the eye,
it even seems to vanish from one's sight,
looking just like the flying atoms that
often appear in the light of sunbeams.[209]

---

[203] Tasso is probably joking (see in fact line 1258); nevertheless, some Gnostic schools ascribed different species to different Creators. In line 1256 there is a clear allusion to Beelzebub, the "Lord of the flies." The pun "a fly / to fly" exists in English but not Italian.

[204] From Dante, *Purgatorio* 18: 46. Noticeably, "naive" creationism was not a dogma.

[205] Eden. Usually, the Dantean phrase *il bel paese*, "the beautiful land/country," meant and means Italy.

[206] *Non* (not) in BB must be edited into *son* (= *sono*, they are).

[207] Eden was commonly believed to contain plants of all climates; see Milton, *Paradise Lost* 4: 205 ff.

[208] Cf. *Mark* 4: 26-28.

[209] Cf. Dante, *Paradiso* 14: 112-115.

Then, being fed by the earthly humors and
irrigated by the dew and the breeze,   1290
it feeds itself, it grows, it colors itself
like the work of some famous painter.[210]
But when God first created the world,
He made all forests perfectly full of leafy
trees, and one might have seen sweet
fruits among the branches: not unripe
as in their beginning, but already ripe
and already inviting the not-yet-made
animals. They would soon entice[211] hunger
and taste towards that unknown sweetness.   1300
Made pregnant by that supreme command,
the Earth gave birth to the roots and herbs
and sweet fruits, in which the native
power of a fertile germ was hidden,
an immortal and nearly eternal seed[212]
that would renew all extinct things.
The animals then, created all together,
were covered with their bristly skins,
or with white, soft and pure wool;
each immediately appeared armed   1310
with its own horns or sharp claws,
each perfect and mature in its age.
None of them, at that time, knew of
infancy and of undeveloped limbs.
    This whole great, newly-formed mass,
indeed, this amazing world, I say,
had no early age, and it appeared
all at once,[213] perfect and embellished.
Were the hideous monsters[214] made by You?
No, not by you, the Father and Master   1320
of Nature; it was rather the flaw and fault

---

[210] The first hyper-realistic *Still Lives* were painted in Renaissance Holland.

[211] Once again, the "myth" of creation crosses the "myth" of evolution. Or rather, as some philosophers of science stress, so-called "atheistic" Darwinism simply secularizes the narrative of *Genesis.*

[212] Suggesting a range of possibilities—from Aristotle's *telos* to DNA to stem cells—Tasso's mysterious "seed" is intriguing.

[213] Following St. Augustine's conception, according to which the universe was created *totum simul,* the six days of *Genesis* had a symbolic meaning—but Tasso usually accepts the "seven-day" pattern.

[214] The Renaissance was deeply interested in unusual natural phenomena, including deformities, etc.

of Matter, so extraordinarily unfitting,
sometimes in default, sometimes in excess.[215]
If the male's seed happens to be weak
and diluted as in a tired, old man,
or sparse as in a boy, it is unable to
overcome—through its shaping power at work
in the hidden cloisters of the female's womb—
the undigested[216] matter, wet and unformed:
so a female is born, who also is needed.[217]   1330
Delivery may be unpleasant,[218] but necessary;
while not necessary is that any hideous monster
should come into the world; it is not born for
any gracious end[219] but has no grace nor end
in being born. But an unconquered Matter,
rebelling against the Best Nature[220]
(who always aims to act for the better)
is the impotent[221] cause of monsters.
But Matter overcome, not rebelling,
not resisting stubbornly, in its womb[222]   1340
obediently accepts the "form," and a male
is born, adorned with every kind of beauty,
in the perfect likeness of his father.
Whoever degenerates and becomes
dissimilar to his father and his old stock

---

[215] From Dante, *Paradiso* 13: 64-78, where the explanation comes from Thomas Aquinas. Dante, however, as a refined Medieval poet, leaves the issue of monsters in the background. Tasso adds "medical data" taken from the Aristotelian school. In general, one may note that this theological solution, in a religious context that is no longer the Greek one, simply shifts or skips the problem insofar as Christianity conceives God as the Creator of matter *too*.

[216] The Italian wording echoes Dante, *Purgatorio* 25: 37-51. The man's seed was believed to "activate" and shape the (passive) matter in the woman's womb, turning it into a fetus. This matter was a special portion that did not enter the bloodstream, therefore did not undergo ("undigested") the processes of metabolism.

[217] The sexism implied in Aristotelian biology was not questioned by Christian authors.

[218] This is a personal remark, not commonplace. As already mentioned, in his tragedy *Il Re Torrismondo*, Tasso introduces a modern-minded female character who refuses pregnancy and subjection.

[219] Against an "answer" that was often given by Christian apologetics; see especially Leibniz.

[220] It may also be rendered as "the best [energies, purposes, etc.] of Nature," but the concept of rebellion implies God, and *miglior natura* recalls Dante, *Purgatorio* 16: 79. Again Tasso's words sound Gnostic, but now not for fun.

[221] In Scholasticism, evil was not considered as a "hideous strength" but, negatively, as the lack of good.

[222] *Materia* (matter) is feminine.

of ancestors, is to the world a monster.[223]
It can occur that a person degenerates
so much, decaying from the glorious root,
that he is almost different from Man,[224]
no longer a man but a hideous being;   1350
out of an ill-sown and ill-conceived seed,
an ill-born[225] animal is born and lives,
called "a monster." Nature herself shuns
and hates and disdainfully abhors him.
As an ancient narrative truly recounts,
a boy was born with the head of a ram,
another appeared whose head was an ox's,
and a newly-born calf displayed a head
shaped like a boy's, and like a bull's was
the head of a humble, docile sheep.   1360
Who does not know about the misshapen form
of the Chimera,[226] in which the goat was
joined to the lion, and this to the dragon?
And who does not know that Fame couples
and mixes the mare with the Griffin[227]
there, on the snowy Hyperborean or
Riphean Mountains,[228] where he watches and defends
the gold so longed for by errant mortals?
Famous and well-known are the shapes that
also were portrayed in Ancient Egypt   1370
or in sandy Africa; there, they stuck the
frightening forehead of an ox to a man
and covered his superb horns with a veil,
calling that false deity Jove Ammon,
and worshiped him in a notorious temple,
which was surrounded by a stormy sea

---

[223] The problem had been raised by Dante (*Paradiso* 8: 93 ff.), but less dramatically than here.

[224] Cf. Dante, *Inferno* 33: 151, against all inhabitants of the city of Genoa!

[225] A literal translation of "mal nato," usually meaning ill-bred, wretched, wicked. A horror parody of the Infant Jesus, with a subtle pun, since the Italian text says "*ci* nasce," where *ci* means "here, there (is, does)," but also "to us." See the Christmas hymn *Puer natus est nobis*, "*Ci* è nato un Figlio," "A Child is born onto us…"

[226] Some medical reports in the Renaissance—probably authentic, as many Web images still nowadays show—remind us of classical mythology, and even of the Holy Scriptures, as we will see later on.

[227] Their offspring is the Hippogriff.

[228] Celebrated places "somewhere" in the North; the particle "or," here, makes things even worse.

of sand in the middle of a forlorn plain.
They pictured and engraved their barking
Anubis[229] with a canine face, together
with another thousand lying idols.   1380
Even Judea[230] made its own simulacrum,
a monster not unlike the African fraud,
when they made sacrifices to Moloch.[231]
And the first origin of this false and vain
error was Nature herself, by erring[232] beyond
her purpose with such hideous creatures.
Moreover, she often bears mixed
monsters with many limbs by joining
several hideous heads on one torso,
or many legs to its lower parts.   1390
Bold Fame, feeling encouraged by such types,
created Biareus and Aegaeon the Giant,[233]
and armed them with a hundred hands and arms;
and she adorned Geryon's forehead with
crowns, giving him a very high and lofty
seat in the ancient territories of Spain[234]
—but perhaps, in this fashion, she depicted
the proud and authoritarian human soul,
in which three powers are joined into one.[235]

   Now, leaving out the hidden senses and   1400
the shadows and mysteries of old fables,
which simply darken the light of truth,
a uniform cause produces monsters by
mixing and marring, in the mother's womb,

---

[229] See the footnotes to Day 1: 106-107.

[230] Here, the OT Hebrews in general; but, strictly speaking, the term only indicates the Kingdom of the South, whose capital city was Jerusalem, after the political split that took place after the death of King Solomon.

[231] Cf. Milton, *Paradise Lost* 1: 392 ff., on the basis of *Leviticus* 18: 21, *I Kings* 11: 5, etc.

[232] The link "error/erring" is in the original text (*errore/errando*). This biology-based hypothesis on the origin of mythological hybrids may originate from Tasso: a sort of reworked version of Euhemerism.

[233] Two names of the same personage; Tasso often uses couples of synonyms linking them by "and." See the following line, however, where apparently he considers them two different creatures.

[234] Here the classical Geryon is meant, i.e. a three-headed man, not its Dantean version. His kingdom was not precisely in Spain, but in some islands off the Spanish coasts in the Atlantic Ocean.

[235] Love, knowledge, will. In his handwritten notes, Tasso ascribes this allegory to Aristotle, but the actual source was a free translation of Plutarch's *Morals* published in the late 16th century (BB).

the soft limbs of the damaged fetus—
be it the bad effect of a mixed seed[236]
or maybe the evil fault and innate vice
of matter—[237] and this occurs more often
with the most prolific animal species.
Such is the rooster's feathery mother;   1410
such is the simple-minded dove as well,
whose chicks sometimes have mixed
and mingled limbs; and with two heads
a frightening serpent was even seen.
To the good, beloved servant of Jesus,[238]
in that divining[239] dream, the strange beast
appeared with seven heads; a lustful
woman, sitting proudly on its back,
attracted kings to[240] her shameless love.
Seven heads had the beast of Lerna,[241]   1420
a horrid plague; and they were believed
to re-grow, having been cut off in vain.
I will omit to describe the uncertain
shape[242] of the beast shut up in the labyrinth,
as I leave out sphinxes and centaurs,
and Polyphemus and the Cyclopes nearby,
and satyrs and fauns and sylvans, and
Pans, Egipans and other wood deities
roaming the solitary, untilled forests:
such ancient marvels comprising the army   1430
gathered by Bacchus in the Orient when
he defeated and overcame the Indians,[243]
then triumphantly returned to Greece,
after an old and legendary report.

---

[236] Hybrids.

[237] Again a statement with a gnostic resonance.

[238] The apostle John, traditionally considered the same John who wrote the *Book of Revelation*. Even the symbolic dragon in *Rv* 17: 3 is here listed among the "freaks of nature," maybe in the wake of Dante, *Purgatorio* 32: 147.

[239] For this sense of the adjective *divino*, not meaning "divine," see Dante, *Purgatorio* 9: 16-18.

[240] The particle *e* (and) in BB must be edited into *a* (to).

[241] The Hydra, killed by Heracles.

[242] In fact, the Minotaur was imagined as a bull-headed man by the Greeks, as a centaur with a bovine body in the Middle Ages and in the Renaissance, and as a man-headed bull in some minor traditions.

[243] This is why in Camões' long poem *Oi Lusiadas*, known and liked by Tasso, Bacchus (the devil) tries to stop his "competitor" Vasco Da Gama.

I will omit the Arimaspians and those who
lay down to shade themselves with their one foot;[244]
nothing about the fabled Pigmies either,
long warring against the cranes, and all such false
images ornamenting the maps of Africa.
In fact, it is not true that such hideous   1440
and odd appearances were ever produced
by Nature; and even if it were partly true,
God did *not* create monsters at that time,[245]
because what causes a "monster" is only
a lack or an excess taking place in matter,
so that it is born different from its parent,
but this seldom occurs: a hateful sight,
that proves a shameful failure of Nature
—though a sign, perhaps, by which the High King
dismays us weak and wretched mortals   1450
by threatening pain, death, and ruin.[246]
   In the primordial creation, the eternal Forger
made no male of female mule, both being
illegitimate progeny, the dubious
offspring of animals coupled by
a natural, unrestrained desire: the strong
mule is thus born of an ass and a mare;
but the she-mule, from a fast-running
steed and a sluggish and lazy mother;
and sometimes, like her brave-hearted   1460
father, she[247] took part in the Olympic games
and won the precious prize by running.
Now they boast of carrying on their backs
the holy, red Fathers about the Vatican[248]
during the great feasts, in sublime pomp,
who proceed to meet noble ambassadors
of other[249] kings, of famous emperors.

---

[244] Unfailing characters in the ancient "reports" from the Far East. In recent times, they crop
up again, e.g., in C. S. Lewis' novel *The Voyage of the Dawn Treader* and in Umberto
Eco's *Baudolino.*

[245] During the six days of creation, when everything came directly from His voice.

[246] Like the comets.

[247] For syntactical consistence, but it might be about a male mule; as well in lines 1463 ff.

[248] See Raphael's fresco *Pope Leo I Repulsing Attila.* It is no longer Dante's decaying
Rome, nor would the Renaissance poets, who were sponsored by the Church hierarchy, ever
dare write—not overtly, at least—something like Dante's *Paradiso* 21: 130-135.

[249] The Pope was equivalent to a king, the Cardinals were called "the Princes of the
Church."

Sometimes a male mule may be born
of a running steed, and the she-ass boasts
a fast, noble filly for a mother;   1470
but the former will ejaculate a sterile seed,
the latter will receive it in a sterile womb.
Therefore, usually no mule begets a mule,
while we very often see a horse being born
of another horse, and in the warring herd
a brave-hearted son succeeds his father.
Many different reasons are given for this.
To deformed ducts it was ascribed by that
old blind man,[250] the famous one—I say—
who used to laugh at the ravings of   1480
the wretched mortals, and welcomed disasters
and catastrophes with a smile of superiority.
While the man[251] who threw himself into the fire
atop high Etna, and chose—the fool!—
to end his life among the smoking flames,
thought that a liquid element,[252] mixed with
another liquid one, would not coagulate well:
the soft and the thick would mix better,
as it happens by breaking and melting
different metals, muddling them up,[253]   1490
when the tin and silver are condensed.
Another[254] whose mind was more eminent,
and who was the Master of those who knew
everything being taught in the world's schools,
rather ascribes a much truer reason
to sterility: the *coolness* of seed.
In fact, the donkey is a cold, slow, lazy
beast, intolerant of the rigors of winter;
therefore, its birthplace is not in the icy
climate of Scythia, on ice and snow,   1500
but in such places as France and Britain.
Born of a donkey, the mule also is cold,

---

[250] Democritus.

[251] Empedocles.

[252] The mule's seed. Tasso apparently devotes an excessive number of verses to the topic, but this is revealing: as a true Renaissance man, he was not so much interested in the rules as in the exceptions—and in the exceptions to the exceptions, see lines 1505 ff.

[253] With a pun between *fondere* (to melt) and *confondere* (to "melt together," mix, muddle, confound, etc.).

[254] Aristotle, once again according to the definition given by Dante.

but, unlike its father, the son does not
produce a cold seed in a cold bosom.
But sometimes the son of a she-mule
is pointed out as a wonderful freak;
and when a mule is seven years old,
he mates with a mare, and she delivers
the unusual issue of a prodigious son.
There, where a hot sun warms Syria   1510
along the coasts of Phoenicia,[255] in old times,
the she-mules were very often fertile,
and mule-like mules were then born,
so that the memory[256] of the ancestors
was passed to the new generations,
and the bastard stock was long honored.
Now that race is no more, its name has died
among the new Syrians and Phoenicians,
Sidon and Tyre can no longer boast of it.

   In the olden times, the mixed foal   1520
of horse and deer[257] also used to exist,
taking the splendor of its long mane
and its wonderful, superb antlers
from both of its parents put together:
illegitimate, yes, but a beautiful,
big, wondrous offspring, nimble and fast;
and when it grew up, its long fleece
hung down from its chin like a beard.
Among the *Aracots*,[258] in the ancient woods
it then freely wandered and pastured,   1530
and there also pastured the wild oxen
with a hooked snout and twisted horns,
with a black hide and strong limbs.
Does anyone still glimpse it anywhere?[259]
In the icy zones, the thickest forests
still nowadays feed wild oxen, and we
still know about aurochses[260] and elks.
But no certain news has been left about

---

[255] In current geographic terminology: "...warms the Near East, along the coasts of Lebanon."
[256] Probably in the sense of the "genetic" memory, the "seed."
[257] Called *hippocervus* (BB), which simply means horse-deer.
[258] Or rather *Aracosii*, Arachosians, a people set by Pliny in India (BB).
[259] Again a modern concern for ecology and animal extinctions.
[260] Which would become extinct very soon, in 1627.

the mixed son of the horse and the swift deer;
nor does the fierce steed mate with   1540
the leopard,[261] letting us see their whelps
as the older ages did then admire them.
So short-lived are the honor and name
and fame of any bastard offspring,
and this occurs because they were not
works of the heavenly, eternal Forger,
who makes the various animal stocks
perpetual, and renews and keeps them.
Also extinct are the strange, mixed, and muddled
shapes of the wild beasts which sunburnt   1550
Africa once engendered along its rivers,
proud of its own horrible novelties;[262]
or they are about to become extinct, for
illegitimate, uncertain stocks of different
seeds are not able to survive for long.
Only legitimate stocks are nearly eternal,
as their Maker willed in creating them.
    But now close to my high, noble goal,[263]
towards which I hasten like a tired runner,
I can realize that I forgot the bison   1560
and the hyena, and[264] that horrible beast
which draws human bones out of their dark tombs,
and copies and counterfeits the voice of man.
I also see the hooked-nosed rhinoceros,
and you,[265] who, with your beautiful horn,
can purge the springs of any poison.
Among the snow and the ice-clad mountains,
I see the *rangifer*,[266] hidden to our world,
which pulls fast wheeled carts in its run.
I see a thousand others, in the cold   1570

---

[261] A fantastic animal called *hippardion*, perhaps to be identified with the giraffe (BB).

[262] Cf. Dante, *Inferno* 24: 85-90.

[263] Adam, who will be dealt with in the very last section of this Day; and even so, just as an anatomical specimen, with no personality at all. From this viewpoint, Milton's *Paradise Lost*, however revolutionary, goes back to the literary tradition. Only some twentieth-century avant garde movements will re-propose an approach like that of *MC*.

[264] For some reason, this animal is distinguished from the hyena. A remarkable example of black humor (see line 1562), immediately after proclaiming Man as the "noble goal" of the whole poem.

[265] The unicorn. It has often been identified with the rhinoceros.

[266] From Danish *rensdyr*, "horned animal," has persisted as the scientific name of the reindeer. See Day 3: 460 ff.

zones and in those that are hotter and burning:
animals we cannot see, but well known
by virtue of an old and perpetual fame.
Nevertheless, I do not slow down my run,
though tired and panting; here I come
where, among shadowy trees in blossom
and a thousand beauties and scents,
the God-made Man waits and calls me.[267]
As a naive[268] son who, in a solemn feast,
after wandering throughout a city   1580
crowded with the common, low populace,
finally glimpses, in some higher place,
the revered face of his own dear father,
there, where from afar, adorned he shines
with crown and purple, a powerful king;
he then shuns the varied and vulgar crowd
to take refuge where he is safe, invited
to join the superb royal Majesty by
a joyful nod or by the well-known,
imperious voice of his old parent;   1590
so throughout this beautiful created world,
the very home of mortals and immortals,[269]
great and sublime, in which perpetual laws
have been fixed from eternity to our lives,
up until now I kept wandering, longing
for so many marvelous things, one by one,
examining and admiring all of them;
I have sometimes stopped my slow pace
among the beasts, which are the mean plebs.
Now that, in paradise, the Ancient Parent   1600
offers himself[270] to me with his revered face,
not yet divided from his supreme King,
forgetting anything else, I turn towards him
and hear a voice resounding in my heart
—not from a statue of lying Apollo,
nor from a coarse oak, nor from a grotto,
neither from a wooden or marble idol,

---

[267] Cf. the final chapters in C. S. Lewis' novel *Perelandra*.

[268] "Esperto" not in the usual sense of expert, but just the opposite, on the basis of the Latin *expers*. A "Renaissance story" like this is found in Lewis' novel *The Horse and His Boy*.

[269] Including the angels as the cosmic movers, but this definition of the universe dates back to the Greeks.

[270] Cf. Dante, *Inferno* 1: 62.

but from Heaven, a truly heavenly one:
"Man, know yourself!"[271] Oh, holy guide
that, along this path, leads us to God,   1610
so that our minds rise up towards God beyond
themselves, and can know and conceive[272] Him.
Not by admiring the beautiful starry courts
nor the course of the all-illuminating sun
will we be able, in the invisible light, to
know the great God who made the world
as perfectly as when we examine our mind,
and, in order to know His mind, we lift
the wings of our quick and fervent thought,
which will not stop at human objects.   1620
As the light[273] of sight, wherever it turns,
wherever it lingers, can see and perceive
meadows and forests and fields, seas and rivers,
rough peaks, steep slopes, and low valleys
but cannot see itself, and only in a clean
mirror will see a true image of itself—[274]
so the human mind gazing at other things,
at the outward things painted and adorned
by the hand and art of the eternal Master,
will not know itself, will not understand   1630
what it is, unless it is enlightened by
the Sun of Truth like a burning[275] crystal;
and unless, once enlightened, it looks
at its own intrinsic form[276] as in a mirror,
and at the Lord, who embellished it with
His image, and made it a model of beauty.
If, therefore, it is dirty with ugly stains,
let it cleanse itself, so as to receive in itself
the pure ray of God, which shines inwardly.

---

[271] Poetry as a sort of time machine carrying us back to Eden, as Dante already did with his *Purgatorio*. Here, the rediscovery of Christian anthropology is strictly and surprisingly linked with classical thought—surprisingly in respect to many of Tasso's premises, although absolutely in line with Renaissance culture.

[272] The Italian verb *intendere* can usually be translated as "to understand," but that would be out of place here. To put it in Medieval terms, and to stay in line with Tasso (see the following lines), we cannot "comprehend" God. *Intendere* in fact comes from *tendere-in*, to tend towards… It can also imply "to (know and) follow His will."

[273] See footnote to 2: 167.

[274] Unlike *I Corinthians* 13: 12 because, in Paul's time, mirrors rendered a blurred image.

[275] The light of crystals was considered an effect of the cosmic fire.

[276] The texts does not say "intrinsic," but "form" must be taken in its Aristotelian sense.

After He had made the earthly animals,   1640
God saw that His works were good, and said,
"Let us make Man as our own image, in the
likeness of ourselves." He had made the earth
and the sky, the sun and the starry courts
without asking for any help or counsel;
now, however, in creating man, He does.
Such a great work it was! O you arrogant,
ungodly Jew,[277] listen to the Lord who speaks!
And whom is He speaking to? To Himself.
Do you, who can only see the light of truth   1650
as a burning sunbeam through a window,[278]
dare disprove, reluctant and rebellious?
Nor know the three different Persons in God,
revealed to us behind a beautiful veil?
Should He be like a smith even working
by night, or a master of a less noble art,
who sits among the tools of its craftsmanship
alone, without the help of any apprentice,
and thinks to himself, and hurries himself
with a hard and hasty command, like: 1660
"Let us make a sword, or—quick!, let us
make a sharp scythe, or a curved plow"?
Nonsense! Or, rather, slanders spoken
by a false tongue accustomed to lying.
Jews deceive themselves when they imagine
such false chimeras in their own minds.
Like horrid beasts, dangerous to man,
that have been closed up in a small cage,[279]
unable to act out their burning rage,
quiver[280] in that jail and, with fierce cries,   1670

---

[277] A theological controversy that, unfortunately, degenerates into anti-Semitism. Another attack will follow later. Probably, the hot-tempered Tasso in that period had some personal reason to express this invective, because he does not show this attitude in his other poems. In *Gerusalemme Conquistata* he also adds Jewish characters to the plot, while none appeared in the *Liberata*. Jewish physicians, especially, had a certain prestige in Italy during the Renaissance.

[278] A modified version of St. Paul's "veil of Moses" (*II Corinthians* 3: 13-15). In fact, common glass—with the exception of the rare crystal—was not perfectly transparent. Paradoxically, in line 1654 the veil will be used as a synonym of *re-velation* (the term itself comes from the root "veil"), as in the works of the mystics. This forced Tasso to find a different metaphor, the window, to mean a lens which is "culpably" imperfect.

[279] The exhibition of exotic animals was quite common in the Renaissance.

[280] Cf. Dante's Cerberus in *Inferno* 6: 24.

show the bitterness of their profound wrath[281]
along with their native inner fierceness;
so the Jews,[282] when they find themselves cornered,
dare affirm that the eternal Father
said "us" with reference to the angels
—to the angels who always surround Him—
and bade His ministering angels to work,
as if He were gathering his servants (who
are fellow-servants to man)[283] for a Council,
making them the Lords of the stupendous   1680
work in which the God-like man is created.
But what craftsmanship could ever be equal
to its master? Oh, the deaf and blind mind,
the foolishness and folly of profane souls!
Should God gather His servants and honor
them with high offices, and reject His Son?
Think about what follows: "Let us make man
in our image." Might God have the same image
as the angels, as one and the same essence[284]
belongs to the Father and to the Son?   1690
Between Man and God the sublime likeness
is not a bodily shape or quality;
that "image" only refers to the divine
mind, by which the human is "in-formed"
and depicts God in its three inward powers.[285]
In fact, God understands himself, and by
understanding himself, He loves himself,
and the eternal Intellect is thence born,
and the eternal Love is equally breathed[286]
by Both, so there are three lights, not three gods, 1700
three Persons who are united in one God;

---

[281] "...de l'ira accolto," reworking Dante, *Inferno* 8: 24 (*ne l'ira accolta*).

[282] BB specifies that the Hellenistic trends are meant; it was, besides, this same cultural milieu which produced Gnosticism.

[283] Cf. *Revelation* 19: 10. The term "conservo," co-servant, comes from Dante, *Purgatorio* 19: 134.

[284] Plato's terminology is here implied: the true essence is the *idea*, originally meaning "shape, image."

[285] Memory, intellect, will, according to St. Augustine's "psychological analogy" worked out in his *De Trinitate*. The first element, corresponding to the Father, was often replaced by "being, essence" in Medieval theology; cf. the quotations from Dante (*Paradiso* 33: 118-120, 125-126) in lines 1696 ff.

[286] Our rendition "is breathed" follows Longfellow's translation of Dante's verses mentioned in the previous note. The Italian verb *spirare* has the same root as Spirit.

likewise, in ourselves, our mind emanates
the will, and, following it, the memory
shapes itself after the fashion of both;[287]
as a consequence, the nature of man,
while being one with three distinct powers,
demonstrates the divine image in itself
and, in itself, knows and loves God.
    The eternal Father also made the soul,
and reason, which is the internal[288] man,   1710
like Himself, who is the divine Love;
such a man, wrapped in the external Adam,
He kept covered and hidden to the senses.
And since He is[289] good, and wise, and just,
merciful and strong in bearing offenses,
for a long time He suffers, not hastening
to take revenge; He calms down and softens.
Such He created the first man, like Him
in his pure love—which is the prime virtue—
and of any other divine, holy virtue   1720
He wonderfully struck the marks upon him.
As a painter[290] keeps adding and shedding
various differing colors and lights to his
beautiful painting in his graceful style,
then adding the shading where needed,
until the figure and outcome are perfect;
so did the Painter of our human minds
color the soul, and made it luminous with
His rays, and with many different colors
ever-increasing its splendors and lights.   1730
And as a sculptor with his iron tools
keeps taking away from the white marble
the superfluous parts,[291] until out from the stone
an almost living and breathing figure emerges,
so, when the eternal and glorious Forger

---

[287] Tasso significantly changes the classic order, placing memory *after* mind (intellect) and will. Was this Tasso's personal theory?

[288] *Esterno* in BB to be edited into *interno*.

[289] Paraphrasing God's revelation (*Exodus* 34: 6-7, *Psalm* 103: 8 ff.), and linking it with man's own essence.

[290] After the technique of holy icons and Baroque art, a description of standard Renaissance art is provided here.

[291] A clear hint at Michelangelo, according to whom sculpting was easy because the statue was "already inside."

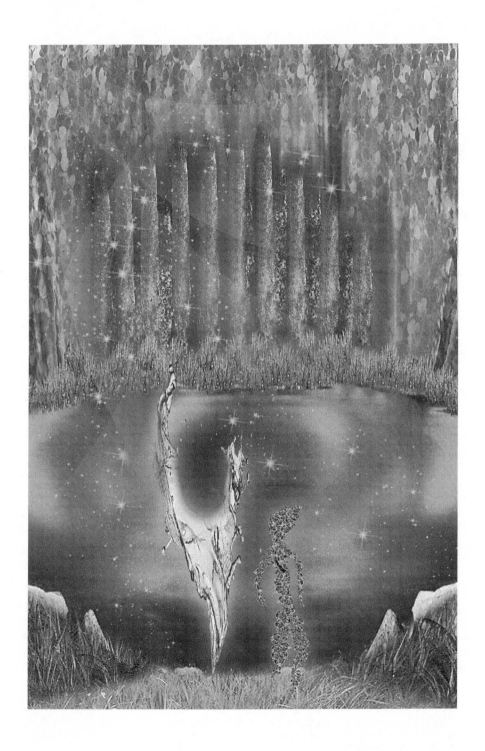

of Nature removed from matter what
was still too hard and too earthly in it,[292]
the Human Form appeared in the clay:
thus man became the image and likeness
of that divinity that shines in God.   1740
But those colors and that wonderful light
are sprinkled and stained with false hues
by the ever-degenerating progeny, which
loses its first likeness and darkens all,
so that our stained, filthy humanity
does not resemble God but rather looks
like a painting made with Hell's brush,
and blackened in Phlegethon or Lethe.[293]
Thus, let Man look at himself and know
that his divine form has been polluted,   1750
and, as long as he can, let Man clean himself
—adding to the soul, depriving the body—
so as to resemble the Primal Example
and prove to be the child of the heavenly
King, the worthy heir of God's Kingdom.

     Finally, God blessed the dear image of
Himself, by Him created, and then said,
"Grow into a numerous, beautiful race;
fill the earth, and render it subject
to your own will, to your command. Have   1760
dominion over the wet fish of the sea,
over the graceful birds in the airy fields,
and let any animal which walks on earth
be not less subjected to your reign."
In this way, as soon as you were created,
Man, you were created[294] a king: the high
command and the imprint of sublime power
was not written for you on dry, frail wood
or between the folds of a piece of paper,
so as to be gnawed by a putrid worm,[295]   1770

---

[292] This conception of "the purest part" of matter chosen to create Adam is not common. Tasso may have taken it from some Church Father, though it usually referred to Christ's flesh—who was the "second Adam," in fact.

[293] In Dante's *Purgatorio*, Lethe is a sweet river on top of the mountain of purgatory, preparing souls to fly to heaven. Here Tasso follows the classical toponymy of afterlife; cf. Milton, *Paradise Lost* 2: 583.

[294] In Latin and Italian, the verb *creare* usually refers to Cardinals rather than kings.

but human nature keeps, written in itself,
God's high voice and resonant sound.
Let him command and spread his natural, just
power over the earth, in the echoing sea,
and over the heights of the wandering air!
In the beginning, you were born to rule:
Why then do you now serve your passions,
despising and thus losing your dignity,
becoming loyal to Sin, enslaved by it?
Why do you make yourself a captive   1780
prisoner of Satan, bound by his chains,
if, while being first made, you were called
the Prince of creation, the earthly King?
Why, as if throwing away, do you scatter
what in human nature was most worthy
of reverence and of the highest honor?
What limits have been fixed to your dominion,
on earth, in the air, or in the sea depths?
If you compare yourself with *that* Man,
won't you see your wings, and soar high?[296]   1790
    Nothing can hold back bold[297] Reason,
which, with its wings, will fly not only
past the windiest fields of the atmosphere,
but also the starry, golden courts of the sky.
The ocean is much less deep at its bottom
than man's rare[298] and marvelous intellect,
that, in the salty kingdoms, is able to pry
into the secrets of the waves, bays, and beds,
and their most hidden wonders; and thence,
triumphantly, it returns to the surface,   1800
rich in knowledge and immortal treasures.[299]
In this way man, by virtue of his mind,
does conquer and subdue all created things.

---

[295] This section mixes *II Corinthians* 3: 2-3 and *Matthew* 6: 19, while "Baroquizing" the worm.

[296] This "sermon" clearly echoes the Catholic way of preaching, as in Lutheran theology man's will is irreparably a slave (*De Servo Arbitrio*), no longer able to regain its freedom—not on its own, at least. Once again, however, we have to remember that this was only one side of Tasso's pendular worldview.

[297] *Arida* (dry!) in BB must be edited into *ardita*. Cf. Dante, *Paradiso* 33: 79.

[298] "Peregrino," once again with a pun suggesting the pilgrim's progress.

[299] Quite remarkably, such "knowledge and immortal treasures" are not heavenly but earthly, or rather undersea.

And again, God spoke:[300] "Lo! I gave you
each herb germinating from a sown seed,
and each plant in which there is the seed
of its progeny. From these you will get your
food, and the aliment will also be provided
to the birds which soar high through the sky,
and to the heavier animals whose   1810
living soul[301] makes them shift on the earth."
In this fashion, in that ancient condition
of innocence, an equally innocent[302]
food, not stained with blood, nor polluted with
ungodly death or with unjust plunder,
was allowed to man and given alike
to the animals—which, without rage or scorn,
were then subject to man's meek command.
No one was killed yet by the evil poison
of harmful[303] herbs or hideous snakes,   1820
but everything that Mother Earth produced
in her womb was healthy and welcomed.
The hungry lion or wolf or bear had not yet
stained its claws and teeth with blood;[304]
nor did the vulture look for its food within
dead corpses, because no one had ever
passed away yet, and out of the dead limbs
there could not be any heavy, reeking smell.
But, pasturing in the green, grassy fields
—as the white, singing swans often do,   1830
or as we may sometimes see the dogs,
whose master is Nature, go and feed
on some hidden medicinal herbs—[305]
those wild beasts also ate spring grass,
who now are greedy for bloody meals.
No harm yet was made by man's hunting;
no hidden snares were laid, at that time,
against those wild, solitary living beings.
All wild beasts, then friendly to[306] Man,

---

[300] An enlarged paraphrase of *Genesis* 1: 29-30.
[301] Recalling the link between *anima* (soul) and *animali*.
[302] That is, without shedding blood, from Latin *in-nocens*. After stressing the power of Man over Nature, Tasso highlights that such power did not mean killing and destroying.
[303] "Nocente," the opposite of *innocente*.
[304] Again the Edenic—or rather, Messianic—descriptions from *Isaiah* 11: 6 ff.
[305] Two charming scenes.

with a happy and benign countenance,   1840
wandered peacefully, humbly, all around,
all obedient to that wholly just power.[307]
Indeed, not only the king of frightening
beasts, and snakes, or high-flying birds,
and of wet "undersea-flying" fish was
the First Man,[308] but, as a Master and Lord,[309]
he even ruled[310] over his own feelings,
and could easily keep his own thoughts in check,
firm and steady, imperious and strong.
But when, rebelling against the holy order,   1850
he despised his Creator's great prohibition,
the fierce beasts transformed into his enemies,
rebels against him; his transient[311] body,
soon to be devoured by horrid Death,
had then to be fed with sanguineous[312] food;
a mortal food given to wretched mortals
as their aliment in a less happy state
after the waters gathered in the Flood
had covered coasts and mountains with waves.[313]

But since Man as the sacred, divine image   1860
still maintains his sublime and primal features,
he has not lost his first, natural authority
over the beasts, and in the name of a just
law—indeed, a just and justly allowed war—
can make of them prey, plunder, food, and clothing[314]
when his weary and stiffened limbs need it.
This is no harmful and no ungodly law,
but a law of Nature; of the High King, rather,
who made the wild beasts as the servants
of Man, as well as the flocks, herds, and birds,   1870
and the inhabitants of the swelling sea.

---

[306] The particle *o* (or) in BB must be edited into *a* (to).

[307] Cf. Milton, *Paradise Lost* 4: 340 ff.

[308] To stress his universal meaning, Tasso almost never calls him by name, Adam.

[309] "Signore e donno," that is a synonym, from Latin *dominus.* Echoing Dante, *Inferno* 33: 28.

[310] Literally, "had the scepter and reign."

[311] "Caduche" includes the concept of falling (*cadere*). St. Augustine linked this verb to the word *cadaver* (corpse).

[312] See above, footnote to line 1022.

[313] *Genesis* 9: 3, marking the beginning of the change in man's diet.

[314] Shifting the viewpoint once again, Tasso justifies the postlapsarian *status quo.*

So it was all done; and God knew and saw
that His works had been fulfilled.[315] Day Six was
here ended, and He rested in Himself.

---

[315] Here Tasso quotes *Genesis* 1: 31, watering it down. The creation of Eve is described only
at the end of Day 7.

291

Day Seven

R ome, after having spread its glorious
  Empire from the West to the East, as well
as across the northern and southern zones,
to its victorious people offered at once
the wonderful sight of two theaters
joined together while turning round about.[1]
Here, the people separated among themselves
—of which one part to the other part had
before remained hidden—now by uniting
in the large shape of a perfect circle,   10
could see one another. Nobody was then
in hiding; indeed, by admiring all around
the flights of steps packed with sitting
people,[2] they all were suddenly amazed
and delighted by that new, unusual sight.
But in this—which the eternal Master made—
greater theater, ever-twirling and rotating,[3]
like the amphitheater of His glory,
though one single sphere includes in itself
two great and different hemispheres,   20
one remains ever hidden from the other,
so the divided and opposite peoples
will never have a glimpse of one another.[4]
We here knew nothing. We were doubtful
whether the world had other inhabitants,
or there was a bare land[5] in some solitary
place, or maybe hidden underwater.[6]

---

[1] "According to Pliny the Elder (*Natural History* 36: 24.102), the Circus Maximus and that of Valerius Ostiensis, because of their elliptic shape, let both audiences see each other" (BB). Tasso's use and elaboration of the configuration is remarkable at many levels.

[2] Cf. Dante, *Paradiso* 31: 46-53, describing the seats of the blessed souls in heaven.

[3] The most Tassean definition of the world. In theory, he did not accept the Copernican revolution, so, *prima facie*, this line refers to the movable scenery of a theater (see line 29), as it happens with the alternating seasons. Or, was he concealing some "heretical" opinion?

[4] Not directly, not while "sitting": exploratory voyages were needed. See lines 35 ff.

[5] The existence of lands in the southern hemisphere had already been theorized by the Greeks. They were usually thought to be inhabited, but Tasso echoes Aristotle's demographic theories; and perhaps he also hints at Dante's island of Purgatory, whose sole inhabitants were human souls.

293

Though the sky always turns around,
the revolving scenery will never show us
those peoples whose feet are always   30
set against our own in that sunny land,
or show them us and our environments
in these quite distinct latitudes, because
of which the Pole appears higher or lower.
But what the incessant turning and tireless
passing of many skies cannot do, *that*
the swift thought of the mind can do, which
(as it were) turns and returns to itself
in a perpetual and varied motion.
Before its eyes the veil of the interposed   40
Earth is taken away: by gazing at God,
it sees in His great light[7] the world gathered,
which grows small to the enlightened soul, which is
ravished out of the world, and nothing can shade
the peoples and kingdoms in the inner light.
Therefore, simply gazing at them, standing
on their stairs,[8] the rare pilgrim-intellect[9]
descries the Finns[10] and the farthest *Biarms*,[11]
and the Ethiopians and Indians, all at once.
On the one side, it sees the cold Plow   50
and lazy Arcturus, and at the same time
the other Pole together with other stars,
not because the world shrinks in its eyes,
but because the mind progresses in God[12]
and becomes so wide that, at one glance,
it can admire the whole universe below
as once did the blessed Father Benedict[13]
(who, when dying, marked a luminous path
of a thousand shining lamps across the sky),

---

[6] Atlantis.
[7] Cf. Dante, *Paradiso* 33: 82-87.
[8] Again like Dante's heaven, see *Paradiso* 31: 46-48.
[9] The words "rare pilgrim" translate the one word *pellegrino*, conveying both meanings.
[10] Curiously called "Finmarchi," from *marca*: land, territory. *Finlandesi* in current Italian.
[11] See *MC* 3: 480 and footnote.
[12] Cf. *Paradiso* 33: 109-112. This whole section reworks Dante's ultimate vision.
[13] St. Benedict, the founder of the Benedictine monks. The episode is told in St. Gregory the Great's *Dialogs* (BB), that for a long time have been the only source mentioning Benedict, which led many scholars to believe he was a fictional character. Here, with a pun, *Benedetto Padre* means both "Father Benedict" and "the Blessed Father." Dante's admiration for this Saint is related in *Paradiso* 22: 28-99.

while following his own sublime thought.   60
Such a mind wonders where the eternal
Cultivator may have placed that gorgeous
Paradise:[14] in what unknown, exotic climate
the new and happy plants blossomed then,
when our father Adam was first created?
    And so, the earth had been completed now,
so had the sky, and beautiful ornaments
had embellished the labor of Six Days,
that sublime and magnificent artwork,
when God, stopping His fresh activity   70
and creation, took a complete repose
the following day, that was the seventh.
Nor would He be creating new beings,
but, keeping the created ones alive,
He took command of them—but without
finding *peace* in the already created things.
He had made the sky, but He did not find
His repose in it;[15] He had made the beautiful
starry circles, the wandering sun and moon,
but He could not rest among the golden   80
stars, nor in the sphere of the royal planet,[16]
nor in the circle of the icy cold moon.
He made the earth, which is solid and firm,
but He did not rest in the heavy earth,
that maintains itself and lies in itself.
Where, therefore, and in whom is the repose
of the Maker of great and eternal things?
Only in what is most constant and heavy
—and reasonably so—would He not disdain
to repose; rest and motion, indeed, never   90
existed without any steady point.
    In fact, the sky keeps rotating precisely

---

[14] It was usually placed in the Far East, or in Ethiopia (see Ariosto, *Orlando Furioso*, Canto 34), which, on the other hand, was often mixed up with India. Dante's Eden lies on top of a mountain—purgatory—on an island at the antipodes of Jerusalem. Milton choose Armenia (*Paradise Lost* 3: 742) "or" Assyria (4: 126). Tasso, in *Gerusalemme Liberata*, Canto 15, "rediscovers" Paradise in the Atlantic Ocean, as was commonplace among Renaissance explorers. But in *MC* he prefers another solution, see lines 647 ff.

[15] Tasso capsizes the famous sentence by St. Augustine, "You [God] made us for Yourself, and our heart finds no rest until it can rest in You" (*inquietum est cor nostrum donec requiescat in te*). Note that Adam was created on the sixth day, not "now" in the seventh.

[16] The Sun, then listed among the seven planets, and not among the stars.

over its fixed Poles, on both sides,
and it would not move without a fixed
center[17] given to its perpetual course.
This is why they told the fable of Atlas,
who made the sky turn around its Poles
while resting his feet on firm ground.
The animals, too, so mobile and wandering,
would not even move if in their bodies   100
there was not a steady part which does rest;
therefore, the part that bends and folds
in their motions works as their center.
So, if the First Mover[18] must be a mover,
not only does He need to be motionless,
but He had to stop his eternal motion
in an immobile point. And He disdained
to stop it on earth: Where did He, then?
Which body may be steadier than the earth?
In Man He stopped it. He chose to create Man   110
after all His works, so that motion may cease;
or—if such was no motion—so that the
Divine Art may make an end of creating.
More constant than earth, thus, is Man
the true image of the eternal Pattern;
he must despoil himself of his heavy
and transitory shell; and, taking on
an immortal form, become eternal on high,
in the quiet of the invisible Kingdom.
In this way God, while creating, wanted   120
to show the deep mystery of His own death
figuratively; to forecast that, indeed,
before the tortures of death, the Son would
have to rest in Man; and in human limbs,
like any mortal, to the sweetness of sleep
would yield his troubled and tired spirits.[19]
So, God found peace in the earthly man.

---

[17] The Earth, according to the Ptolemaic model.

[18] It usually means the celestial sphere communicating the motion to all other spheres, but here God himself is meant, as in Dante, *Purgatorio* 25: 70 (quite fittingly, because Dante deals with the creation of the soul in man).

[19] These lines may have some Patristic source (BB quotes St. Ambrose: *Christus requiescit in homine*, "Christ rests in Man"), but are Tassean to the bone. Representations of Jesus sleeping—as an adult, not as an infant—are very rare; see William Blake's illustrations for Milton's *Paradise Regained*.

Won't man have quiet or peace in himself?
No inward quiet can weak mortals enjoy;
no work of Nature ever rests in itself,   130
but the fire turns in its perpetual course
through the sky, forever restless and wandering;[20]
the air, agitated by contrary winds,[21]
forever parts from within itself and divides;
and the waters roll and pass, peacelessly.
And this terrestrial mass, which seems heavy
and firm to us, even shakes and staggers
from its foundations, crushing the cities
and leveling lands as high as mountains,
and the peaks themselves. Her bosom splits: 140
through those deep chasms the Earth sometimes
shows Pluto's kingdom and his blind gulfs,
menacing the ultimate ruin of all.[22]

But created things do have peace and rest
in their Creator, while He finds peace
in Himself, not needing any external
glory nor any good except Himself, since
He is the Supreme Good; and with eternal
rest He rules the happy, immortal Kingdom,
there where He calls us, away from our troubles.   150
He looked for peace in Man on earth
so that Man, in Him, may finally rest.[23]
So, when in such a wonderful way He
joined humanity to his divine nature,
he finally gave sweet repose to himself
in his troubled and tired life; together
with glory and grace, by which our nature
is fulfilled and blessed, seeing itself in Him
exalted so high. Thus, in that evening,
the sixth day put an end to His works,   160
nor would He create any new progeny,
any new stock. Very fittingly did He

---

[20] The "sphere of fire" hovering between the air and the moon.
[21] "Da contrari venti," from Dante, *Inferno* 5: 30. Another quotation from Dante is found in line 135, "senza pace" (peacelessly), see *Inferno* 1: 58.
[22] In Medieval and Renaissance art, hell is often shown as the enormous mouth of a monster emerging from underground. The very term *voragine* (chasm) comes from the Latin verb *vorare*, to devour.
[23] Cf. the ancient concept of *admirabile commercium*, the "wonderful exchange" between God and Man.

cause the birth of the great world, and all
the species which in itself it includes,
by using the most fecund number, Six.[24]

Let him who knows the science and art[25]
of numbers tell the pregnancy of Six,
which, as perfect and fulfilled in its parts,
can beget out of itself varied figures
of numbers; and let him add everything   170
that the world teaches in its schools.
Let him tell the barrenness of Seven,
as it will produce nothing out of itself
and is the product of nothing, and cannot
boast as if it owned some hidden treasure.
Now let us despise and leave behind
that which makes earthly wisdom[26] so
puffed up with pride, and give prime importance
to the ancient, sacred custom of the faithful,[27]
who added honor to the seventh day: 180
the Hebrews honored it in the sixth day
when they happily pitched leafy tents
and took shelter in those wild dwellings.[28]
They again honored it on that famous day
full of sounds and joy from trumpets[29]
and celebrations: a propitious day, which
gave no less worth to the number Seven.
The seventh year,[30] too, for the ancient Jews
deserved all kinds of reverence and honor:
for in the six preceding years it was   190
lawful for anyone to furrow the soil

---

[24] Tasso follows the ancient Jewish exegete Philo of Alexandria (BB), but, as is often the case when he translates from a specific source, he focuses on it so closely that he neglects the other sides of the problem. Here, praise of the number Six against Seven does not take into account the fact that Seven is one of the most sacred numbers in Christian tradition— while Six is often associated with the devil, on the basis of *Revelation* 13: 18. The fact that Philo is among his favorite sources (Tasso expressly includes him in his hand-written notes to *MC*) rescales his former attack against the Rabbis' theology.

[25] For this couple of concepts, cf. Dante, *Inferno* 4: 73.

[26] The number 7 was sacred to Athena, the goddess of Wisdom (BB).

[27] The Biblical festivals. Tasso will mix things up by identifying the number 6 (and the *sixth* day of Catholic calendar, the Saturday) with the *seventh* day of the Hebrew week.

[28] Actually *Sukkot*, the Feast of Booths, has a completely different timing, see *Leviticus* 23: 34 ff. But, as BB highlights, Tasso is following St. Basil, or rather a Pseudo-Basil.

[29] The first day of the seventh month? See *Leviticus* 23: 24.

[30] The Sabbatical Year (*Leviticus* 25: 1-7).

with hard plows, and in the plowed fields
sow the fertile seeds in generous handfuls;
but in the seventh, they would be content
to reap out of the untilled womb of Nature,
what she voluntarily produces.
Six years would the ancient Jew serve;
but freed from toils and servitude would he
be on the seventh.[31] And the hard yoke of
the proud Assyrians beyond Orontes,   200
beyond Euphrates, in Babylon, oppressed
the wretched prisoners for sixty years
and nine more;[32] then the pristine freedom
shone very bright to the enslaved people
when number Seven was multiplied by Ten.

   Let us now pass without delay to our own.[33]
Seven times a day the just man will fall
and rise again, struck down by Adam's
heavy burden and his own frail nature;
but God's grace lifts him, and in this way   210
we will be companions in that number.
Seventh in line from the First Parent, Enoch[34]
did not meet death: his mystery foreshadows
the immortal and holy Church that still
lives, and outlives the extinct Empire.[35]
The seventh in line from father Abraham,
Moses, received the Law. Hence, conversion
chased away injustice, the door opened
to Justice, and God descended to us
in human form, lo, nearing, and coming,   220
and wonderfully teaching the world
a holier virtue, and bringing a new law:
all this is partly prefigured by Moses.
Then, multiplying the Seven by Ten
and adding Seven,[36] from ancient Adam

---

[31] Another mistake. This happened—or was supposed to—every fiftieth year, in the Jubilee (*Leviticus* 25: 8 ff.).

[32] It is not clear why not ten; see *Jeremiah* 25: 11 and here below, line 205.

[33] The popular phrase "i nostri" is employed, usually meaning "our folks," "our heroes," even "the goodies."

[34] This section corresponds, *mutatis mutandis*, to Book 12 of *Paradise Lost*.

[35] Two centuries and a half after Dante, the dream of rebuilding the Roman Empire was definitively gone.

[36] According to Jesus' genealogy in *Luke* 3: 23 ff.

the Son of Mary at last appeared.
Later old Peter[37] also learned a deep
mystery referring to the number Seven
as the sign of forgiveness and peace;
but he did not fully grasp it, at first   230
doubting it; he would understand it
when revealed by his Lord and Master,
who, by forgiving us, opened the bosom
of his graces and eternal treasures;
he teaches mankind to forgive not only
seven times, but seventy times seven.
And so, the punishment of unjust Cain,
already stained with his brother's blood,
is now matched by Peter's forgiveness
as the extreme opposite to that sin.   240
The Lord's forgiveness even overcomes
the ancient fault of the blamed Lamech:[38]
to a light mistake, a narrow forgiveness
seems to be given, but when sin abounds,
God's grace abounds beyond measure.[39]
To those who receive a great forgiveness,[40]
much fervent love is freely given by
Him who is the true, not-dissembling lover.

    Thus, a sign of forgiveness and rest is
the seventh day, in which the eternal   250
Father, by reposing, gave an example
of repose to the ancient Jews—now in vain
reposing in their lazy works and faith.[41]
That Seventh Day had a morning and dawn
but did not see any evening and night,
which has not yet come: unshadowed is the Day
that is illuminated by perpetual light;
while Time's turns[42] and runs and circles
close our days between morning and night,
during which we all work and then stop,   260

---

[37] *Matthew* 18: 21-22, though at that time Peter was not old—another example of an Homeric epithet, characterizing a person in any situation, past or present. In Christian art, Peter is traditionally portrayed white-haired.

[38] *Genesis* 4: 24.

[39] *Romans* 5: 20. Compare "Great sins do draw out Great Grace" (Bunyan).

[40] Cf., in part, *Luke* 7: 47.

[41] Another gratuitous gibe.

[42] *Voci* (voices) in BB to be edited into *veci* (turns).

and alternate fatigue with repose,
until, frightening to see, that seventh day
comes, that will consume both the earth
and the sky, as it has been threatened
most horribly.[43] Then, the lofty walls
of this ancient and luminous mass,
taken by storm, will turn into heaped ruins.
Then, the victorious fire,[44] preying upon
the sea's kingdom and the black, smoking
fields of the burning and dry earth—it will   270
appear that everything is in flames,
so that the incinerated remains of the now
destroyed world will be hardly made out,
becoming a trophy to eternal Justice.
In the beginning of that hideous day,
while waiting for those impending fires,
no weddings or feasts will be celebrated;
no precious goods will be exchanged[45] between
India and North Africa,[46] or icy Schythia
and Ethiopia. No, the fear of fire   280
rather than the tilling of the fecund fields
will then be the sole concern of mortals.
The Earth will show a wholly amazed face,
astonished; all trembling will appear
the beings that had been created by God,
out of a sudden, unprecedented terror.
The very righteous will be afraid of
the Last Judgment. Our father Abraham
will then fear no fire or torment, but enjoy[47]
the honor to which he was destined[48]   290
by the Providence of his heavenly King
—in this Order of the Just, the divine Justice
reserved for him the reward and the seat,
be it the first, or the second, or the third.[49]

---

[43] "Orribilmente," an adverb employed—or coined—by Dante in *Inferno* 5: 4.

[44] Classic(al) imagery, from the Stoics to *II Peter* 3: 7, 10.

[45] Cf. *Revelation* 18: 11 ff.

[46] "Mauro" meant an inhabitant of NE Africa or Africa in general, not strictly of Mauritania. Cf. Moor.

[47] The verb is missing in the original text (not in BB, but in Tasso's text itself), with the paradoxical consequence that Abraham seems to "fear" his own honor and glory. The poet apparently didn't have the poem edited.

[48] "Sortillo," from Dante, *Paradiso* 11: 109, in a similar context.

And flashing[50] on high the heavenly King
will appear enveloped in a white cloud;
and like a cloud or veil which is torn asunder,
the sky, opened and split before Him, will
then overtly reveal the Supreme Power.[51]
Thousands and thousands of flaming phalanxes   300
and squads of the divine army will appear,
shining with light and weapons aloft;[52]
there, gold and fine *electrum*[53] will be flaming
among the dark and frightening clouds,
seen wandering from nimbus to nimbus.
More frightening than thunders, shrill
and terrifying trumpets will be heard;
all the beautiful starry courts will be
seen shaking because of that great blare;
the whole creation will tremble, upset   310
and overcome by horror; the very angels
will fear, while standing reverent on high
and encircling the thundering King.[54]
What Persian, or Assyrian, or Indian king
was ever crowned by such dreadful squads
in a conquered city, which fire and blood
horribly flood and ravage with their raids,
while the swords fill the streets with
mutilated bodies and scattered ruins?[55]
Or, what image of superb, proud Ilium,   320
which was utterly burned[56] by Greek fire,
what of the ruinous fall of high, imperious
Carthage, or again, of what ruin and havoc

---

[49] The role of Abraham in the Christian "economy of salvation" was discussed in Medieval theology. On the basis of *Luke* 16: 22, the "Bosom of Abraham" was seen as the place where the righteous dead went before Christ's work of salvation was accomplished, waiting to follow him in heaven after the resurrection. This now forgotten subject was engraved on the portals of cathedrals and other structures. It was essentially the same thing as Limbo; in some miniatures of the *Divine Comedy*, the "Bosom of Abraham" is pictured; Dante never mentions it.

[50] "Folgoreggiando," flashing because of lighting; from Dante, *Purgatorio* 12: 27, where Satan is described falling.

[51] "Alta possanza," again in Dantean parlance.

[52] Baroquizing *Matthew* 26: 53 and ideally paving the way to Milton.

[53] An alloy of gold and silver, used in antiquity.

[54] Cf. Milton, *Paradise Lost* 6: 734-735, 824-826. Here Tasso vies with the Masters of Baroque art.

[55] Cf. the final Cantos in Tasso's "bloody" *Gerusalemme Conquistata*.

[56] "Ilion superbo . . . combusto," from Dante, *Inferno* 1: 75.

of such cities as Corinth and Numantia[57]
—of all these, what (I say) blurred, mixed,
pitiful, bloody, hideous image may
be compared to the vast world when it is
destroyed in the midst of smoking fires,
the pyre and grave of itself by itself?
The just will be abducted[58] through the air,   330
the clouds will turn into flying chariots
to carry them; the holy angels, chosen as
their charioteers, in those cloudy vehicles
will carry them in motion swift and high.
And then the righteous will shine like
sparkling stars,[59] while, bound by the heavy
weight of their sins and of their transgressions,
oppressed by it, the wicked will fall into
the eternal chasm,[60] and none of them will
ever rise up from that hateful burden.   340
    Oh, that great, frightening, horrid day![61]
Will it really have a dawn and morning,[62]
with no evening putting an end to that
horror? Or will a limit be fixed upon that
great day[63] of reward and punishment
in that last evening? Then will a new light
shine, wonderful and eternal, on the
Eighth Day, enlightening the minds?
As Rome,[64] the noble and celebrated work
of great Romulus and then of Augustus,   350
the founder and father of the Empire,
was hit and defeated by barbaric hands
and collapsed, thus lying buried under
itself among ruins and dead bodies;

---

[57] The former was sacked in 146 B.C.; the latter, in Spain, was stormed in 133 B.C., both times by the Romans (BB).

[58] The word *fiano* ("they will be" in old Italian) is missing in BB. Heavenly chariots and vehicles have a long tradition all over the world, from Hinduism to the Bible, to Greek mythology; a more direct source was the *Aeneid*. But, as he also does in his Jerusalem-poems, Tasso prophetically emphasizes their likeness to twentieth-century UFOs.

[59] *Matthew* 13: 43.

[60] Possibly with Michelangelo's *Last Judgment* in mind.

[61] Echoing the famous Medieval hymn *Dies irae, dies illa*.

[62] The seventh day of creation is identified with the Latter Days.

[63] The word *dì* (day) is missing in BB.

[64] It is interesting to compare this section with the history of Rome as summarized by Dante in *Paradiso* 6: 35 ff.

then, with Christ's Vicar,[65] it rose again
more beautiful to the mind's inner eye,
greater than before, greater than the world,
which cannot limit its holy and sacred
kingdom, founded on a firm rock;[66]
so—by comparing the part with the whole—   360
this perishable worldly mass will come
to an end, and after all of Time's turns,
the revolving theater will fall and crash
to the ground, turned to ash and sparks.
But then, remade by the eternal Forger
and rising in a more wonderful shape,
it will not be subject to the varying ages,
it will no longer be afraid of collapsing.

But then the sky's temple, now so variable,
and the sun will stop; even the curved course   370
of the wandering stars will finally still.[67]
So that the Saved will constantly dwell
in the place of eternal, quiet peace,
never stirred by any tempest or twister:
a pure, invisible light, and a stable day,
not limited by any horrid night.[68]
Nor will the light run from dawn to evening,
nor in alternation with the dark,
nor will four seasons turn any longer;
up there, the noble souls[69] will be rewarded   380
with rest and glory simultaneously,
their supreme honor will be supreme calm.
There, with crowns and palms, high and shining
seats will be given to the glorious souls.
Those who were warriors in such a long war
as is the life of wandering mortals
on earth—and through their victory earned
a thousand glorious and sacred spoils over

---

[65] The Pope, or rather the—Renaissance—Papacy.

[66] *Matthew* 16: 18. A strong allusion to the Roman Catholicism. This verse from *Matthew* is written in *very* large letters on the inner ring of the dome of the Basilica of St. Peter.

[67] The Medieval Scholastics had combined the "new heaven" promised by the New Testament with the Aristotelian cosmos, so that an eternal universe had to remain perfectly still, since motion causes corruption.

[68] But he loved nocturnal landscapes…

[69] Meaning the saints in general, because all this will happen after the resurrection of the flesh.

the enemy Satan in a hard campaign—[70]
will be seen triumphing in formation   390
with the great eternal triumph, crowned,
following the flag of the powerful King
of Kings.[71] And God's very hand—in that
shining temple of eternity whence
the rebellious angel, hurled headlong,[72]
fell—will raise on high all the sublime spoils
and trophies of the Cross. O happy day,
holy, merry day, in which the triumphal
pomp, the glory, the singing, the stillness
will become eternal! Then the swift, twirling   400
minds[73] will enjoy quiet and peace after
the many thoughts and the many motions
—they now come out of themselves, straight,
inclining towards the low and transient
things, and with crooked turnings they
sometimes shift obliquely,[74] sometimes turn
towards themselves and make a circle,[75]
or turn about that divine, motionless center
of which the longing soul is like a sphere.[76]
Then even the frantic wheel of Fortune   410
will remain still, since it turns with the sky.[77]
Our desires also will find their rest,
which against the sublime, divine Mind
take backwards steps[78] and a crooked path,
in the same way as against the highest sphere[79]
Jupiter and Saturn steadily turn,
as well as the stars Mars and Venus.[80]

---

[70] As the symbol of Christian life, John Bunyan chose pilgrimage; Tasso war.

[71] Against Dante's slothful in *Inferno* 3: 52 ff.

[72] The translation draws on Milton, *Paradise Lost* 1: 45.

[73] BB reads Tasso as referring to the angels, but they are in bliss even before the world's end, and the connection with lines 412 ff. shows that this section deals with the inward powers of humans: the mind first, then feelings.

[74] When they sin; cf. Dante, *Paradiso* 1: 130-132.

[75] By "reflecting."

[76] The Medieval *mens* or *apex mentis*, the "part" of the soul that is in direct "touch" with God.

[77] Cf. Dante, *Inferno* 7: 73-81.

[78] "Ritrosi passi," from Dante, *Purgatorio* 10: 123.

[79] The *Primum Mobile*, moving contrariwise to the other celestial spheres. See *MC* 4: 787 and footnote.

[80] Unusually called "stars" because of their appearance in the sky.

It is suitable that, when the motions
of the wandering and fixed stars stop,
so cease the motions of the human mind 420
and soul, which are similar to the sky's course.
All will have peace in the fixed point[81]
of the Godhead. Eternal rest will then
be our understanding and our love,
which currently change in many ways[82]
with so many gyrating turns and returns.
Eternal rest will come from grace and merit,[83]
in an eternal seat. Let those who grow old
in waiting for that day suffer and hope,
and resist the hard blows of Time and Fate[84] 430
by simply enduring, and commit a just
outrage against ruthless and horrid Death.
While the great Clement reshapes the Church
according to its model[85] and God's Idea,[86]
let all of us welcome God in the pure
temple of his or her own serene mind,
and form an inner simulacrum of Him
with devotion. Let the soul be the altar,
the burning heart the innocent victim,
and charitable love the fire and flame.[87] 440
So, let the soul prepare a home in itself,
still changeable and yet constant in its
uncertain turns, until the naked spirit
flies to that sublime and eternal Palace—
there where priesthood joins with royal crown.[88]
    But, where, oh, where am I led by my
fervent thoughts? From this Last Day, let us

---

[81] Cf. Dante, *Paradiso* 28: 16.

[82] Echoing Dante, *Paradiso* 5: 99.

[83] But Tasso offers no further investigation of the thorny relationship between the two.

[84] Echoing various sentences by Dante, e.g. *Paradiso* 17: 24, 106-108.

[85] God, according to BB; the apostles, in our opinion—but to the same effect. The Pope was Clement VIII.

[86] Not only His "concept" of Church but His very *Logos*/Word and Son, Christ. Clement VIII is not remembered among the great Catholic Church reformers; indeed, under his papacy Giordano Bruno was sent to the stake (it would happen five years after Tasso's death, however).

[87] The Biblical "manifestos" of inward worship are such texts as *Psalm* 50 and *John* 5: 21-24, but Catholic writers—let alone Tasso—can hardly be expected to follow the implication of an *exclusively* inner cult to its final consequences.

[88] Probably in the sense that the Saved are spiritual "kings and priests" like Christ.

go back to the day in which the earthly
Father was created by the heavenly One.
God had not yet sprinkled rain upon   450
the dry face and arid womb of the spacious
Earth, and the good tiller of fields[89] was
not yet born to perform that tiring job,
but from the soil there sprouted a clear spring
that irrigated it all,[90] and sometimes bathed
the craggy mountains and the rough cliffs,
as the Nile inundates the green plains
of fertile Egypt, and thus makes the happy
fields loamier, covered with dark mud.
Whether an airy cloud or a spring,   460
it rose so high[91] that, murmuring, it sprinkled
even the steep slopes with running water.
A spring, a spring this was, which however,
in the beginning of the still young world,
was like a rainy cloud to the mountains,
not only to the lower and dusty soil.
    So, the Lord, the eternal Father, eternal
God, shaped Man with earthly mud.
In order to make this sort of living
statue of humankind, He chose a pure   470
and genuine material,[92] that had just been
divided from the water; He squeezed and drained
it dry, then He added, in every part,
the best selected portions of earth
—in fact, there was no vice or flaw at all
in that primordial matter out of which
He made the home, the temple, indeed,[93]
for the noblest soul endowed with reason.
Malice would later prove the flaw and fault
of matter in man's corrupted seed,[94]   480
from which hunger would issue, and vexing
thirst, and the bloodless army of weakening
diseases, and finally the pallor of death.[95]

---

[89] Adam (*Genesis* 2: 5).
[90] Cf. Milton, *Paradise Lost* 4: 229-230.
[91] Cf. *ibid.*, lines 226 ff.
[92] See *MC* 6: 1736-1737 and footnote.
[93] Cf. *I Corinthians* 6: 19.
[94] Tasso seems to follow the Augustinian doctrine of original sin being transmitted through man's seed.

Good was the Forger, good were the matter
and the craft, so that our father Adam's new
body was well formed, nimble and tall,
wonderfully shaped, at the same time
handsome and strong; his cheeks and hair
had the fine hues of the clay-red earth.[96]
From the clay[97] he would receive his name,   490
a symbolical name which expressed
that he was born on earth as the Lord
of the East, and of its opposite, the West,
and of the lands in the North and South.[98]
In his soul also God worked wonderfully,
following in the making no created pattern
but He alone and his Word, of whom
a divine image He instilled in Man.
Into his face He breathed a living spirit,
that was not a divine part of Himself,   500
as some[99] maintain, but a created spirit,
exhaled by Him so that it may enliven
and give a soul to that noble body.

As, later, Phidias,[100] sculpting a famous
portrait of the unconquered Alexander,
made his magnanimous forehead turn
to the sky, and bending[101] his proud neck
expressed his noble character, as if,
dissatisfied with an earthly empire,
he aimed at the stars and asked for the sky;   510
so the Primal Forger lifted Man's eyes
and forehead towards the starry spheres,
so that he may see the heavenly origin
of his immortal soul and ask the eternal

---

[95] Cf. Milton, *Paradise Lost* 11: 466 ff.

[96] As to the perfection of Adam—surely not an "ape man"—according to ancient theology, from the Church Fathers to the Renaissance, see C. S. Lewis, *A Preface to Paradise Lost*, ch. 16.

[97] *Adamah* in Hebrew.

[98] In the wake of St. Augustine (BB), who linked the four letters A.D.A.M. to the Greek words *Anatolè* = Dawn, Orient, *Dysis* = Sunset, *Arktos* = Bear (the North Pole), *Mesembría* = Midday, South.

[99] In his handwritten notes, Tasso refers to St. Cyril of Alexandria on the basis of a text by St. Thomas Aquinas. But this—the soul as a "part" of God—was rather a Gnostic doctrine.

[100] Lysippus, actually: Phidias lived one century earlier (BB).

[101] Upwards. Cf. the heroism of Milton's Satan, but softened by lines 515 ("by grace") and 522 ff.

312

Father for an eternal kingdom, by grace.
While all other animals He made prone
and bent towards the ground, forever forced
to look at the common, ignoble Mother,[102]
as beings born to obey their own bellies
since their only purpose is food and repasts, 520
and earthly joys entice and soften them.[103]
But if man unreasonably happens to
aim too high, without any grace or merit
aspiring to heaven, bragging and daring,
let him behold the earth and ponder over
the fact that he was born of dust, and dust
will become; so let him erase any self-
aggrandizing thought in his arrogant heart.
As a man, whom a lowborn maid brought
into the world from a noble parent,[104] 530
breathes the paternal pride, wrath, and glory
of his ancient stock, and may generously
venture into some illustrious enterprise,
then, recalling his maternal descent,
he curbs the excess of his boldness;
let man examine his humble beginnings
from that old, base Mother, and think about
the womb he came from—he tramples on it
with his proud, bold and irreverent feet,
as if he had drawn his face and limbs from 540
a celestial matter, even from heaven.
Let him remember: he is an earthly beast,
he walks on the earth, on the earth looks
for his food, and on the earth he also rests;
because of the earth, he often starts conflicts
and wars, and rushes raving to arms.
He cannot undertake any enterprise
except on the earth, so as to stifle his
wrath and appease his burning desires.
This thought, which sometimes bends him 550
to humility, can also lift to heaven his

---

[102] The postural and "therefore" essential difference between man and animals was already stressed by classical writers, but what Tasso says here against Mother Earth challenges everything he has been saying so far.

[103] Rather than a brief treatise on zoology, this might be an encrypted sermon; cf. e.g. *Philippians* 3: 19.

[104] It was a widespread phenomenon.

immortal spirit,[105] whose intrinsic end
is not on earth, nor in the golden stars,
but in the Lord, before Whose sublime seat
the "heaven of heavens" is like the low
earth, so far away from the divine height.
    But not only in the face and forehead
was the eternal Master's art wonderful,
since it penetrates all parts in depth,
and shapes and forms even the hidden ones.   560
As in a stronghold or a lofty tower,
the sentinels are placed all around
so that, safely from night ambushes,
the enemy can be made out from afar;
thus the eternal Forger placed, as guards,
the quick and alert senses in the head.
He made the eyelids and the hairy brows
as the eyes' wall, and opened a way
to the voice, so that, like a messenger,
sound may pass through and enter, and from   570
the outside carry news to the heart.[106]
But through these high places God made
a narrow pass, twisting its wet ways
like a labyrinth;[107] and opened a swifter
and double path for the pleasant smells.
A wet, soft tongue He gave to taste,
that distinguishes flavors; He diffused touch
throughout Man's body. Round the head,
God made a natural crown for him with
his beautiful locks, letting Man adorn   580
his own body, whose bones are kept bound
by means of the nerves—the strings and knots,
hard and soft, by which he bows and bends.
God also made the heart as a living spring
of blood, as well as other inner springs,[108]
and the veins[109] that, like rivers of running

---

[105] An excellent synthesis of the swinging anthropological dualism of the Renaissance.
[106] That was considered the spring of feelings not only in a metaphorical sense.
[107] Milton, in exalting Adam's and Eve's bodily perfection (*Paradise Lost* 4: 288 ff.), does not take the inner organs into consideration.
[108] The other three basic "humors" of ancient Medicine: yellow bile, black bile, phlegm.
[109] There was no distinction between veins proper and arteries (cf. Dante, *Purgatorio* 25: 42). Modern understanding of artery-vein function was discovered in 1628 by William Harvey.

humor, from the heart to the other limbs
carry the blood which irrigates the body.
In the body He diffused and spread the soul,
all in all, and all in each part of it,   590
though three[110] are in one, and the two mortal
ones are joined to their immortal sister.[111]
In order that "she," enveloped in the body,
may not disdain to have an earthly home
until the Lord calls her back to heaven
from that watch He had assigned to her,
He placed her in the high fort of the noble
head as in a palace suitable for her;
there, of Man who is a small cosmos,
He granted her the honored reign.[112]   600
The other souls, as the subjects to a just
reign, the Maker placed in the lower parts,
and by removing places and seats, He
divided the sacred power from the
profane ones.[113] Wrath, fervently and hastily
burning with flames and with greed for revenge,
He set in the middle of the breast,
within the blood-filled heart; it will not,
however, remain in those narrow beds
—but it also freezes and shrinks out of fear.[114]   610
God then added the windy lungs, which,
like bellows, gather and again turn
the air out, so as to temper and cool
the inner heat with their sweet breathing.[115]
Concupiscence left the upper organs
for the others, and, as if forcefully pushed,
retired to the lower ones: there it settled.
The girdle[116] that crosses man in the middle

---

[110] The irascible, concupiscible, and rational soul, according to Plato.

[111] *Anima* is feminine. The debate on whether the soul was immortal, and/or which "part" of it was, caught fire in the Late Middle Ages with the rediscovery of Aristotle's anthropology. Cf. Dante, *Convivio*, Part II, ch. 8; *Inferno* 10: 13-15 and *Purgatorio* 25: 61-66. See also Adam's doubts in *Paradise Lost* 10: 782-786.

[112] Tasso wittingly reworks the typical Renaissance conception of man as a microcosm.

[113] The mind from wrath, and especially from sexuality. Cf. the structure of Dante's hell that recalls an overturned man, with sins progressively connected with the "lower senses" (eating, sex), wrath (Canto 8), and the intellect.

[114] Causing pallor, which was interpreted as the effect of the blood "retreating" towards the heart.

[115] This was considered the function of breathing.

315

then divided them: cupidity would
remain there as a beast tied to its manger,   620
and there it keeps feeding greedily; famished
and ravenous, it cannot satisfy
a thousand rabid and burning desires.[117]
In fact, now a greedy thought tortures it
as with a hard whip, now it burns with the
torch[118] of a thousand loves, all aflame.
That is what currently occurs, now that
lust and greed have shaken off the yoke and curb
of reason as its enemies, and rebels;[119]
but when God created them at first,   630
no tumult, no war was inside the soul,
but supreme peace; united in deep love,
obedient to the mind's just commands.
The mind's will was the firm law of the soul,
which was still a close friend of Justice.[120]

    In this fashion did the divine Hand shape
the First Man, then not subject to death
but immortal by grace—though not by nature
like the angel, who is purely mind.
God shaped him on the sunny soil   640
of ancient Damascus, as old fame
(provided it is trustworthy) still has it.[121]
Then He carried him to His delightful
paradise,[122] which the art and work of
the eternal Tiller had made, wonderfully[123]
adorned with shady and fecund trees.

    There is a place in the Orient[124] in which
the sun, coming near, inflames and burns
that very great and blazing cosmic belt[125]

---

[116] The diaphragm.

[117] Echoing Dante, *Inferno* 1: 98-99, and providing his own interpretation of the She-Wolf. Ariosto (*Orlando Furioso* 26: 31 ff.) had seen the beast as the symbol of the greed for money and power, but not of unrestrained sex.

[118] In Renaissance art, it usually symbolized wrath, feuds, and the desire for revenge; cf. the classical Furies.

[119] Augustinian anthropology. Cf. Milton, *Paradise Lost* 9: 1011 ff.

[120] As a virtue, and as a synonym of God.

[121] Milton does not venture geographical hypotheses, see *Paradise Lost* 8: 270.

[122] *Genesis* 2: 8; *Paradise Lost* 8: 300 ff.

[123] The Dantean adverbial phrase *a maraviglia* also suggests "in great number."

[124] Its features allow us to identify it with the Phoenix's plateau (Day 5), though Tasso does not make this clear.

placed between the circle whence the sun,   650
as if stopping, turns its wandering course
from the home of Cancer, and the other
turn, in which it leaves Capricorn behind.
There a lofty and sacred mountain rises,
crowned with trees and with shadows,
never reached by vapors condensing
into fog or rain, or hovering in clouds,
and no storm, no curved, thick twister,
no thunder and lightning ever appear,
neither do diverted sun rays hit it   660
so as to inflame and boil up the air.[126]
Although the sun makes the land red-hot
in the plain, and warms up the woody slopes
of the beautiful mount, its fiery heat
cannot spoil the green grass at the peak
or cause annoyance by changing the seasons,
nor spoil its happy, flowery forehead.
The mountain's painted and scented glory
and its high domes are always in bloom;
the dew from the sky, in big drops   670
looking like pearls, bejewels the crowns
and silvers the mountain's shoulders and chest.
Here, in fact, the cold and wet shadows
always match the hours of clear light,
so that, if the hot day lowers them,
the chilly night increases them again.[127]
To all this, add the crystal clear spring which
with abundant wetness irrigates the mount,
and pours a wide torrent of delights.
Add, further, the shade and the breeze—not one   680
of the impure, mixed breezes, exhaled
from a heavy, smoky earthly vapor
which disperses in turbid flight their
spirits through the air, always to and fro,
then drops by losing motion and wings—
but (we can believe) a celestial breeze
is this, born from the turns of a serene sky,
moving from the Orient and bending

---

[125] The Equator.

[126] Echoing Dante, *Purgatorio* 21: 40-52. Cf. *Paradise Lost* 10: 651 ff.

[127] Milton equips heaven itself with similar climatic benefits, see *Paradise Lost* 5: 628-629.

the branches and leaves contrariwise,
blowing gently and unceasingly.[128]   690
   Here did the eternal Father place Adam,
making him worthy of that happy seat,
in which He produced the most beautiful
vegetable species, the sweetest to taste.
In the middle of paradise, He planted
the Tree of Life, and alongside,[129] the Tree
that teaches how to discern evil from good.
The river of delight[130] irrigates the flora,
then overflows out of paradise,
running fast, and divides into four: 700
The first is called *Phison*[131] (now Ganges),
emulator of the sea, which encircles
the sunny and fecund land of Indians
with its veins of shining gold,[132] where
the carbuncle flames and overcomes
the tenebrous night with its splendor,
and the green *prasius*[133] happily sparks,
with a thousand other dear and shining gems.
Similar to the more famous olivine,
the shady-leafed *bdellium* can be found,   710
which exudes scented drops like shed tears
that are bitter, but shining to our sight.
Gebon[134] is the second river, called the Nile
not only nowadays but long of old;
this runs all about the Ethiopian land
and enriches the fields of the green Egypt.
The third watercourse was called the *Tiger*[135]

---

[128] From Dante, *Purgatorio* 28: 7-12, 103-108.

[129] The "spatial" difference between the two Trees is not clear in the Bible: both seem to be in the middle of Eden (*Genesis* 3: 9). Milton clearly distinguishes them (see *PL* 4: 424). Dante sees with his own eyes a tree "born of that which was bitten by Eve" (*Purgatorio* 24: 116-117) and a tree associated with Adam (*ibid.*, 32: 37-42), whose features recall the Tree of Knowledge but whose height is the same as Milton's Tree of Life (*PL* 4: 195). According to some Bible interpreters, there should be one tree with twofold effects.

[130] Cf. *Psalm* 36: 8.

[131] But pronounced *Pison* [pee-son] in Hebrew. Milton neglects this whole section of *Genesis* (PL 4: 233-235).

[132] India had become better known to Westerners: its riches had been the goal of Portugal.

[133] A kind of quartz (BB).

[134] *Sic.* Spelled *Gehon* in the *Vulgate* (*Genesis* 2: 13), and, more correctly, *Gichon* in Hebrew.

because it runs as fast as an arrow;
it has kept its ancient glory and fame;
the fourth, Euphrates, runs towards Assyria.   720
Both—which first join, then depart again,
and finally mix with one another—[136]
mark the borders of Mesopotamia.

   O Most Holy Tiller[137] of the sacred mount
—beside which Parnassus would look
humble and low, and would immediately
bow its double forehead and ridge,
in spite of the laurel that crowns it—
I will not say: "You be Apollo to me,"
but: "Oh, unmask the numberless lies   730
of fallacious Apollo,[138] and reveal the truth
which lies hidden in Antiquity[139]
and occult in Your deep mysteries."
You, who made Eden beautiful and happy,
strewing it with coolness and shadows;
You, who poured the urns into pure springs,
and to the rivers opened the hidden ways;
show me the place and hidden origin of
the waters,[140] and their ever-changing courses!
You made it. You could re-make the earth   740
and the heavens, but the heavenly breeze
of your burning Spirit hardly reaches me.
Is it true that[141] the "third heaven," to which
the flying-minded Paul[142] was abducted,
was paradise? Are there worlds in the sky?
In the sphere of the opaque Moon, is
there any land,[143] and even caverns

---

[135] In the original text, its name—*Tigri*, Tigris—is wrongly spelled as *Tigre*, Tiger, in connection with the two meanings of *corso*: course (as in current Italian) and run (in old Italian; *corsa* in current Italian).

[136] A brief but substantially accurate description of their courses.

[137] God.

[138] Cf. Dante, *Paradiso* 13: 25-27; but also 1: 13-36.

[139] Cf. Dante, *Purgatorio* 28: 139-147, concerning the parallelism between Eden and the classical Golden Age.

[140] As we have mentioned, this was a fixed idea of his.

[141] An interesting list of conjectures concerning Eden is provided. The "extraterrestrial hypothesis" will have a modern sequel in C. S. Lewis's Space Trilogy.

[142] *II Corinthians* 12: 2-4.

and woods? Do true seats and green cloisters,
up there, encircle wild, shady temples?
But if earth and heaven are not mixed   750
together, why does the Moon shade its face?[144]
Or do the errant minds stain it by looking
for earths and paradise in the universe?
Do bold voyagers,[145] also in vain, long
for it by searching either north of Cancer
or, on the contrary, beyond Capricorn,
in more temperate zones? Do they fruitlessly
explore the Nile's sources,[146] where ancient fame
used to place paradise, in the wide bosom
of the Moon Mountains?[147] Or the Ganges' sources   760
in the Caucasus,[148] or in Armenian mounts,
whence the *Tiger* and *Euphrates* run off?
Provided they discovered it over there,
how could Eden host the living sources
of four such rivers, famous worldwide?
Was maybe Your paradise the *whole* globe
of fertile and not yet cultivated soil,
in that primordial state of innocence?[149]
Or, are the river beds and courses changed,
now following a different path than then?   770
Could ancient times have changed so much?[150]
Might the primordial sources have sprung
in Eden, murmuring, to the sky;
then, plunging into the deep bosom
of the gloomy Earth, in full darkness,
roam the blind kingdoms underground,[151]

---

[143] An ancient hypotheses that survived, at least, up to the 18th century in official science, then revived by alternative science in the 20th century. Cf. Ariosto, *Orlando Furioso* 34: 71-72; Milton, *Paradise Lost* 3: 460-462. As for Dante: in the Moon he met *nuns*.

[144] Another very ancient question slips in: the nature of the "spots" and the "seas" on the face of the moon.

[145] During the Renaissance, finding Eden was *an* aspect of some expeditions.

[146] In fact, Ariosto (*OF* 34: 48 ff.) placed Eden right there.

[147] In central Africa; they were considered the Nile's place of origin.

[148] The Caucasus is a very broad term, but this conjecture hits thousands of miles off the mark. On the other hand, according to Indian tradition, the *Ganga* (feminine) has a "mysterious" source in addition to the visible one.

[149] An interesting opinion. Cf. C. S. Lewis, *Out of the Silent Planet* and *Perelandra*.

[150] Again, Tasso's precocious interest in geology; cf. lines 785-787.

[151] He apparently reworks Dante's description of the origin of hell's four rivers in *Inferno* 14: 112 ff.

until again they appear in the clear light,
and create new and visible sources
among the steep rocks of the mountains?
    But You shelter and hide the primal springs   780
from the vain studies of the errant mortals,
not only from their longing and weak sight:
thus hidden is the major underground
origin of the pure "river of delights."
When the great Ancient Mother lay
submerged under the gathered floods, it was
this source only that was not dispersed;
safe from the waters was the sacred
mount of paradise,[152] the place chosen
for humankind, its dearest home,   790
which rises so close to the Moon's sphere.
But You expose those ancient mysteries,
and reveal the truth[153] that sheds light on our
modern books[154]—You, who enlighten the mind,
O most holy Tiller of our intellects,
turning the soul into a rich paradise
whose trees are sublime thoughts, fed
and cultivated by contemplating You,
and creating four rivers out of one
source, with their four respective virtues.[155]   800
You, indeed, are that source, the living source[156]
which sprinkles the minds with eternal joy,
and whence all noble virtues derive.
You appear in the shadow,[157] in the breeze;[158]
or burn in the bush,[159] and in a living flame
and blazing light You manifest yourself.
    God carried Man, as if transplanting a tree
—for man is a tree[160]—into paradise, the place

---

[152] Milton does not agree: *Paradise Lost* 11: 829-835.

[153] Starting from such NT passages as *Letter to the Hebrews* 10: 1, the Christian tradition calls the Jewish Scriptures "shadow" not in the sense of darkness, but as the blurred shape of the "body" or "truth," i.e. Christ.

[154] "Carte" may also mean maps.

[155] The classical "cardinal virtues": prudence, temperance, fortitude, and justice. Dante also associates them allegorically with the earthly paradise, see *Purgatorio* 1: 22-27, 37-38 and 29: 130-132.

[156] Cf. *John* 7: 38.

[157] Probably the "cloud" that led the Israelites out of Egypt and through the wilderness.

[158] To the prophet Elijah in *I Kings* 19: 12.

[159] *Exodus* 3: 2, obviously.

of delight, away from that fertile land
where He first created him. There, He set   810
him to guard[161] that happy, sweet place, indeed
to work, since he had not been created
in vain to lead a life of laziness;
although no toil or work was needed
from that ancient and more fecund Mother[162]
—from the tireless mother of all offspring,
whose mammae were springs and rivers,
whence she abundantly poured sweet waters.
A true, wonderful, life-giving Pandora,[163]
whose large box was full to the brim   820
of all gifts that may delight and be useful.
But better works, and the cultivation
of a better soil would befit Man,
who had to adorn his noble mind with
precious intellectual gifts and sublime
virtues, among them piety above all:
the true religion by which the soul
devoutly worships the heavenly King.
   An old, sacred belief among the Jews[164]
has been handed down by the fathers   830
to their sons as a legacy; it increased
then, and now flies, still great and resounding.
According to it—which has many tongues
and carries news with a thousand wings—[165]
when Man still lived alone and single,
without his frail and errant[166] wife
(not yet created by God), the sweet place
of his joys, the delightful paradise
of his pleasure was not like our woods.

---

[160] An unexplained allegory from Pseudo-Basil (BB). It may also echo *Mark* 8: 24.

[161] In *Paradise Lost*, this specific task is assigned to the angels, not very successfully.

[162] Milton draws the opposite conclusion, see *Paradise Lost* 9: 205 ff.

[163] Milton, *Paradise Lost* 4: 714-716, compares Pandora to Eve not only as the Great Mother, but also as a fallen creature.

[164] Regaining his temper, Tasso now praises the Rabbis' *midrashim*. BB quotes Philo of Alexandria, but actual interfaith exchanges took place in the Renaissance Courts. This also allows the poet to retrieve the dimension of fantasy (lines 850 ff.).

[165] The classic(al) portrait of Fame. The word *fama* appears in line 830, here translated as "belief."

[166] *Errante* could also be rendered as "wandering," and this perhaps influences the first section of Book 9 of *Paradise Lost*, since the episode of Eve departing from Adam does not date back to *Genesis*. Dante was even more of a male chauvinist, see *Purgatorio* 29: 23-27.

Here, in fact, untilled forests also   840
happily rustle, but the trees are not
endowed with senses. Some perpetually
keep the honor of their green leaves,
while others put forth their green gems
only when the year's age is still tender,
and Spring, looking like a young girl,
happy and proud, walks with her wreaths;
others produce those sweet fruits so dear
to men, others the food for wild beasts.
But in the Lord's adorned paradise   850
the superb trees were animated, all
endowed with language, senses, and mind.
Oh, the sublime marvels of the Lord,
in which nothing is false, and no fiction
simply veils the hidden and concealed truth![167]
They[168] also maintain that the new world[169]
was to Man (then just born of the earth)
like a large city, which no base master[170]
made with rough wood and rough stone,
surrounding it with perishable walls,
digging moats filled with stagnant waters   860
all around. There, safe and joyful, Man
lived as the Lord and master of the beasts
produced by the earth and the sea,
and him all would necessarily obey;
under his sweet command, many learned
to serve willingly, in perfect peace.
That large city followed divine laws
written in nature, much firmer than those
on metal and marble. Its ancient   870
citizens were noble, divine indeed:
the angels—I mean—and the upper minds,[171]
who had received in heaven[172] vast fields
of pure light and eternal splendor[173] as

---

[167] Cf. Tasso's poetics as it had been expressed in *Gerusalemme Liberata* 1: 3: fiction works as "sugar" to make the "medicine" of truth more pleasant, therefore longed for; sweetness must not be an end in itself.

[168] The Jewish Rabbis.

[169] With a hint at the New World.

[170] Architect, etymologically meaning "the arch-carpenter." Cf. Dante, *Inferno* 15: 12.

[171] "And" should simply be a hendiadys. Cf. Milton, *Paradise Lost* 4: 677-678.

[172] Milton develops this concept in depth, see *Paradise Lost* 5: 461-518.

the inhabitants of the starry mansions.
Man, then happy, led a peaceful, still
fully honest life as the young child
and immortal heir of heaven's King,
full of His zeal and of His Spirit,
forming his thoughts to please God, his steps[174]   880
following God's tracks that led him upwards
along the pathways of noble Virtue
—the only one allowing the souls, who
wish to return to God, to reach up there.
And insofar as Man had been granted
in this world a hereditary power
over the beasts with life and soul,
and as it belongs to a king to know his
subjects and servants by name, and name
them, allotting the various tasks   890
according to their virtues and merits;
his Lord and Father led all the animals[175]
in Man's presence at the same time,
because it was up to him to give them
proper and naturally fitting names.
And he—as a true teacher who awakens
the inner attitudes of a young soul[176]
so as to test the quickness of his brain—
he, our father Adam, did not stray
from truth in giving so many names;   900
he, indeed, expressed the hidden qualities
and inner habits of the animals,
so that in the very first articulate
sound of Man's language,[177] each nature
was comprehended, or rather, was moved,
and calmly obeyed, swiftly and readily,
the sublime, imperious words from him.

---

[173] Cf. Dante, *Paradiso* 28: 53-54.

[174] His behavior, with a Hebrew expression taken from the Bible.

[175] Except fish (Milton, *Paradise Lost* 8: 345-348).

[176] This interesting remark on Adam giving animals their names comes from St. Ambrose (BB). "Education" comes from Latin *e-ducere*, to lead/draw (the truth) out of (the pupil's mind/soul).

[177] Usually during the Renaissance identified as Hebrew. According to Dante, who says that Adam in person informed him about this (in *Paradiso* 26: 124-132, but in what language?), all human phenomena are so transient that Man's native tongue had disappeared long before the Tower of Babel caused the well-known confusion. These verses by Dante are echoed a little below, in lines 926-927.

If those many animals that the sea,
rivers and lakes produce in flowing wombs,
and the multitudes that the wide earth hosts   910
were known by the First Man, moved and drawn
by his voice alone—and they came, meek,
humble, setting aside their great pride,[178]
their native fierceness, disdain, and rage,
obedient and prone to his just command—
would it be a wonder if some recount
famous examples from Adam's descendants?[179]
They speak of Themistocles, of Cyrus
the Persian Emperor, and the Moor[180] Chief,
who knew all the names, not of camels,   920
or elephants—and a thousand hideous
African beasts, varied in shapes, natures,
and habits—but of their loyal warriors.
So much Nature, even at her best, loses
and degenerates from her primal model.[181]
But since not one of the mortal things is
constant and firm—they transform and change,
and more often so where royal honor
lifts and exalts the fervent thoughts—it was
fitting that the first Man and first king,   930
who in himself expressed the outer image
and picture of the newly-created world,
even the image of the heavenly King,
He who had shaped his mind and his soul…
it was fitting for Man, it was necessary
that he gave the first example of error
and misery to his earthly descendants.[182]
A woman[183] was the cause of such a sin,

---

[178] From Dante, *Purgatorio* 2: 126, describing the behavior of scared pigeons.

[179] A noteworthy remark, especially in the Renaissance: Man is *not completely* fallen.

[180] Improperly designating Hannibal, who, moreover, the ancient sources do not record among the men with the strongest memories (BB).

[181] Adam. The personages just listed were only exceptions.

[182] A very daring interpretation of the original sin. It is not even an invention of Tasso: he found it in the book *De Paradiso* by St. Ambrose (BB), but it surely does not belong to the "common doctrine." The Medieval concept of *felix culpa* is quite different; it states, in fact, that the original sin had been a "happy" event insofar as it had the Son of God in person as its Redeemer (*quae talem ac tantum meruit habere Redemptorem*, as Catholic liturgy sings on Easter Eve).

[183] Eve's creation has not yet been described; it will in lines 1020 ff. Nothing about the Serpent.

of so many evils, and of death itself;
a woman, by her blandishments, led him   940
to despise God's supreme prohibition.
    After the eternal Father had placed Man
in that beautiful and pleasureful paradise
—until he (as it was due) would be transferred
into the glory of the heavenly Kingdom—
He commanded not through His servants[184]
or dreams, nor in an ecstasy; nor did
His voice resonate from a cloud, a burning
bush; but He himself talked to father Adam
as to His angels, since Man could   950
understand those sublime, divine words;
and He then moved his mind in such
a wonderful way that we cannot guess.
"Take, Adam," He said, "the food you need
from any plant that grows in paradise,
because all I give you, but I forbid you
the Tree of Knowledge, the one teaching
how to distinguish evil from the good.
In fact, the day you should eat of it, you
will die of death."[185] Oh, the threatening command!   960
Oh, the dreadful sentence, the harsh penalty!
But Man, simple-hearted in that pure
state of pure and spotless innocence,
did not know evil (hidden, unknown, not
yet committed) *ab experto*;[186] nor realize
that God is the soul's very life—so, if
He ever abandons the soul, it dies
in its sin, in its unjust transgression.
Yet a double[187] fierce death was threatened
by the heavenly King in His prohibition.   970
As a white and simple-minded dove,
when newly born and not yet accustomed
to deadly dangers, within its own soul
already carries a native, inward fear

---

[184] The angels.

[185] "Morrai di morte," translating literally from the *Vulgate* (*Genesis* 2: 17): *morte morieris*. More properly, according to the Hebrew syntax, it should be rendered as "die, you will die," where the first infinitive strengthens the action: "You will surely die" (cf. KJV). But the "wrong" *Vulgate* translation is still deeply fascinating.

[186] By experience; in Latin in the original text.

[187] Physical and spiritual.

that makes it afraid of fierce death,
so that, seeing a bird of prey from afar,
it opens its wings and flies away;
Man had that threatening voice and
great prohibition instead of instinct,
so as to be afraid of death albeit   980
unknown; add, later, the fault that came
out of knowledge, or rather of action,
since there is no fault or vice in knowledge.[188]
    And yet that fear was finally overcome
by pleasure and blandishment:[189] he then
daring tried the sweet taste of unknown
knowledge, and thus broke the first law.
By means of sin, Death[190] would find an open
way letting him come into the world
through a large gate; he now occupies   990
all of its parts, so that the earth and sea
are the dark, woeful kingdom of Death.[191]
Here, he would not only triumph by force
and usurp the empire from father Adam
and his degenerating, decaying race,
but also from all beasts housed by the world
—until Life took back Death's undue
war spoils and triumphed over Hell.[192]
As a weak, sick person is often greedy
with food that, though sweet to his palate,   1000
is bad for his health, so that his burning
fever gets worse, and he, finally dying,
is guilty of causing his own death[193]
because he disobeyed the strict recipe
that the physician prescribed to his senses;
so by that sweet, delightful delusion,
Adam was overcome and became the first
cause of frightening death to himself

---

[188] Cf. Dante, *Paradiso* 26: 115-117 (Adam speaks); Milton, *Paradise Lost* 4: 514-518 and 7: 111-130.

[189] Tasso seems to imply that Eve convinced Adam by means of a sexual approach.

[190] Milton mythologizes this formula though Satan's affair with his daughter Sin; the issue of that incestuous union is Death. The story is recounted by Sin before Hell's gates (*PL* 2: 746 ff.).

[191] Cf. Milton, *Paradise Lost* 10: 264-271, 298-305, 591-606.

[192] Echoing Dante, *Inferno* 12: 38-39.

[193] Cf. *Paradise Lost* 9: 792, but Tasso sees it from Adam's point of view.

—not God,[194] for divine Goodness did not
create death and evil, but our error did;   1010
He did foresee the fall of our sin,
and He consented, for if there was no sin
there would be no virtue of mind or soul.[195]
In order that the soul, wavering in this
bitter sea of stormy and dubious life,
might not founder among rocks and shallows,
as a helm to steer the soul's course, He
gave it the Law for direction to the
port of salvation and eternal peace.

   But God saw[196] that Man should not lead   1020
such a long life lonely, without a mate,
like a wild and solitary beast.
So, He resolved to give the one Man
a Mate, a helper in his very likeness;
and He infused a sweet sleep into Adam,
and irrigated with placid quiet all
his limbs while he was asleep and relaxed.
Out of one rib, God built the soft body
of Man's consort,[197] and after that, He
himself led the new bride before him.[198]   1030
And in a placid countenance, Adam said,
"Bone of my bone, flesh of my flesh is
this *wo-man*,[199] who has been made of me."
Hence man, leaving his mother and father,
will be co-joined to his own consort.

   The bodies of both were then wholly nude,[200]
but they felt no shame yet because of it,
because in their perishable limbs there was
not yet that counter-law rebelling against
the sublime and just law of reason.[201]   1040

---

[194] Cf. *Paradise Lost* 1: 1-4, 24-26.

[195] Another interesting perspective on the "necessity" of the Fall.

[196] The poem possibly diverges from the Biblical narrative insofar as Adam's helpmeet is not intended to be simply his companion in Paradise, but as well after the fall.

[197] *Con-sorte*: "sharing the same destiny."

[198] Another detail not present in *Genesis*, and that is found in Milton (*PL* 4: 467 ff.).

[199] The original text has "donna e virago." The former term means woman, but it has no etymological connection with *uomo*, man, so Tasso added the quite inappropriate term *virago*, which comes from Latin *vir* (male human person), but indicates a mannish woman, i.e. one who "acts like a man" (*vir-ago*).

[200] With a solemn Greek accusative in the original text: "they both were naked-their-limbs."

They, therefore, wanted no veil or cloak
for those naked and later hidden parts,
because of which the new era[202] would look
for gold and purple—for rich and varied
attires with endless precious, golden frills.
In this manner, the eternal Father made
this wonderful worldly construction,
and He created Man, himself a small world,
and He finally shaped a mate for him,
and He put an end to His noble works.   1050
    Then, not only the supernal minds
—angels and celestial powers, I say—
praised and exalted the eternal Father,
but so did the sky, and joyfully[203] together
the waters He had gathered over the skies
celebrated Him with high, clear sounds.
The Sun, and you shining stars, praised Him;
you also praised Him, O white Moon;
you, the clouds, you dark clouds and nimbi,
and you snows and frosts, as well as you   1060
blazing thunderbolts celebrated Him.
Night and Day also resounded with
His great Name: their one powerful echo
was heard in the clear, serene light
and in the dark and gloomy shadows.
The Earth, surpassing herself, exalted
the Lord in heaven with lofty praises;
above their peaks, the hard, rugged mountains
exalted Him; so did the green, shady hills,
as well as the murmuring, resonant sea.   1070
The springs and the wandering rivers
whispered His holy and glorious Name;
the birds in the air, the wandering fish,
and all beasts, both wild and meek,
intoned a clear song of His praises.
    In the adorned temples, the priests would

---

[201] From St. Paul's *Letter to the Romans* 7: 23, where, however, the rebellion is against "God's Law" (line 22); Tasso—like many authors from the Late Middle Ages on—tends to Aristotelize the issues of theology and salvation.

[202] The post-lapsarian one, i.e. the whole of human history. Cf. Milton, *PL* 4: 312-315, 740.

[203] "A prova," literally: in competition, a phrase often used by Tasso to enliven the effects of an action. The main source for this section is *Psalm* 148, reworked by Milton also in *PL* 5: 153 ff. and 7: 558-563.

later praise Him with resonant hymns;[204]
nor would the souls of the just, the naked
spirits,[205] omit to praise the eternal God;
so that to Him a concert of three worlds[206]   1080
echoes evermore with His high glory.
But[207] this corporeal frame, old and weary,
and the other, as well aging and weak,
after such a long turning of the centuries,
praises[208] and sings Him at the world's end,
and says, "O my Lord and eternal Father,
who once, out of nothing, created me
wonderfully adorned, then saved me
from the great Flood and from fires,[209]
I, for one, am a heavy and frail mass,   1090
destined to collapse, not only to quake.
But Your hand supports me so that
I will not fall,[210] and turns my[211] still
perpetual course around the firm Earth.
Therefore, though now so old and tired,
I still look like myself as a young boy;
nor did I lose or change my adornments:
not one of so many shining, golden gems
is missing. But if I were detached from You,
I would suddenly turn into nothingness.   1100
As best as I can, I join You in love,
and in all my parts, I humbly worship
and look for You, I long for You only;
and sometimes mourn for You, dripping
in a thick rain, blaming my own Fall.[212]

---

[204] The Baroque hymns are among the masterpieces of Roman Catholic music.

[205] The narrative time has jumped to the present, to the "universal liturgy" involving the blessed souls.

[206] The cosmos, man, and heaven.

[207] The most important "But" in the whole poem, marking, as it were, the passage from the "song of innocence" to the "song of experience." The first "weary" subject that will be mentioned is Tasso himself, and/or man in general; the second is the universe (cf. *Romans* 8: 19-22); not so heaven, of course.

[208] In the singular: it is the one voice of the macro- and microcosm.

[209] It might simply be a general symbol of danger, in order to enrich one term (Flood) by linking it with its opposite, according to Baroque aesthetics; cf. Dante, *Inferno* 3: 87. *Genesis* 19: 12 ff. is another possible comparison.

[210] See the tension between Entropy and Negentropy at the beginning of the poem.

[211] The sky's.

[212] Nature being "hurt" by man's original sin. Cf. Milton, *Paradise Lost* 9: 783.

In mourning and singing, as far as I can,
I sanctify myself to You[213] lest You may
disdain Your divine image in me,[214]
the picture imprinted by Your hand.
But I look for You outside, and weep:[215]   1110
Where are You? Where? Who is hiding You?
Who stole You, O my Lord and Father?
Wretched me! Without You, I am nothing,
alas, hope nothing, alas, long for nothing.
What shall I long for, when All is nothing,
O Lord, without Your grace?[216] To You, again,
I flee beyond myself, and pray, so as to
join You in love by transcending myself.
I am consumed and languish in loving;
if another fire were to destroy me,[217]   1120
Your love can make me anew, more shining
and in a different shape, freeing my now
weak, sick nature[218] from toils and motions.
Let the aging and weary World
rest in peace, at last, and become eternal
in You: it will not be a frail temple forever,
but, at last, the steady seat of Your glory."

    So speaks the cosmos, and deaf is the soul
which does not listen to its sound and song,
and does not add its own cries and prayers.

THE END

---

[213] Like Christ himself, see *John* 17: 19.

[214] In *Genesis* the cosmos as a whole is not defined as an "image of God," but Medieval and Renaissance theology is echoed here.

[215] The crisis of any easy "find God in yourself."

[216] Renaissance Catholics were much closer to Protestants than they were ready to admit.

[217] *II Peter* 3: 7, 11.

[218] Contradicting line 1096.

Contributors

Tiziana "Selkis" Grassi is an international tour leader based in Italy. Her interests include archeology, astronomy, Japanese comics and computer graphics. www.tizia fra.wix.com/the-magic-trio

Carter Kaplan has pioneered the application of poetry and fiction to the study of analytic philosophy, as presented in his book *Critical Synoptics: Menippean Satire and the Analysis of Intellectual Mythology*. In addition to a number of academic articles and reviews, he is the author of the Aristophanic comedy *Diogenes*, and a novel of intellectual life in trans-Atlantic culture, *Tally-Ho, Cornelius!* His Afterword appears in the International Authors edition of Nathaniel Hawthorne's *The Scarlet Letter*.

Salwa Khoddam, PhD, is Professor emerita of English at Oklahoma City University and founder of the C. S. Lewis and the Inklings Society (CSLIS). She has co-edited three anthologies on the Inklings entitled *Truths Breathed through Silver: The Inklings' Moral and Mythopoeic Legacy* (Cambridge Scholars Press, 2008), *C. S. Lewis and the Inklings: Discovering Hidden Truth* (CSP, 2012), and *C. S. Lewis and the Inklings: Reflection on Faith, Imagination, and Modern Technology* (CSP, 2015). She is also the author of *Mythopoeic Narnia: Memory, Metaphor, and Metamorphoses in The Chronicles of Narnia* (Winged Lion Press, 2013). Her other interests are Dante, Tasso, and Milton.

Eva "Nivalis" Nieri lives in Lucca (Tuscany, Italy) and works in the field of decoration. Inspired by Japanese *anime* and *manga*, she is interested in making illustrations inspired by popular fiction. www.tiziafra.wix.com/the-magic-trio

Dario Rivarossa was born in Italy in 1969. After studying philosophy, theology, mass communications and comic art, he started working as a journalist. Currently a translator: English or German to Italian: sci-fi novels, historical essays, articles for specialized magazines, etc. Lecturer of the Dante Alighieri Society and online essayist, and he is emerging as an illustrator. He is the author of *Dante was a Fantasy Writer*. Blog: www.tassonomia.blogspot.com

Torquato Tasso (1544–1595) was an Italian poet known across Europe for his poem *La Gerusalemme Liberata* (*Jerusalem Delivered*, 1581). His late masterpiece *Il Mondo Creato* (*Creation of the World*, 1607) is an exposition of early-modern sensibility emerging from the turbulence of the late Counter-Reformation. Scholars have suggested Tasso influenced John Milton, whose *Paradise Lost* reflects elements of Tasso's style, themes and genius.

About International Authors

A consortium of writers, artists, architects, filmmakers and critics, International Authors publishes work of outstanding literary merit. Dedicated to the advancement of an international culture in literature, primarily in English, the group seeks new members with an enthusiasm for creating unique artistic expressions.

www.internationalauthors.info